Shipwrecks

of Southern
California

Shipwrecks

of Southern

California

by Bonnie J. Cardone and Patrick Smith

Menasha Ridge Press
Birmingham, Alabama

Printed in the United States of America

Published by Menasha Ridge Press

First edition, first printing

Library of Congress Cataloging-in-Publication Data
Cardone, Bonnie J.
  Shipwrecks of southern California.
  Includes bibliographical references.
  1. Shipwrecks—California, Southern. I. Smith,
Patrick, 1950- . II. Title.
G525.C324   1990   910'.9164'32   89–37758
ISBN 0–89732–094–8

Menasha Ridge Press
Post Office Box 59257
Birmingham, Alabama 35259–9257

To Beverly, Pamela, and Michael
B. J. C.

For Kathy, Jed, and Zack—the best parts of my life.
P. S.

Contents

Acknowledgments

Rare is the endeavor that one or two people can accomplish by themselves. Such is the case with this work. Though there are but two names on the cover, the help, information, and advice from many people contributed to its completion and accuracy. We wish to thank all who were a part of it: Kramer Adams; Vestal Arnold; Chris Barclay; Dr. and Mrs. Jerry Bastian; William Beebe; Herbert Beckwith, National Maritime Museum, San Francisco; Skip Dunham; Steve Giles; Patrick Gibson; Jean Haviland; Louis Hough; Captain Harold Huycke; Peter Jensen; J. Joblotz, Steamship Historical Society; Captain Mike Johnson; the Allen Knight Maritime Museum; Steve Lawson; Dr. William "Pete" Lee, Director, Los Angeles Maritime Museum; Ernest Marquez; Pat McFerran; Jack McKenney; Herb Miller; Fletcher Nash; Daniel Purdie; Mike Reis; Mike Redmon, Santa Barbara Historical Society; Al Rowe; Woody Treen; and Victor C. West.

A thank you also to Kathy McGuire, whose patience, insight, and support have been counted on since the beginning.

Introduction

In recent years the general public has been having its collective consciousness raised in regard to shipwrecks. Advances in technology have made possible not only the location of the *Atocha*, lost in 1622, but the recovery of her very precious cargo. In 1985, when Mel Fisher's divers began bringing up gold disks, silver bars, emeralds, and assorted other wonderful treasures, the entire world paid attention.

Another incredible shipwreck was found that year. A French-American team located the *Titanic* two and a half miles beneath the surface of the Atlantic Ocean. The *Titanic* sank in 1912 on her maiden voyage, and her tragic journey inspired books, movies, poems, songs, and the creation of societies that study her demise even today.

Diving was very much involved in the discovery of both the *Atocha* and the *Titanic*; and, without diving, there would have been no recovery of items from either ship. They were two different kinds of diving, however. The *Atocha* divers used scuba; the *Titanic* divers, a small submersible.

No matter how a wreck is dived, those who participate in this activity are stepping back into history. No doubt this is why so many of us find it so intriguing. Although some the wrecks we've included here are covered in other books, our volume is unique in that it is written by divers for divers. (The initials of the author of each chapter appear at the end.)

Southern California Shipwrecks

Southern California waters do not contain shipwrecks that rival the *Atocha* or *Titanic* in either riches or fame. The stories of many of their sinkings, however, are no less dramatic. There were the seven destroyers that went aground at Honda; the luxury yacht that burned off Catalina; the gold-rush era paddlewheeler that ended her days at Anacapa, to mention a few. Each ship has a life, a story, a drama of its own. Our intention was to produce a factual work that is enjoyable to read. We want to put you on those ships— and then on their wrecks—but in your mind's eye first.

We have not included every wreck to be found from Point Conception to the Mexican border. One of several considerations was depth. Since 130 feet is the maximum depth limit for recreational divers, a large part of any wreck we covered had to be above or at that level. Some wrecks were included because they are fascinating to dive; others because they are fascinating to read about. In the interest of getting this book published in our lifetimes, we decided to limit the number of wrecks included to 50.

Our research yielded a great deal of material on some vessels, with almost nothing on others. When we found conflicting accounts, we tried to choose those that either seemed the most logical (to us!) or that could be supported by other sources. This had to be done for the sake of clarity. Of course, there is danger in re-creating a long-past event; the sinking of the *Titanic* illustrates this very well. The majority of the survivors of that wreck insisted it sank in one piece; only a handful said it broke in two and sank. Since the majority contained some highly regarded people and the "experts" said the ship couldn't have broken in two, the majority was believed. However, when the ship was found 73 years later, it was in two pieces—separated by one third of a mile. It had obviously broken in two before sinking.

We hope our choices will better withstand the test of time.

Artifacts

When we began working on this book, divers were routinely removing artifacts from wrecks not within the boundaries of the Channel Islands National Park and National Marine Sanctuary. This protected area encompasses the land area of Santa Barbara and Anacapa islands and the sea for six miles offshore, as well as the sea six miles offshore San Miguel, Santa Rosa, and Santa Cruz islands. Recent events, however, have made artifact salvage from many wrecks questionable.

With the passage of the Abandoned Shipwreck Act (Public Law 100-298) and its signing by President Reagan in April 1988, the states acquired jurisdiction over all shipwrecks in waters up to three miles from their shores. This encompasses all the wrecks we have included in this book, with the exception of the *Moody*. Even before the Abandoned Shipwreck Act was passed, however, California had the State Antiquities Act, which protected "historical resources 50 years and older" on state lands and in state waters. To comply with this law, anyone recovering any kind of artifact 50 years old or older from public lands or waters is required to obtain a salvage permit from the State Lands Commission.

By the time you read this, the state will probably have either altered existing laws or instituted new ones concerning shipwrecks in its waters. Whatever these may be, it seems wise not to take artifacts from ships that were 50 years old or older when they sank or from those that have been down 50 or more years. If there is any doubt as to the age of the vessel, don't take anything other than photographs. All of the artifacts shown in this book were taken before the legality of this activity was in question.

Shipwrecks

of Southern California

Surf to Point Conception

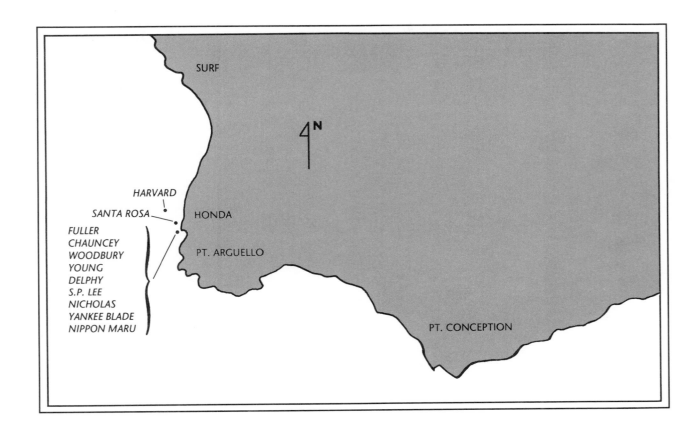

Harvard: Shipwreck Deluxe

A shipwreck under any circumstances is a serious and sometimes deadly event; when the vessel involved is a passenger liner carrying nearly 500 passengers, and the area is that ship-killer known as Honda, then the odds are against a happy ending of any kind. But in May of 1931 such a liner did crash ashore at Honda, and instead of a life-or-death fight for survival by the 497 passengers on board, the result was a grand adventure the likes of which few would ever again experience.

Designed by William Denny & Bros. of Dumbarton, and built by Delaware River Shipbuilding Company of Chester, Pennsylvania, *Yale* and *Harvard* were launched on December 1, 1906, and January 30, 1907, respectively. They were built for the Metropolitan Steam Navigation Company for the New York-to-Boston run, and run they did. Measuring 403 feet in length and 51 feet in width, and powered by three 10,000-horsepower Parsons turbines that pushed their 3,737 tons along at over 24 knots, these well-favored sisters delivered their passengers in speed and luxury unmatched by rival vessels.

In 1910, the owner of the Metropolitan Steamship Company, Charles Wyman Morse, earned a prolonged visit to the federal penitentiary for his creative financing techniques, and under intense pressure from jealous competitors, the *Harvard* and *Yale* were sold to the Pacific Navigation Company.

Departing New York on October 22, 1910, they arrived in Los Angeles on December 16, via the Strait of Magellan, and were established on the San Diego–Los Angeles–San Francisco run. They immediately proved to be very popular, bringing new standards of luxury and speed to the Pacific Coast.

Both *Yale* and *Harvard* were chartered by the Pacific Alaska Steam Navigation Company in 1916, and later in the year when the company merged with the Pacific Coast Steamship Company, the sleek "White Sisters" were part of the deal. They were so popular and so well known that they remained on their San Diego–Los Angeles–San Francisco run until the United States' entry into World War I.

With America's entry into the war, both *Harvard* and *Yale* were commandeered by the U. S. Navy and taken to Mare Island Navy Yard, San Francisco, for refitting as troop carriers. All their luxurious interiors and fine fittings were removed and stored, replaced

Coastal liner Harvard *entering floating drydock. Photo from the Los Angeles Maritime Museum.*

with tiers of metal-framed bunks. Their exterior appearance changed also; their sleek, white exteriors were covered by the garish Dazzle camouflage, and their bridges were surrounded by splinter mats.

On April 9, 1918, when all work was completed, the *Harvard* was commissioned into the U.S. Navy and placed under the command of Commander M. F. Tarpey, USNRF. Two days later *Harvard* was renamed U. S. S. *Charles* and, some six weeks after that, departed Mare Island for Hampton Roads, Virginia, where she loaded troops for transport to Brest, France.

After an 11-day crossing, the *Charles* arrived in Southhampton, England, on July 27 and reported for duty as a cross-channel ferry for troops. She continued in this capacity until May 5, 1919. During this period, she made more than 60 voyages between Southhampton and Le Havre, carrying cargo and troops of all nationalities headed for action at the front or for the occupation duty after the armistice.

After embarking passengers for the United States at Rotterdam and Brest, *Charles* arrived in New York City on June 15, 1919, and, after unloading her passengers, sailed for the Philadelphia Navy Yard where she was decommissioned on July 24, 1919. Five days later she was given back her original name, *Harvard*, and on October 14, 1920, she and her sister ship, *Yale* (which had served in much the same service as *Harvard* during the war), were sold to the Los Angeles Steamship Company (LASSCO).

After reaching the Pacific Coast via the Panama Canal, both vessels underwent massive and extensive refitting at San Pedro, and in August of 1921, they once again resumed their old coastwise route of San Diego-Los Angeles-San Francisco. In the times of prosperity after the war, the two "White Sisters" were more popular than ever. They continued on the run for many years until, by 1930, they each had completed over 1,000 round trips up and down the coast with a train-schedule-like punctuality.

By this time, though, they were being pressed hard by competitive lines, and times were tough anyway; the Depression cut deeply into all types of businesses, including steamship lines.

For Memorial Day Weekend 1931, LASSCO offered special holiday fares; and, as a consequence, the *Harvard* was carrying nearly a capacity load on her final voyage, including nearly 200 delegates returning home from a Parent-Teacher-Association conference in San Francisco.

The passengers' mood was festive as the *Harvard* departed San Francisco for ports she would never reach. Despite the post-holiday enthusiasm and numerous "departure parties," however, most every passenger had retired to his cabin by 12 o'clock that evening, as the *Harvard* headed south through the calm night sea at a steady 20 knots.

But instead of making a punctual 10 A.M. arrival at Los Angeles as her passengers expected, *Harvard* arrived at her ultimate destination—a rocky area just north of Honda—a little after 3 A.M. with a slight jolt and grind.

At 3:29 A.M. the foggy, early-morning airwaves crackled with the first SOS from the stricken *Harvard*, and within moments several vessels had responded to her plea for assistance.

One of the first to respond was the U.S. Navy's newest cruiser, the U. S. S. *Louisville*, which was conducting sea trials in the Catalina Channel off Los Angeles. Abandoning her test cruise, she put on steam and raced 133 miles for the beleaguered passenger liner at 33+ knots, arriving on the scene shortly before 8 A.M. On her arrival, the *Louisville* found the freighter S. S. *San Anselmo* fully engaged in rescue operations, having already taken many of the *Harvard*'s passengers on board. There began an immediate retransfer of passengers to the *Louisville* while the *San Anselmo* stayed on the scene to receive most of the passengers' baggage.

By this time there were three Coast Guard Cutters and the freighter S. S. *Marsadak* standing by as well to offer assistance if required.

Harvard passengers boarding lifeboat after stranding near Honda on May 30, 1931. *Photo from National Maritime Museum, San Francisco.*

When the news had arrived in Santa Barbara, the local Red Cross, with the enthusiastic support of the Southern Pacific Railroad Company, put together a relief train that was to carry a score of doctors and nurses, medical supplies and blankets, as well as enough food to serve over 500 people, north to the wreck site. By herculean effort all this was accomplished in under an hour, but shortly after it had left Santa Barbara, the relief train was called back; with all the other assistance already there, further help was unnecessary.

As soon as the last *Harvard* passenger was on board the cruiser *Louisville,* Captain Hillsinger of the *Harvard* radioed the following message: "All passengers kept their shirts on and enjoyed themselves immensely. All safe on cruiser *Louisville.* No one got their feet wet."

When questioned by newsmen about the wreck and rescue after their arrival in Los Angeles, *Harvard* passengers were quite enthused by the whole event. Said one, "It was a shipwreck deluxe. No one was hurt—it was a genuine thrill and it earned us a ride on the Navy's newest cruiser."

Not only a ride home, but a special Memorial Day dinner on board consisting of turkey, cranberry sauce, and all the trimmings.

Although the wreck itself didn't claim any casualties, the resultant publicity of the affair did, as evidenced in this excerpt from a June 2, *San Francisco Chronicle* interview with the San Francisco general passenger agent for LASSCO:

> A certain man of prominence told his family he was going to Los Angeles on the *Harvard,* but his name did not appear on the list when the vessel grounded, and now he is beseeching me to tell his wife he actually was on the *Harvard.*
>
> Another man who registered on the liner with his wife bore the same name as a prominent San Franciscan, or used a fictitious name. . . Fortunately the man whose name was used was at home with his family, but the wife fears the neighbors will misunderstand.

Salvage operations were begun almost immediately by the Revenue Cutter *Tamaroa* and the *Peacock,*

The liner Harvard, *aground near Honda, with salvage vessels attempting to pull her free. Photo from P. Smith collection.*

Homer and *Commissioner,* three salvage tugs of the Merritt-Chapman & Scott salvage company. Some 350 tons of cargo and equipment were saved and for a short period of time there was some hope that the *Harvard* might be towed free, but the heavy ground swell soon put an end to any such attempts.

Just four days after the stranding, Merritt-Chapman & Scott's senior salvage expert, Captain John Johnson arrived on the scene and described the situation he found in a dispatch to company headquarters:

> On arrival on board of the wreck we made an examination. The vessel was full of water all over. The heavy sea was breaking over C-Deck and into the vessel. Midway between the foremast and the forward smokestack on the port side was a crack in the shell plating about 4" wide at the D-Deck line and extending in a wedge shape opening down to and under the waterline. All the superstructure had been broken and started by the seas breaking over the vessel and by the working of the hull. She was a perfect wreck.

As the *Harvard* began to break up, residents from the Point Arguello area "reaped a rich harvest from the *Harvard,*" according to the *Santa Barbara News Press.* "Citizens who were willing to shed their shoes and socks, roll up their trousers and skim from the oily surface of the Pacific floating foodstuff, were able

From right to left: dolphin light fixture, dolphin chandelier, and deck washdown pump cover salvaged from the Harvard *and restored. Photo by Bonnie J. Cardone.*

to stock their larders with canned goods, cheese, flour, salmon, coffee, and coconuts."

Further benefits were derived by Adam Sykes, an enterprising rancher whose land overlooked the *Harvard*'s ultimate destination. This home-grown entrepreneur garnered a substantial profit by collecting a 50 cents-per car parking fee from each of the estimated 20,000 or 30,000 automobiles that crossed his land to view the stricken liner.

Once the sea began to tear the *Harvard* apart, her destruction was amazingly quick. Within five days she had broken in two and her colors, which had been defiantly flying from her stern, were struck, signaling her surrender to the sea. Within three weeks all trace of the *Harvard*, except for a small portion of her stern that was visible at low tide, had been battered beneath the surface.

In hearings carried out in San Pedro before officers of the United States Steamboat Inspection Service, volumes of testimony were taken from passengers, crew, and even the operator of the radio compass station at Point Arguello.

Many causes of the accident were suggested: fog, magnetic anomaly, unusual currents, drunken crew, and even deliberate grounding so the owners could collect insurance on the vessel, though this was never proven. Despite all this input, an exact cause for the stranding and loss was never revealed. Eventually Captain Hillsinger was completely exonerated, but the three watch officers on duty at the time of the wreck had their licenses permanently suspended.

Diving the Harvard

The *Harvard* is probably the least dived of any known shallow-water wreck in southern California; for this reason she is a veritable cornucopia of artifacts. There are three reasons the *Harvard* has been able to maintain its nearly unsalvaged condition: the distance and remoteness of the site from shelter and launch facilities, the large seas caused by the usually unsettled weather in the area, and the shallowness of the site. These factors serve to keep all but the most determined divers away from her. Even though the *Harvard* lies less than one mile from Honda, the open, exposed nature of the area along with the shallow depths over the site generate conditions that prevent diving the site even when it is possible to get in on the nearby destroyers or the *Yankee Blade*.

During an 18-month period between 1986 and 1987, it was judged that there were only a dozen days calm enough to dive the *Harvard*. Unfortunately for those of us who work for a living, those calm days north of Point Arguello rarely seem to occur on weekends.

Depth on the *Harvard* ranges from 18 to 25 feet with visibility varying from 5 to 40 feet. Surge is a constant companion on the *Harvard*, even on the so-called flat days. There are two interesting effects of this nearly constant movement of water across the wreck. The first is that the shifting of sand constantly covers and uncovers various areas and artifacts on the wreck. This ever-changing bottom provides new discoveries, experiences, and artifacts with every dive, making each visit seem as though it's a visit to a new wreck.

The second effect of the surge is the gleaming shine given to every exposed piece of brass or bronze on the wreck by the continual burnishing produced by the moving sand. One of the most impressive sights I've ever experienced underwater was coming across the *Harvard*'s three propellers, immense and gleaming through the murk, during my first dive on the wreck. Visibility wasn't good enough to see all three at once, but after I discovered the first, the second and third were just a few strokes beyond. Each looked nearly new, bright, shiny, and perfect. But they had turned their last revolutions some 45 years before; the ship they once drove was long dead and they remained as most appropriate markers.

Like any of the wrecks in the Honda area, patience, common sense, and caution are the bywords for any safe visit to the *Harvard*. The precaution of always leaving someone on board to check on weather changes and sea conditions is a good one and should always be practiced. Aside from these caveats, a dive on the *Harvard* is a rare and unique experience that is well worth the time and effort a visit to this proud old steamer requires.

P. S.

Santa Rosa

A 326-foot steamship, the iron-hulled *Santa Rosa* was launched in 1884 in Chester, Pennsylvania. She carried passengers and cargo for the Pacific Coast Steamship Co. On July 6, 1911, the *Santa Rosa* was on a regular voyage heading south along the California coast. Captain O. J. Faria had asked his crew to awaken him when the Point Sal light was sighted but the thick fog obscured it. Although the crew must have realized the light had been passed, they neglected to wake the captain to tell him. Thus, he was asleep when his ship went aground at the mouth of Honda Creek, just north of Point Arguello, in the early hours of July 7.

The ocean was flat and the *Santa Rosa* was undamaged by the grounding. Earning a place in history, Captain Faria became the first man to use the wireless to ask a ship's owners if he should abandon ship. The owners decided against this, feeling sure that at high tide the ship could be pulled free and would continue on its journey.

This decision was to have fatal consequences, as conditions deteriorated with the arrival of high tide.

The steamer Santa Rosa *dying at the mouth of Honda Creek. Photo from P. Smith collection.*

A large wave lifted the ship as she was about to be pulled free and smashed her upon a reef, breaking her in two. Now her passengers and crew were forced to abandon her and go ashore in high surf and strong winds. In the process, four of them died.

The remains of the *Santa Rosa* are still to be found at the mouth of Honda Creek. In 1923, seven destroyers joined her, running upon the rocks directly south. Although their remains are divable on the rare occasions when the seas are very calm, the area is treacherous, more so for the *Santa Rosa* than for the destroyers because she lies directly within the surf line. Those who attempt diving here are very likely to end their days the same way as those four crew members and passengers did in 1911.

B. J. C.

U. S. Destroyers at Honda

It was a stunning loss: In less than five minutes on September 8, 1923, seven destroyers worth $13 million sailed into the rocks of Honda and were lost forever. Twenty-three crewmen died; the military career of the squadron commander was ruined.

Whole books have been written on this, considered the greatest peacetime tragedy in U. S. Naval history. There is Elwyn E. Overshiner's *Course 095 to Eternity; Last Hours of Seven Four Stackers*, by Charles Hice; and *Tragedy at Honda*, by Charles A. Lockwood and Hans Christian Adamson.

Squadron 11 of the Pacific Battle Fleet consisted of 14 Clemson Class destroyers. They had various nicknames. They were called Greyhounds of the Sea because they could cruise between 33 and 34 knots; Four Stackers (or Four Pipers) because they had four smokestacks; and Tin Cans because their steel-plate hulls were only three-eighths-inch thick. Three hundred and fourteen feet long, each had a beam of 32 feet, and displaced 1,215 tons.

There were 300 Four Stackers built for America's New Navy, a project initiated by Woodrow Wilson, Secretary of the Navy Josephus Daniels, and Assistant Secretary Franklin D. Roosevelt. However, with the end of World War I came The Naval Limitation Treaty among the United States, Great Britain, Japan, France,

The twisted remains of the Delphy *give some idea of the power of the seas in the area. Offshore, the capsized* Young, *and, beyond her, the* Woodbury *and the* Fuller. *Photo from P. Smith collection.*

and Italy. Plans for the New Navy were scrapped, along with hundreds of brand-new vessels. Among these were 150 Four Stackers.

Of the remaining 150 destroyers not scrapped, 38 were assigned to Squadrons 11 and 12, stationed in San Diego, California. The nineteen Squadron-11 destroyers had been constructed by the Bethlehem Shipbuilding Corporation. All of those that ended up on the rocks at Honda—with the exception of the *Delphy*, built in Quincy, Massachusetts, in 1918—were built in San Francisco and launched between 1918 and 1920.

In the summer of 1923, Squadrons 11 and 12 sailed to Seattle for fleet exercises in Puget Sound. Then there was Fleet Week in San Francisco, reviewed by the president of the United States, Warren G. Harding. For seven of the ships and the president there would be no more reviews: Harding died in San Francisco on August 2, before he could return to Washington. Thirty-seven days later, while on their way back to San Diego, seven of Squadron 11's vessels would be on the rocks at Honda.

Tragedy

Squadrons 11 and 12 left San Francisco at dawn on September 8. Each squadron consisted of three divisions and each of these was assigned six vessels. DesRon 11, composed of Destroyer Divisions 31, 32 and 33, was commanded by Captain Edward H. Watson, aboard the *Delphy*.

Two of the casualties at Honda. S.P. Lee (DD 310) in foreground and the Nicholas *(DD 311) in background. Photo from P. Smith collection.*

Ship's bell recovered from the flagship of DesRon 11, the U.S.S. Delphy *(DD 261). Photo from P. Smith collection.*

DesDiv 31, commanded by William S. Pye aboard the *Farragut* consisted of the *Somers, Fuller, J. F. Burnes, Percival,* and *Chauncey.*

DesDiv 32, Walter G. Roper in command, consisted of his flagship, *Kennedy,* along with the *Thompson, Paul Hamilton,* and the *Stoddert.* Two ships were missing from Roper's division.

DesDiv 33, commanded by Robert Morris aboard the *S. P. Lee,* consisted of the *Young, Woodbury,* and the *Nicholas.* Two ships were also missing from this division.

The *William Jones* (DesDiv 33), *Farquhar* (DesDiv 32), and *Melville* (flagship of the commander of Squadrons 11 and 12), along with the *Selfridge* and *Farenholt* of Squadron 12—all of which had mechanical problems—had left at midnight, limping to their home port under considerably less than full speed. Squadron 11's *Reno* (DesDiv 32) was already under way, making her annual smoke-prevention and full-speed run. (She would rescue survivors of the *Cuba,* which ran aground San Miguel Island.) Missing from the dawn caravan as well was the *Zeilin* (DesDiv 33), which was in dry dock in Seattle. While escorting the *Henderson,* carrying President and Mrs. Harding through Puget Sound to Seattle, the ships were enveloped in a dense fog. Somehow the *Zeilin* ended up in front of the *Henderson* and was hit by her. Although the *Zeilin* was cut nearly in half, the much larger *Henderson* was undamaged.

Two things contributing to the Honda tragedy were the orders to maintain a speed of 20 knots and, except for the flagship *Delphy,* to maintain radio silence. Only the *Delphy* was allowed to request Radio Direction Finder bearings, although those in charge of one or two other ships were worried enough to do so. The others intercepted bearings intended for the *Delphy* or other vessels. Since RDF bearings were relatively new and not considered by many to be entirely accurate, dead reckoning and celestial were the standard methods of navigation used by the fleet. Dead reckoning consisted of estimating distance traveled by knowing the time that had passed and the speed of the vessel. While this may seem simple, such things as wind and currents could skew the results. Celestial navigation, the means of determining position by measuring the altitude of certain celestial bodies, is highly accurate. Unfortunately it requires clear skies, something *DesRon 11* didn't have on that voyage.

In much the same way fighter planes flying in formation have followed the leader to their deaths, the ships in Squadrons 11 and 12 followed the *Delphy.* Her navigator and her officers were wrong. They did not believe the RDF bearings they were receiving were accurate. Because they wanted to maintain speed, they decided not to stop and take soundings, which would have shown how shallow they were. Although no one ever saw the Point Arguello light—the fog could have obscured it—and they didn't hear its foghorn, either, those in charge aboard the *Delphy* assumed they were south of it. At 21:00 on September 8, Captain Watson gave the order to head 095 degrees true, thinking he'd be heading straight into the Santa Barbara Channel. Instead, he had headed his ship and those following it directly toward the shore.

Unfortunately, he was several miles farther north than he thought. First, the *Delphy* became enveloped in a thick fog. Then she ran aground. Following in tight formation behind her, only 250 yards from foremast to foremast, came the *S. P. Lee, Young, Woodbury, Nicholas, Farragut, Fuller,* and *Chauncey.* Captain John F. McClain managed to reverse the *Farragut's* engines and backed his ship to safety, although the *Fuller* ran into her in the confusion. The *Fuller* might have escaped, except a rock had already left a four-foot hole in her port side. With her engine room flooding she was helpless. In four minutes, the seven ships were aground.

It is remarkable that more men were not lost. The surf was high and the fog pea-soup thick. There were many heroes that night. Only two ships suffered fatalities: 3 from the *Delphy* died. The *Young* capsized, taking 20 of her crew to their deaths: 14 of these were firemen who were trapped below decks.

Court Martial

Immediately after the disaster, a Court of Inquiry was convened, and on October 31, it let its findings be known. Eleven officers were recommended for trial by General Court Martial. When the trial was over,

Remains of the destroyer Chauncey *(DD 296) at Honda. Photo by Patrick Smith.*

Artifacts recovered from the Chauncey *on display at the Lompoc Museum. Photo from P. Smith collection.*

Memorial to the 23 sailors who lost their lives at Honda, September 8, 1923. Photo from P. Smith collection.

found guilty of culpable inefficiency and negligence were the *Delphy*'s Captain (and Squadron Commander) Edward H. Watson and Lieutenant Commander Donald T. Hunter. The ship's navigating officer Lieutenant (jg) Lawrence F. Blodgett, was found not guilty: Commander Watson had assumed full responsibility for the navigation of his vessel. Lieutenant Commander J. O. Roesch, of the *Nicholas*, was found guilty of negligence, but his conviction was later set aside.

Epilogue

On September 11, 1923, salvage operations began at Honda. From that day until September 25, Navy personnel removed or fired torpedoes from the destroyers and recovered what they could of their confidential papers. Guns and assorted other gear were removed. Salvage was difficult because of the rocks and high surf. Those items brought to shore had to be pulled up a cliff, on a sled, by a tractor and then towed to the railroad a short distance away.

After September 25, Merritt, Chapman & Scott was hired to continue salvage operations. On November 28, 1923, the Navy put the seven destroyers up for sale. The terms of the sale indicated that salvage work could not begin until Merritt, Chapman & Scott was finished, about December 1. One of the provisions also was, "It is agreed that the removal shall be completed in 180 calendar days after award and that there shall be at the conclusion of the

removal no trace or vestige of these vessels or any part thereof above ground or above water at mean low water." The Navy wanted no visible reminders of its greatest peacetime disaster.

The Ring

The shallow waters at Honda do not encourage divers. Exposed to the weather, they are often surgey. The jagged rocks have been responsible for the deaths of several ships other than those of Squadron 11 and are dangerous to divers as well. At times, however, the Honda's seas can be millpond calm. On those days they are a wreck diver's dream.

Such a day occurred late one September. Several southern California divers had dived all day Saturday bringing up artifact after artifact from the destroyers. Today, their boat was anchored right over the *Young*.

The greatest loss of life occurred on this vessel during the Honda tragedy because when she capsized, 20 of her crewmen were trapped below decks. Her captain, William L. Calhoun, was one of the heroes of the day. It was felt that his courage, calmness, and discipline had prevented a much greater loss of life aboard the *Young*. He was recommended for a

The Annapolis class ring of Captain William Lowndes Calhoun, found on the wreck of the Young *in 1984. It was later returned to his wife Rosalie. Photo by Bonnie J. Cardone.*

From top left: silverware retrieved from the Woodbury; *the ship's clock from the* Young; *various artifacts from the* Fuller, *the* Young, *and the* Woodbury. *Photo by Bonnie J. Cardone.*

citation by the Board of Inquiry. The crew members of the *Young* presented him with a sword as a token of their appreciation. Calhoun spent 44 distinguished years in the Navy, retiring in 1946 with the rank of four-star admiral. He died in 1963 at the age of 79.

The divers did not know all this when they were diving Honda that day. All they knew is that this was the last dive of the second day. One diver in particular hadn't found anything significant: only a pocket watch in poor shape, recovered the day before. He'd decided to return to the spot he found it and look around some more. He found the small mound amidships quickly. It was six to eight inches high and about four to five inches wide. It was an aggregate that resembled a clump of asphalt, formed when pieces of the wreck started to rust. As the diver examined the little mound he noticed "something glittery, that looked like spun copper wire." With his hammer he tapped behind the object and it popped out. It felt heavy. He rubbed the conglomerate off and saw what looked like a ring.

The diver's air ran out before he could examine the object further. That had to wait until he was once again aboard the boat. It turned out to be a 14-karat gold ring in like-new condition, even after 61 years beneath the sea. It cleaned up easily. Engraved inside it was: "William Lowndes Calhoun, United States Navy." It was the distinguished admiral's 1906 Annapolis class ring.

Calhoun's second wife, Rosalie, was still alive and living in San Diego. They had married in 1946. The diver who found the ring drove down to meet her several times and eventually returned her husband's ring to her.

Diving Honda Today

Honda today is part of Vandenberg Air Force Base and the Naval Missile Facility, Point Arguello. No diving is allowed from the beach. The only access is via boat. Because the area is exposed to the weather, it is rarely divable. Diving depths range from 35 feet to the shoreline. Visibility ranges from 10 to 40 feet. Because the area is shallow, it is surgey.

The Navy got its wish: Not a trace of the ships can be seen topside. Underwater, however, Honda is a wreck diver's dream. Wreckage is everywhere. Perpetually buffed by sand and surge, pieces of brass gleam like gold. Many of the more delicate pieces of ships' fittings and machinery have been crushed, bent, or twisted by larger debris or rocks. Some artifacts survive in remarkably good shape: Admiral Calhoun's ring; the handle of an officer's sword; and a San Francisco policeman's badge, #574. How the badge got to Honda is a mystery. The owner has been identified as Royal W. Hollingsworth, now deceased. The badge was found on the *Delphy*, and

A porthole from one of the Honda destroyers. Photo by Bonnie J. Cardone.

there is speculation that it was acquired by a crew member while on shore leave in San Francisco. Exactly how this occurred we'll probably never know.

B. J. C.

Yankee Blade

In 1961 a unique piece of maritime history was rediscovered in the foothills above Santa Barbara. The item, a large carved wooden eagle, was found atop the entrance gate of a San Marcos Pass ranch. The significance of this impressive bit of woodwork dated back more than 100 years to 1854, when the eagle proudly adorned the pilot house of the crack steam side-wheeler *Yankee Blade*. The eagle, which was recovered by a fisherman on Santa Rosa Island in 1856, some two years after the *Blade* wrecked, was brought to Santa Barbara where it passed from person to person until it disappeared from sight in 1923. Its rediscovery in '61 and subsequent transfer to the Santa Barbara Historical Society Museum provides the public with the only easily seen memento that remains of the fabled gold-rush treasure ship. In the museum, the eagle, as an object designed to catch one's attention, seems to have found a fitting, final port of call after a long, tragic voyage that began in San Francisco in September 1854.

On September 30, 1854, at four o'clock in the afternoon, four steamers released their lines and backed from their berths along San Francisco's bustling Embarcadero. The vessels were the *Yankee Blade* and *Sonora* bound for Panama, the *Cortes* bound for Nicaragua, and the coastal packet *Goliah* bound for San Diego with intermediate stops along the coast. Because of the low fares brought on by the competition among the Isthmus steamers, each of those three vessels carried capacity-plus loads of passengers.

Many of the *Blade*'s passengers were reported to be miners returning to their eastern homes. A great number of the Argonauts were broke, homesick, and disappointed and had begged, borrowed, or by some other means managed to gather the fare to get them home. By the same token, there were some gold seekers upon whom the fates had smiled. On their persons they wore money belts heavy with yellow gold from the mother lode. Additionally, the *Blade* carried a $153,000-consignment of gold for the San Francisco bankers, Page, Bacon & Company. This shipment was securely locked in the *Blade*'s below-deck specie tank.

One account in the San Francisco *Daily Alta California* described the departure of the four vessels and the subsequent procession as they moved past the city toward the Golden Gate as a "gala scene." Further reports in the same issue of the *Alta California* said that as the *Yankee Blade* reached Fort Point she "stopped her engines, and, allowing the *Sonora* to pass her, raised her flag as a challenge of speed, and then getting again headway, passed the *Sonora* at the bar. It was understood at San Francisco that a bet of $5,000 was pending on the race to Panama."

Thus, what was to be the *Yankee Blade*'s last voyage began. It started with pomp, excitement, and anticipation, and would end almost exactly 24 hours later with destruction, suffering, and death.

As the four steamers crossed the bar, they immediately encountered dense fog. On the *Goliah*, Captain Robert Haley immediately ordered the engines of his vessel slowed and watched the other three steamers disappear into the mist.

For Captain Randall of the *Yankee Blade* the fog was of little importance. He had a race to win and the limited visibility certainly wasn't cause enough to order his ship's paddle wheels slowed even by one revolution.

At nine that evening, as most of her passengers were preparing to bed down for the night, the *Blade*, still traveling at high speed through dense fog, passed another steamer. Though the vessel was believed to have been either the *Blade*'s fleet sister, the *Uncle Sam*, or the Pacific Mail steamer *John L. Stephens*, the visibility was so poor that an exact identification could not be made.

Meanwhile, Captain Haley of the *Goliah*, some miles astern of the *Blade* found the fog so heavy that he hove to in hopes that the visibility might improve before he attempted his approach to Monterey Harbor. After several hours with no change he continued on, slowly. The *Goliah* finally groped her way into Monterey the following morning. After discharging and unloading passengers and cargo, the *Goliah* cautiously departed Monterey about three in the afternoon. Just about the time Captain Haley was turning the *Goliah* southward toward her next port of call, Santa Barbara, Captain Randall and the *Yankee Blade* were, quite literally, running into big trouble.

The *Alta* published a letter on October 10, from the *Blade*'s purser, Samuel Vought. In it he gave his description of the wreck of the *Yankee Blade*.

> Oct. 1st, at 3 1/2 P. M., being encompassed in a dense fog and steering S.E. by S. course, and supposing ourselves at least 10 miles from shore, we struck a reef of Point Arquilla, about 15 miles above Point Conception, upon which the ship run upwards of 60 feet, while her stern swung in 9 fathoms water, which in less than 25 minutes sunk below the promenade deck, but so firmly was the forward part imbedded in the rocks, that up to the time we left the ship, (about 4 P. M. on the 2d inst.), she had not receded an inch, as soon as we were discovered to be in danger, the officers of the deck launched and manned the boats and, proceeded at once to get the ladies and passengers ashore.

As soon as the *Blade* struck, confusion reigned, as might be imagined, but order was quickly restored. Immediately, Captain Randall ordered the engines stopped and them attempted to back the *Blade* off the rocks. It is probably fortunate that this attempt was unsuccessful for when he went below to check the damage, he discovered a hole a foot wide and several feet long with the remainder of the ship's bottom being badly stove in. Had he been successful in backing off the rock, undoubtedly the *Yankee Blade* would have plunged to the bottom taking hundreds of her passengers with her.

Captain Randall directed the first officer to begin loading women, children and other passengers into the starboard-quarter lifeboat. When the craft was filled and being lowered from its davits, the aft tackle was accidentally released. As the stern fell, all those aboard the small boat were dumped into the churning sea. Only a few were saved. Some of the *Blade*'s crewmen—who had been oarsmen on the lifeboat—managed to

The steamer Yankee Blade. *Photo of a drawing by Heyl, 1949.*

clamber aboard the boat after it had fallen into the sea. After bailing out the small boat, they began rowing for shore where the boat was caught by the large surf and once again swamped. A second boat, which had been successfully launched with a full load of passengers, met the same fate in the breakers just a few minutes later. Total losses for the two landing attempts: perhaps as many as 30 men and women were drowned and two of the *Blade*'s three remaining lifeboats destroyed (one of the *Blade*'s boats had been smashed by large seas soon after she struck).

At this point Captain Randall felt that finding a safe place to land his passengers took precedence over the seafaring tradition of the captain being the last to leave a doomed vessel. The *Blade*'s jollyboat was launched, with Captain Randall in command. Though it was a small craft capable of carrying only 8 passengers, the Captain, with luck and skill, negotiated the churning surf and safely brought his boat and passengers ashore. He landed them on a small protected beach sheltered slightly by the rocks that had impaled the *Blade*. A short time later, the *Blade*'s last remaining lifeboat, guided by the steamer's third officer, safely brought its load of humanity to the small beach, too. Over the next few hours Captain Randall and his third officer used the two boats to ferry about 150 passengers to the safety of the tiny rock-rimmed beach.

During the time Captain Randall and his third officer had been transferring passengers to shore, the situation on board the *Blade* had seriously degenerated. When Captain Randall had personally begun handling the jollyboat and overseeing the rescue operations, he had left his teenage son in command of the *Blade*. Almost as soon as the captain left the ship, hoodlums made up of ruffians from steerage, as well as some members of the *Blade*'s own crew, had broken into the ship's liquor supplies and proceeded to help themselves. In short order, groups of drunken roughnecks were running wild throughout the ship. They broke into cabins and ransacked the belongings and luggage of the other passengers; anyone who attempted to stop them was attacked by the heavily armed pack and threatened with death. There were rumors that one or more passengers had been murdered below decks. Even the captain's cabin was breached. When he returned, he found his quarters plundered, with some $1,800 stolen from his

desk. Despite the hooligans' vigorous attempts, the gold cargo and the purser's vault were untouched since they were located in the stern section of the *Blade*, and that had sunk beneath the water and beyond their reach shortly after she had struck. Well before darkness fell, the entire promenade deck and all structures aft of the paddle wheels had been torn away by the violent seas.

The terror on board continued until approximately 10 o'clock that evening, when Captain Randall and the third mate returned to the ship. The captain's presence—and his revolver—helped calm the situation. As the remaining passengers jammed together in the *Blade*'s forward section and rigging, and prepared to settle in for the night, their hymns and prayers were punctuated by the tolling of the *Blade*'s bell as the swells rolled the ship on her rocky perch.

For the 150-or-so passengers who spent the night onshore the situation was only marginally better for, there too, ruffians held sway. Though the passengers who had been ferried to shore were mostly women and children, some of the rowdies had made it also. Once there, the hoodlums had commandeered all the baggage plus the provisions and materials that were brought ashore to provide shelter and sustenance for the castaways. Once they had the provisions under their control, they would release such items as extra clothing or blankets to keep off the foggy night chill, or a few cups of water to slake a castaway's brine-induced thirst, only after they received a substantial payment in gold, jewelry, or other valuables.

With the coming of dawn, Captain Randall and his staunch third officer commenced shuttling the remaining 800-plus passengers still on board the *Blade* to the beach. They had been at the task less than an hour when the steamer *Goliah*, under the command of Captain Haley, appeared on the scene.

On board the *Goliah* was passenger Major Horace Bell, who documented the *Yankee Blade* incident in his book, *Reminiscences of a Ranger* (1881). He describes the discovery of the *Yankee Blade* that morning with great feeling.

> . . . early on the second morning (we) ran
> into a heavy fog bank, and were feeling our
> way along carefully, when all at once we
> heard the roar of breakers on our port
> quarter, which created quite an alarm. (Cap-

The fatal rocks that are the final resting place for nearly a dozen ships, including the Yankee Blade. *Photo by Patrick Smith.*

tain) Haley at once commenced to change our course more to starboard, when, above the roar of the breakers, which was not heavy, we heard the cry of a thousand human voices for help. . . . Nothing is more solemnly terrifying than to be on shipboard near the breakers and in a fog bank, but add to this the knowledge of being in close proximity to a wreck is awe added to terror, and is paralyzing to the bravest heart. About the time we were headed off, the fog lifted almost perceptibly as the raising of a curtain, and lo! within a cable's length lay a large steamer, which proved to be the *Yankee Blade*, a hopeless wreck, her deck swept by the breakers and the hundreds of passengers in the rigging on the roofs and bridge, clinging to the rail and shrouds, presenting one of the most awful pictures one can well imagine.

When Captain Haley stated his intention to attempt a rescue of those aboard the unfortunate *Blade*, nearly all his officers advised against such a risky endeavor. But Captain Haley would not tolerate any dissenting opinions. His reply to the naysayers, according to Major Bell, was "There are over a thousand of them while there is less than a hundred of us, and if they are lost then we will go together."

Captain Haley's plan, though simple, required great skill and was not without considerable danger. After dropping the *Goliah*'s anchors, he backed the steamer down through the heavy seas and jagged outlying pinnacle rocks, to a point as close as possible to the *Blade*. Then a light line was floated across to the wreck. Those on board the *Blade* attached a large hawser to the line, which was then pulled back aboard the *Goliah* and made fast. By judicious use of his paddle wheels and by heaving in slack on the anchor windlass, Captain Haley created a taut hemp link between the wreck and the ship. Immediately, a shuttle of small boats began between the *Goliah* and the *Yankee Blade*. Much to Captain Haley's amazement the first boatloads of survivors were not women and children, but men--the toughs who had controlled and terrorized the passengers and crew of the *Blade*. Despite repeated pleas through his speaking trumpet for the women and children to be sent first, for the first hour of the rescue, the bullies commandeered every seat in each boat to the *Goliah*. When they assembled on board the little rescue steamer, they immediately attempted their old tricks. Major Bell described what happened:

> . . . those who had come on board took possession of the cabins, including the ladies', and when requested by Captain Haley to vacate in favor of the rescued women and children informed him that they had commanded "the *Yankee Blade* and while on board the *Goliah* would do as they thought proper."

Captain Haley called on some of the armed male passengers of the *Goliah* (several of which, like Captain Bell, were California Rangers) to attack the ruffians and drive them from the cabins into the confinement of the forward steerage compartment. The attack was carried out quickly and with complete success.

Since the *Goliah* was only one-third the tonnage of the *Blade*, she didn't have the capacity to carry all the wreck's survivors. In order to accommodate as many women, children, and men not associated with the troublemakers, as possible, Captain Haley had several of the armed California Rangers who had assisted with the toughs' capture transfer the ruffians from steerage to the small landing area on the beach. There they were deposited along with supplies, while the women and children landed the day before were gathered up and taken to the safety of the *Goliah*. Major Bell described the transfer thusly:

> All day the transfer of passengers went on, without an accident; all day the gallant *Goliah* groaned, labored and creaked, with waves sometimes breaking over bows and washing her decks. . . . at sunset the last soul on board the wreck had been safely trans-

ferred to the *Goliah*, nearly half of whom had been retransferred to the land, with water and provisions enough landed with them to do them for a day or two. . . . by this time the wind had commenced to blow, and by dark had become a gale, and by the time the *Goliah* was well clear of her dangerous neighbor, and before dark obscured our vision, the gallant *Yankee Blade*, with her golden treasure, broke in two amidships, and sunk. . . .

The *Goliah* beat her way south that stormy night and finally made the safety of Santa Barbara. After dropping part of her human cargo at that port she continued to San Pedro where more of the survivors chose to disembark. The remainder of the *Blade* passengers were taken to San Diego and placed ashore on October 4, while the doughty little *Goliah* resupplied, then headed north. Delayed 24 hours when the *Goliah* ran around in heavy fog coming out of San Diego Harbor, Captain Haley returned to the wreck site early on the morning of October 7. All those who had been landed on the beach—361 people—were rescued, then taken to San Francisco. As far as can be determined, there was no prosecution of any of those involved in the robberies, terrorism, and perhaps murder that occurred aboard the *Yankee Blade*.

Less than three weeks after the rescue, the Pacific Mail steamer *Carolina* was at the *Blade's* grave with divers and salvage equipment. High seas and foul weather thwarted this, the first of many salvage attempts on the *Yankee Blade*. But the lure of gold is strong, and within 13 months, San Francisco papers were reporting that the last of the documented gold had been recovered from the *Blade*. One of the retrievers of the *Blade's* gold? Why, none other than the *Yankee Blade's* old captain, Henry Randall! Despite the stated recovery of all the registered treasure from the wreck, the Santa Barbara and San Francisco papers periodically printed articles over the next several years mentioning the successful recovery of considerable sums of gold from the old hulk. Gradually, interest in the steamer waned and the *Blade* was pretty much left in peace until the Honda disaster of 1923 brought her name once more to the newspapers.

Ship's bell recovered from the Yankee Blade. *Photo from P. Smith collection.*

A brass signal gun, identified through serial numbers as having been the *Blade*'s was recovered by Captain G. H. Carlisle of the Santa Monica-based Fyhn Salvage Company. Captain Carlisle had been working under a Navy contract to remove all visible remains of the seven destroyers that had stranded there in September when he discovered the old muzzle loader and brought it to the surface. Though it is rumored that the old gun still survives and is somewhere in the southern California area, its location is unknown.

The *Yankee Blade* was built in the Williamsburg, New York, yard of Perine, Patterson & Stack, in 1853 for Edward Mills. She was a 1,767-ton wooden sidewheel steamer with three decks and three masts. The 274-by-34-foot vessel with her pair of 38-foot-diameter paddle wheels was powered by a single side-lever steam engine built by the Allaire Iron Works of New York City.

After her launching, the *Yankee Blade* made a single round trip from New York to Aspinwall (Panama) for the Independent Opposition Line, then sailed for the West Coast on February 2, 1854. With her arrival in San Francisco on May 4, 1854, she went into alternating service opposite the other Pacific representative of the Independent Opposition Line, the *Uncle Sam*. The *Yankee Blade* ran the San Francisco-Panama route

until she was lost north of Point Arguello in October of that year.

Diving the Yankee Blade

Because Honda is one the roughest and most remote dive locations in southern California, the myriad shipwrecks there don't receive the amount of attention wreck divers would like to give them. It is an area of jagged rocky shoreline, large violent seas and winds, and numerous dense, clinging fogs. Fogs of one-half-mile visibility or less occur twice as often in the Honda-Point Arguello area as they do at Point Conception, just 12 miles to the south. And these fogs have been the major factor in nearly every ship loss in the area, including the *Yankee Blade*. Nearly 60 miles northwest of Santa Barbara and 35 miles south of Port San Luis, Honda lies just about in the center of an area known as the Pacific Graveyard. And in the center of Honda, on its most exposed, outermost fang, lie the remains of the *Blade*.

A silver fork and spoon recovered from the Yankee Blade. *Photo from P. Smith collection.*

When Captain Randall drove the *Blade* onto those rocks more than a century and a quarter ago, he really did a job. Except for those cabins and deckhouses that were torn free and floated down coast, and those items that were eventually salvaged, everything else—machinery, anchors, fittings, baggage, coal, and engines—stayed right there. As the seas tore her hull apart, everything that made up the ship tumbled down the rocky pinnacle and came to rest on the sandy bottom some 60 feet below. While the engine and other large machinery tumbled to a stop slightly north of the rock, smaller items stayed on the base of the pinnacle. From about 30 feet on down to the bottom, the face of the rock is encrusted with conglomerate that is made up of all manner of *Blade* paraphernalia. Fastenings, keys and key tags, coins, pulleys, valves, hinges, drawer pulls, buttons, silverware, glass and china items, and so on are all embedded there like walnuts in a brownie. Higher up on the pinnacle lies one of the *Blade*'s huge anchors. Wedged in upside down, the flukes on this massive artifact span nearly 10 feet and its shank almost 12.

In early 1987, a survey boat for one of the oil companies in the area was running bottom-sample collections down coast from the *Blade* and perhaps discovered the final resting place of the deckhouses that were torn from the ship the night she struck. According to several sources, rotted wood, gold coins and nuggets were removed from the sampling device after a collection was made near Point Arguello. Requests by the oil company to run diving operations on the site were supposedly denied by the Air Force, which controls the area.

Even when conditions are calm enough to allow divers to reach the *Blade*, there are no guarantees as to visibility in the area. Honda Creek (which discharges just a few hundred yards north of the site) can play a major role in affecting visibility on the wreck. Often times, after rains, the creek will spew a muddy plume one-quarter mile offshore and several miles down coast, reducing visibility throughout the area to zero. Plankton blooms and surge also affect visibility, but despite all these factors visibility on the *Blade* averages about 10 feet with exceptional days ranging up to 40 feet.

Two aspects of the site that should be considered are the outlying pinnacle rocks and the rather stout currents that sometimes sweep the area.

Two portholes recovered from the sidewheel steamer Yankee Blade. *Note the wear on the ports caused by over a hundred years of sand and surge. Photo from P. Smith collection*

Though I have never heard of any diver's boat being lost at Honda, I have seen and heard of some close calls. It is a good idea before motoring into the area to hang offshore and observe a good number of the wave sets passing through. Many times it is possible to watch a half-dozen swells pass through and not see any indication of rocks. Yet in the wake of the next swell will be the telltale swirl that marks a hidden pinnacle. Because it so rare to be able to dive Honda, many divers whip their boats right in and anchor. But, beware: Without some careful observation before you drop that hook, you may come up from a dive to find that your boat has joined many other vessels in the Graveyard of the Pacific.

Though not encountered on every visit to Honda, the area rather commonly receives northerly currents of some strength. Velocities of over one knot are not unusual and create the kind of diving situation that could turn into an emergency very quickly. It has to be remembered that common sense in large doses and a lot of open-water diving experience are the keys to safe diving at Honda.

In the nearly three decades that the *Yankee Blade* has been dived regularly, many interesting artifacts have been recovered and saved from destruction (though most were badly worn by the constant sandblasting of the surge). Coins of gold and silver, portholes, silverware, cannons, fittings of all types, and a beautiful engraved bell nearly two feet high with the ship's name on it are just some of the interesting pieces recovered from the remains of the old paddle wheeler. But the funny thing is that after their initial visits, most of the divers who put out the time and effort to make the long difficult trip to the *Blade* (which usually is scrubbed because of rough seas or weather), seem to care less about the artifacts than about the experience of diving the old girl. Knowing her history and being able to swim through her remains is like reaching out and touching the past. Diving the *Yankee Blade* is a rare and heady episode for the experienced diver.

    P. S.

Nippon Maru

The evening of May 28, 1933, found the California coast from Point Piedras Blancas to San Pedro Harbor cloaked in heavy fog. As could be expected, the fog was especially dense between Point Conception and Point Arguello, in the area that marks the western approach to the Santa Barbara Channel. For the lighthouse keepers at Point Conception, the events of that night must have been like *deja vu*, for it was the same type of conditions that had preceded so many other maritime mishaps along this treacherous stretch of coastline.

It was just two days shy of two years since the posh coastal liner *Harvard* had plunged ashore and died on the reefs near Honda. Now the stage was set for the Pacific Graveyard's next victims to participate in its maritime *danse macabre*. So well hidden were the dangers of that jagged coast that on this night the Graveyard would claim three vessels. But no lives would be lost, and luck and hard work would allow two to escape. Only one ship would leave its bones to rust on the reefs of the Pacific Graveyard.

For Captain T. Oni of the Japanese oil tanker *Nippon Maru*, there was no warning of danger. One moment his vessel was moving slowly but steadily through the fog, and the next she was grinding across the reefs of Honda.

At 9:20 P.M. the *Nippon Maru*'s first distress call went out through the ether and was received by vessels and shore stations up and down the coast. The first vessel to respond to the SOS was the *Eyio Maru*. Though her position off the coast of British Columbia precluded her being of any assistance to a sister Japanese ship, response from other vessels closer to the scene was quick in coming. The Standard Oil Company tanker *D. G. Schofield* responded immediately after the *Eyio Maru*, reporting that she was only 12 miles away but involved in another emergency situation.

Just before the *Schofield* had received the distress signal from the *Nippon Maru*, she had been hailed from the fog by the damaged steam schooner *J. B. Stetson*. The *Stetson*'s captain advised the *Schofield* that he had just been involved in a collision with the steam schooner *Chehalis*. The *Stetson*'s captain went on to say that, although his vessel was damaged, it was in no danger of sinking. However, he felt that the *Chehalis* was in much worse shape and probably in danger of going down. Since neither the *Stetson* nor the *Chehalis* had wireless, the *Schofield* not only acknowledged the *Nippon Maru*'s call for assistance, but announced to the world the maritime mishap between the two lumber-carrying steamers as well.

At 9:25 P.M. a second call came from the *Nippon Maru*—"Quick relief please"—and then her signal faded away. This indicated to rescuers a loss of power and perhaps indicated the sinking of the vessel.

The Coast Guard immediately dispatched three cutters—the *Colfax*, *McLean*, and *Tamaroa*—to the *Maru*'s location. The *Schofield*, too, headed toward Honda after learning that the *Chehalis*'s captain had managed to beach the steamer within the relative safety of Cojo Anchorage. Ultimately, the *Chehalis* was removed intact from the beach, repaired, and placed back in service. The *J. B. Stetson* managed to limp down the coast and make port safely at Long Beach. She, too, was repaired and placed back in service, but her days were numbered. Just over one year later she stranded on Cypress Point, Monterey, and became a total loss.

Although the Coast Guard estimated they would arrive on the scene by 1:30 A.M., the dense fog slowed them considerably, and it wasn't until the next morning that help arrived for the *Nippon Maru*. The Coast Guardsmen and the crew of the salvage tug *Peacock* were amazed at the scene that greeted them when they finally discovered the *Maru*.

Because she had been traveling in ballast and drawing little water when she struck, the *Nippon Maru* had slid up and across the outermost reefs at Honda and practically dry-docked herself. She was sitting perfectly upright with nearly 70 feet of her keel completely out of the water and her bow jutting some 10 feet above the rocks. Reporters who arrived at Honda at about noon on the day following the wreck reported the ship appeared to be in good condition and holding up well. Aside from the obvious fact that she was on the rocks, the only other things of note that they spoke of were one lifeboat swung out amidships and prepared for launching, as well as a rather colorful red flag, quartered by a white cross, flying from the mast. None of the reporters realized that that flag was the International Code flag for the letter "V," whose meaning (an obvious understatement in this case) was: "I require assistance." Even though it didn't appear too bad to the reporters

from atop the shore cliff some 400 yards away, on board the *Maru* the situation was very bad.

Even with the calm sea conditions, there was considerable fear that the vessel would roll off her rocky roost into deep water, taking all on board with her, As a consequence, 35 of the *Nippon Maru*'s crewmen were transferred to the salvage tug *Peacock*, leaving only Captain Oni, his first mate, and two engineers on board to assist with any salvage attempts.

Within a few days, after the salvage crews and underwriters had a chance to evaluate the situation, a decision was reached: Since removing the *Nippon Maru* from the reef and refloating her were not possible, her equipment and fittings would be salvaged from her where she lay. Over the next few months, when the seas and weather allowed, salvors worked to remove any fittings and machinery of value from the battered *Maru*. This effort apparently went along rather well, for several months later a newspaper story revealed the salvors' intentions to begin cutting up the hull for steel. Their attempt lasted only one month, for on October 7, 1933, the tanker slipped from the rocks and joined numerous other ships in that watery graveyard known as Honda.

Inquiries into the cause of the wreck revealed that a rather severe error in navigation was the cause of the loss; in the fog, Point Arguello had been mistaken for Richardson Rock—an error of some 30-plus miles.

The *Nippon Maru several days after going aground and being abandoned. Note the absence of lifeboats. Photo from the Steamship Historical Society.*

The *Nippon Maru* was launched in 1919 from the Port Glasgow yard of R. Duncan & Company as the *Noma.* She was built for the Imperial Japanese Navy and, for her time, considered quite large. Her length and beam were 400.3 by 52.2 feet respectively, with her gross tonnage 5,842.

Sometime during the course of her career, she was passed to the Tokyo-based Iino Shoji K. K. Line, for whom she was working at the time of her loss.

Diving the Nippon Maru

Since she is considered less exciting than the Gold Rush-era steamer *Yankee Blade* and the seven United States destroyers that are wrecked nearby, divers rarely visit the *Nippon Maru.* Even though her bow is within a few feet of the props of the U. S. S. *Fuller,* seldom do divers venture the few extra feet to explore the rusty remains of the ex-Imperial Japanese Navy tanker. Precisely because she is less visited, the potential for discovering a unique or unusual artifact should be greater.

The *Nippon Maru* is an interesting dive with many areas of note. On the bow, some of the more obvious structures are her two huge anchors and piles of immense bar-link anchor chain. The individual links are about 18 inches long and must weigh 75 pounds apiece. This section lies in 25 to 30 feet of water and get quite surgey with any kind of a swell. Farther aft, in about 40 feet of water, the engine and boilers of the tanker can be found; these are always prime areas to look for unusual artifacts. One of the first things divers on the *Maru* usually find are the exposed hull plates with rows of portholes on them. Curiously, for a ship of this vintage, most of them are steel, not brass.

Conditions on the *Nippon Maru* are the same as those found on the *Yankee Blade* or the destroyers. Visibility ranges from 10 to 40 feet, with the average—20 feet—somewhat higher than the other sites because most of the wreckage is on a rocky bottom. Swells and surge, currents and offshore rocks, are all things to be considered when diving the *Nippon Maru.* The cautious diver can have a memorable visit to a prominent member of the Pacific Graveyard coterie.

P. S.

Point Conception to Santa Barbara

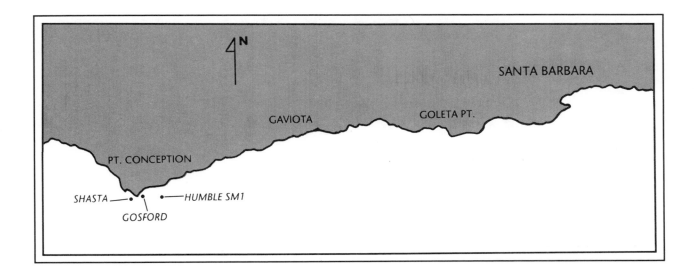

Shasta

Rocks, fog, and strong currents—the proven ingredients for maritime disaster—displayed their deadly efficiency once again in the early-morning hours of October 5, 1906. The victim this time was the 722-ton, two-masted, wooden steam schooner *Shasta*. Part of the E. K. Wood Lumber Company fleet, the steamer was northbound in ballast after discharging her cargo of northern California-redwood lumber at San Pedro. The trip had been uneventful until, upon reaching the western end of the Santa Barbara Channel, she encountered thick fog.

The Santa Barbara Channel is both the boon and bane of coastwise shipping; this 90-mile stretch of coastline runs east-west as opposed to the remainder of the California coastline, which generally runs north-south. This geological quirk requires northbound coastal traffic to bear to port (left) to enter the channel at the eastern end and requires a hard 90-degree turn to starboard to exit the western end at Point Conception. Any mistake in navigation made while transversing the eye of this nautical needle means disaster either on the rocks and reefs of the Channel Islands or on the coastal beaches.

The winds and weather of the channel can change rapidly, and they are always considered by cautious mariners when taking the "inside route." This phenomenon of quickly changing weather is most pronounced at the western end of the channel, in the Point Arguello-Point Conception area. It is not unusual to have calm seas with no wind at the eastern end, yet have Point Arguello reporting winds to 35 knots with 8- to 15-foot seas. I have seen the Point Conception area go from dead calm to 30+-mile-per-hour winds in less than 30 minutes. Add to this the dense channel fogs common much of the year, and one begins to see how the Santa Barbara Channel can sometimes be a very dangerous shortcut.

If the aforementioned problems aren't enough, there are the channel currents to consider. These are strong and change direction seasonally, making safe navigation quite difficult. For Captain Hansen, the skipper of the *Shasta*, the fogs and currents of the channel proved too much for even his years of coastal navigation experience. At 5 A.M. in one of the heaviest fogs seen in the area in some time, the *Shasta*

crashed ashore just a mile and a half east of the Point Conception Lighthouse.

Responding to the vessel's distress signals, the lighthouse keepers soon arrived on the scene but were unable to provide any assistance to the stranded ship or her crew. But soon thereafter, the southbound steamer *Roanoke*, also responding to the *Shasta*'s distress signals, arrived at the wreck site.

Setting about immediately, the *Roanoke*'s crew began a heroic but unsuccessful attempt to save the grounded *Shasta*. After twice managing to get cables aboard the crippled ship and breaking them each time, the attempts at saving the ship were temporarily abandoned. Instead, all of the *Shasta*'s crew members, except for two who remained on board to assist with further salvage attempts, were transferred to the *Roanoke*.

With the coming of daylight and a slight lifting of the fog, it became obvious that the *Shasta* had

Steam schooner Shasta *aground at Government Point. Photo from National Maritime Museum, San Francisco.*

reached her final port of call. Aside from a large hole gouged into her hull amidships, her back had broken and she was badly hogged; the tide moved freely through her hull. Toward evening, with the arrival of a salvage tug from Port Harford, it was decided to remove the remainder of the crew since it appeared as though the wreck might go to pieces at any moment.

With the last of her crew removed and the ship abandoned, one would think this would be the end of the *Shasta*'s story, right? Wrong!

It happened that at the time of the *Shasta*'s stranding the U. S. Navy's Pacific Fleet was anchored off Santa Barbara waiting for clear weather so that sea trials of the U. S. S. *California* (Armored Cruiser No. 6) could continue. Like men of action everywhere, the sailors of the fleet were bored with the inactivity forced upon them by the lingering, heavy fog. So when word came down coast of a ship in trouble, there was a clamor from the fleet's captains to be allowed to go to the rescue of the beleaguered vessel and its unfortunate crew. The ship chosen to make the run for glory was the destroyer U. S. S. *Preble*, commanded by Captain Freeman. Unfortunately for the good captain and his crew, word of the *Shasta*'s abandonment and the safe removal of her crew failed to reach them before they left on their mission of mercy. Nonetheless, it would prove to be an interesting voyage. The incidents experienced by the U. S. S. *Preble* and her crew are best related by the individual who played such a major part in them, Midshipman Pond.

He gave the following statement to the *Santa Barbara News Press* on October 9, 1906, some four days after the grounding of the *Shasta*.

After we worked off the sandbar on which we grounded soon after leaving Santa Barbara, the weather cleared somewhat, and by keeping close to the shore we managed to get inside the fog bank and work our way up the coast. It was very dark, however, and when we finally located the wreck we were not sure for a minute whether it was really the vessel or a large rock. She looked more like an overturned freight car than anything else, but I finally made out her masts, and Captain Freeman ordered me to take a boat and see if anyone was aboard, and whether we could be of any assistance.

At that time the fog had lifted, and the stars were plainly visible, but we hadn't got more than a few strokes from the ship when the fog closed down, snuffing everything out like a candle. We had no water or provisions in the boat, and no compass, but we managed to grope our way through the darkness and finally found ourselves right in the face of a heavy surf.

The water round us seemed fairly smooth, and I noticed that there was a great deal of floating oil. We thought that this came from sunken wells, but it afterwards turned out to be the overflow from the *Shasta*'s tanks, and to this we probably owe our safety, as the surf was running very high on the rocks.

All of a sudden, the hull of the schooner loomed up through the fog right ahead of us. She was what we call "hogged," that is, her keel was broken upwards. When we were right aboard she gave a lurch, and I thought for a moment she was going to roll off the rocks and swamp us, but she righted, and by going to the shore side we were able to climb aboard. I sent two men aboard, but after waiting several minutes and hearing nothing from them, I followed to see what was the matter.

The *Shasta* was fast breaking up on the rocks, and her timbers were being ground like matchwood. I saw at once that she was a hopeless wreck, and after seeing for myself that no one was aboard, I annexed a compass which I found aboard and we took to the boat.

All this time the moon and one star showed dimly through the fog, and I was able to make some kind of a line with them. The tide was so strong, however, that we were carried off the course I had laid, and it was some time before we located the *Preble* by her siren, which Captain Freeman had kept going all the time the boat had been away.

So the *Preble*'s run for glory came to naught, and, seemingly, the only one to benefit from the whole episode was Midshipman Pond, who came away with his "annexed" compass. Logically, one might assume that now, with her going to pieces on the rocks, no cargo on board, and the crew all safe, the *Shasta* would be left to die in peace; but tragically this was not the case.

Soon after her abandonment another salvage effort was attempted from the beach. Huge timbers were sunk into the low cliff just above the beach to act as anchors to support the salvage lines rigged out to the ship. The price for the few metal parts and fittings salvaged before the enterprise was called off would be very high: a man's life.

Every day at high tide, members of the salvage crew would row out to the remains of the *Shasta* and remove any thing of value they could find and send it to shore via the salvage lines rigged between the ship and the beach. One day, when the channel waters were particularly nasty, the rowboat overturned; one of the men was trapped beneath it and drowned. He became the only casualty of the shipwreck.

After this tragedy, the *Shasta* was finally abandoned to the harsh elements of the area. In a short time the sea removed any visible traces of the wreck.

Early in the 70s, while researching shipwrecks in the Santa Barbara area, I had the opportunity to speak with some of the old-time commercial abalone divers. Though most of these guys have vast amounts of knowledge and information concerning locations of wrecks and reefs, for the most part they are unwilling to divulge any information. I finally located one laconic old salt, who, though he wouldn't provide specific locations, would confirm wreckage or debris in certain general areas.

"Wreckage? Yah, I've seen wreckage, sort of around Point Conception."

So, with "confirmation" like that combined with previous research, a group of us scheduled the Santa Barbara-based charter boat *Hurricane* for an early-November dive.

Our plan was to explore the exposed coast between Point Conception and Government Point early in the day. Later, when the wind picked up in the afternoon, we would move inside Cojo Anchorage and look for the remains of a barge rumored to lie in about 50 feet of water.

On our arrival at Point Conception, we found calm seas with clear, bright blue skies and a current of several knots. Deciding to forgo the experience of diving in currents of that velocity, we turned and headed eastward, scanning the rocky beach for some indication of shipwreck, while searching for an area protected from the screaming current. We had covered the entire distance from Point Conception to Cojo Anchorage and were just coming around Government Point when some heavy timbers were spotted protruding from the top of a low cliff just behind the point. These indicated that we had found the wreck of the *Shasta*. Being so close to the beach and in the lee of the point seemed to reduce the current to an acceptable level. After carefully metering the area to find a safe spot to anchor, we dropped the hook. As soon as the engines were shut down, eager wreck divers began hitting the water.

On entering the water, I was delighted to find visibility of nearly 30 feet and a slight surge—just about the best conditions one can expect in the area.

Since the *Shasta* had grounded and then pounded to pieces on the rocks, we snorkeled in and began our search in about 15 feet of water. Within a few minutes, as we picked our way toward the beach, we began finding remains. The bottom was composed of coarse sand and gravel with many large and medium-sized boulders strewn about. As I moved through the area I could see many pieces of iron and brass piping wedged among the rocks. The brass and bronze pieces of wreckage were especially noticeable since the constant sand movement caused by surge had polished them to a bright golden hue.

I found what appeared to be the *Shasta*'s firebox; it now served as a cozy home for a homely group of monkeyface eels. Farther along, a large portion of the ship's propeller lay in the rocks. Apparently the force of its striking the bottom had shattered it into many pieces, for I found several pieces of surf-worn bronze scattered about. As I was re-examining the larger piece of the prop, I noticed that there was writing under the light sea growth on one side. I marked the piece with a popper float and went to recruit lift bags and bodies to help get the piece back to the boat.

Diver Alan Davis with engine builder's plate from the steam schooner Shasta. *Photo by Patrick Smith.*

Back at the *Hurricane* one of the divers, Alan Davis, had recovered quite a find. Searching the surgey shallows, he had noticed a sheet of brass sticking out of the boulder-strewn bottom. When he tried to drag it loose, he found that he could move it only slightly before it wedged in against the imprisoning boulders. After an hour and 40 minutes of prying, cursing, digging, and lifting the smaller rocks out of the way, he pulled the brass free and shook off the sand. It had been worth the effort; through the light verdigris he read:

Marine Engine No. 190
Built By
Fulton Iron Works
San Francisco, California
1904

It was the builder's identification plate from the *Shasta's* main engine, a fantastic piece of California's maritime history.

I recruited Mike Johnson and Larry Akers along with their lift bags for the assault on the prop piece. Just as we were ready to go, Mike pointed out my float and two lift bags in convoy back toward the *Hurricane*. We shucked our gear and moved down on the swim step to lend a hand getting the piece aboard. Pat Gibson, Bill Wilson, and Steve Giles had wrestled the 170-pound chunk of prop under the lift bags and swam it more than 100 yards back to the boat, because, they explained, "it was on the way."

By this time the tide had dropped and the surge over the *Shasta's* final resting place was becoming too strong. The anchor was pulled and the *Hurricane* moved inside Cojo Anchorage in search of the barge wreck.

Diving the Shasta

Though there is not much left of the *Shasta* structurally, she is an interesting dive and quite typical of a shallow water, rocky-coast-type wreck. Because of her exposed location and the sand-and-gravel bottom, fittings and artifacts are uncovered with each storm or period of large swells that hits the area. This circumstance makes each dive on the *Shasta* interesting and exciting—almost like diving a new wreck on each visit.

And so the *Shasta* lies, her remains scattered along a hostile rocky coast, forgotten by all save a few hardy souls who visit her when wind and weather allow.

P. S.

Gosford

More than 300 miles from the nearest land, and your ship is a raging inferno below decks: hardly an enviable position that was faced by Captain William Chatman of the barque-rigged ship *Gosford* in November 1893. She was bound for San Francisco from Birkenhead, England, with 3,600 tons of coal, consigned to the Spreckles Company. Whether the coal was to power Spreckles's steamers to the Hawaiian Islands or to be sold locally to heat the mansions of Nob Hill and the bordellos of the Embarcadero hadn't been decided, but now it was a moot point—the coal, the vessel that carried it, and the crew that manned the vessel were all at risk.

The voyage had been a fairly easy one, with no thought of disaster so near the end of it. But on Saturday, November 18, 140 days out of Birkenhead, smoke was discovered seeping from one of the cargo areas. The hatch was unbattened and the covers removed, revealing a scene akin to something from Dante's *Inferno*.

This type of situation among vessels carrying cargoes of soft coal was quite common. Soft coal has a disquieting habit of spontaneous combustion when it becomes the least bit damp. As can be imagined, the holds of most vessels could be expected to be exposed to more than a little dampness.

The handsome British barque Gosford. *Photo from Allen Knight Museum.*

There were two ways to handle a fire in the hold. The first was to keep the hatches sealed, perhaps pumping chemicals into the area, in an attempt to smother the fire. For vessels like the *Gosford*, which had flammable wooden decks, there were obvious drawbacks to this method. The second way was to open the hatches, dig down among the coal until the burning area was located and staunch the fire with water or chemicals. The problem with this method was that it required the crew to work in restricted areas filled with poisonous gases and to move tons of coal by hand.

Acting quickly, Captain Chatman ordered a skeleton crew to handle the sails and steer the ship, while the remainder of the crew was split into two work parties: one formed a bucket brigade to halt the spread of the flames and the other group manned the pumps. The *Gosford*'s course was changed to due east so as to make landfall as soon as possible, and, as a precaution, the ship's boats were lowered and supplied with provisions and water so as to be ready to leave at a moment's notice.

A fire at sea with flammable cargo aboard is the nightmare of all mariners. Captain Chatman and the crew of the *Gosford* valiantly fought the flames for several days almost without rest, but the situation only worsened. Although the flames were still contained below decks, some portions of the hull were glowing cherry red; it would probably be only a short time until the flames broke out on deck and began consuming the thousands of square feet of sails and cordage, or until the seams of the ship opened from the intense heat.

Then, when it seemed all hope was gone, the situation took a turn for the better. Almost at the same time that the *Gosford*'s lookout sighted the unique silhouette of Point Conception, the steam schooner *Caspar* hove into sight and offered assistance, which was readily accepted. Since the *Caspar* wasn't set up to fight the fire, she accepted a line from the *Gosford* and towed her to the only shelter within 35 miles, Cojo Anchorage, just a mile and a half east of Point Conception.

It was Wednesday, November 22; the fire had been raging within the *Gosford* for five days with the crew unable to gain any advantage. But now that help was at hand, there was hope that perhaps the *Gosford* and most of her cargo could be saved.

With the smoke pouring from her hull, the *Gosford* made a highly visible beacon, and even before she got her anchor down in Cojo, two other ships arrived on the scene to offer help: the steam schooner *McArthur* and the passenger liner *Santa Rosa*. As the crew of the *Gosford* gathered whatever personal items they could and began transferring to the *Caspar*, the captain of the *Santa Rosa* sent a boat over to offer Captain Chatman assistance. Captain Chatman declined, saying that his vessel was in shallow water where, should she sink, she might be saved; but until tugs with fire-fighting equipment arrived, he and his crew would do what they could.

With the *Caspar* and the *McArthur* standing by, Captain Chatman and his crew returned to the *Gosford* and continued their efforts to control the blaze. At about 10 o'clock that evening, the tug *Monarch* arrived on the scene after receiving the word from the *Santa Rosa* on her arrival in Santa Barbara. She, too, offered assistance, but it was too late; the flames were out of control, and there was no hope of subduing them. By 1 A.M., Captain Chatman and his crew had abandoned ship; the *Gosford* was left to burn. When the *Monarch* headed for Santa Barbara later that morning, the third mate and 20 of the *Gosford*'s crew went with her, leaving Captain Chatman, the first mate, seven apprentice seamen, three AB's, and the boatswain on the *Caspar* to watch over the furiously burning *Gosford*. Later that day the tug *Fearless*, dispatched from San Francisco, arrived on the scene and began pouring water on the blazing ship.

A message from the small village of Gaviota, ten miles east of Point Conception, reported that on the evening of the 23rd, "the flames and smoke were rolling out fiercely at 5 o'clock . . . the masts were still standing, but the deck had gone in and all the sails and rope rigging had burned off." It continued, "The tug *Fearless* had pumped water into the vessel for three hours, with no apparent result, then hauled off and anchored in the vicinity."

On the morning of the 24th, the fire in the main cargo hold began to die down. As the hull plates started to cool, they began to contract, creating openings along every seam of every plate. The sea began filling her hull and within a short time the *Gosford* had sunk in six fathoms of water, with only her masts and a small portion of her bow visible above the surface.

Prowling the Gosford. *Photo by Patrick Smith.*

The *Gosford*, hull number 299, was launched on December 7, 1891, at Greenock, Scotland, by Scott & Company for Francis Briggs of Edinburgh, managing owner of Briggs, Harvie & Company. One of three identical sister-ships, she was a handsome, steel, four-master involved in general cargo trade. She had yet to complete her second voyage when she was lost at Cojo. She was a good-sized vessel, her dimensions being 281.6 feet in length, 42.3 feet in breadth, drawing 24.4 feet of water, and 2,251 gross tons. She was well built with the best materials available by skilled Scottish shipwrights; this was verified by Lloyds of London who issued their highest rating, +100A1, to the *Gosford*.

Since she was built at a cost of $150,000 and was less than two years old, salvors on the *Monarch* felt it likely that the *Gosford* could be raised, refurbished, and placed back in service. The plan for raising the *Gosford* involved building a wooden cofferdam around her sunken hull, pumping it out, applying patches or seals enough to float the vessel, then towing her to San Francisco for repairs.

The project started with a lot of enthusiasm. Two tugs, the *Fearless* and the *Monarch*, along with divers, equipment, fastenings, and timbers brought up from Santa Barbara began the job. However, problems arose, and when funds began to run out, the project of salvaging the entire ship was abandoned. Seven months after she went down, the following announcement appeared in the Santa Barbara *Morning Press*, "Preparations are being made near Point Concepcion (sic) to blow up the wreck of the *Gosford* with dynamite. The Spreckles tug *Fearless* has been sent down. Captain D. H. Haskell will superintend the work."

So, like her two sister vessels—the *Gifford*, lost in 1903 at Mussel Rock, near San Francisco, and the *Gunford*, lost at Cape San Roque in 1907—the *Gosford* became a total loss.

She was pretty much forgotten, except for those freelance salvors who, throughout the remainder of the 1890s and into the 1900s worked the *Gosford* along with the *Goldenhorn* and the *Winfield Scott* for whatever they could find of value. After the early 1900s, almost all interest in the *Gosford* disappeared. By the early 1970s her name and how she came to be in Cojo were totally lost.

A few people, mostly commercial ab divers, were aware of the wreck in Cojo, but speculation was that it was a scrapped oil barge; or, one rumor was that it was a barge full of Honda motorcycles that had been lost after being towed over from Japan.

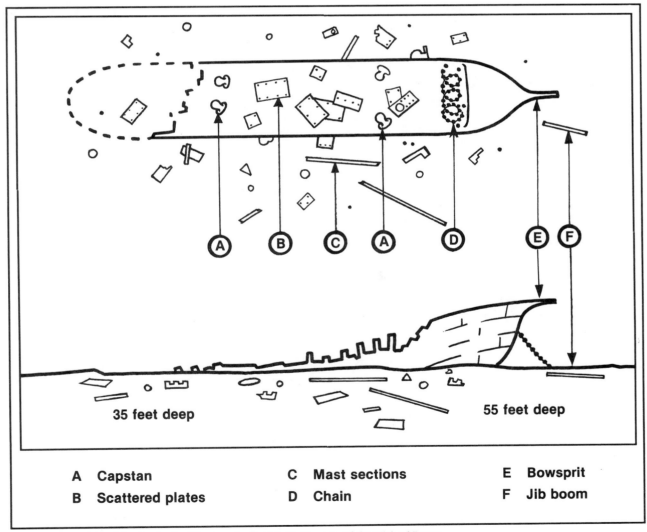

A	Capstan	C	Mast sections	E	Bowsprit
B	Scattered plates	D	Chain	F	Jib boom

Shipwreck diagram of the Gosford. *Diagram by Patrick Smith, redrawn by Michael Brown.*

Diving the Gosford

I first dived the *Gosford* in November of 1973, almost 80 years to the day of her loss. A group of us had chartered the dive boat *Hurricane* from Santa Barbara to check the Point Conception and Cojo Anchorage areas for wrecks. The "old barge" in Cojo was one of the wrecks we were trying to find.

The first part of the day went well with the discovery of the steam schooner *Shasta* on Government Point. When the wind and swell began to pick up later in the morning the *Hurricane* moved into the protection of Cojo and we began metering for the barge. Within ten minutes we came across a good reading near a large kelp bed. Centering the *Hurricane* over the spot, the captain suggested that a buddy team go down and make sure that the reading wasn't just a reef.

Steve Giles and I were chosen to be the gofers. We hit the water, and as the bubbles cleared we found we had nearly 40-foot visibility. The area indicated by the captain had a heavy canopy of giant kelp (*Macrocystis pyrifera*) that shadowed the area beneath it. We had snorkeled nearly to the edge of the kelp before our eyes could penetrate the dimness. What we saw when our eyes adjusted is a memory that will stay with me forever. There, less than 20 feet below us, was the bow of a sailing ship so beautifully intact that her bow sprit, dolphin striker, and cat heads were still in place. After announcing the discovery to the rest of the group waiting anxiously on board the *Hurricane*, Steve and I began our descent.

We quickly surveyed the bow section, then began moving toward the stern to determine how large and intact she was. Through the screen of kelp-filtered light, it wasn't hard to imagine her as she once was; her hull was surprisingly intact, though inside she was mostly rubble and thousands of long abandoned shellfish homes. The masts and yards lay strewn about the hull, some of them lying nearby on the sand bottom. On the port side of the hull we came across what looked like a convention of cauliflowers. In a ten-foot square area were dozens of the huge,

fluffy, white *Metridium* anemones, all leaning toward a central point as if in conference about the bubble-blowing intruders who had invaded their domain.

Examining the interior of the hull in greater detail, we discovered pieces of the ship's cargo strewn about. Many of the larger pieces of coal provided support for the kelp holdfasts; but in some cases when a plant grew too large for its coal anchor, it would float the piece off the bottom and the coal would hang suspended, looking like the fruit of these undersea redwoods.

From the information obtained from this trip, it was possible to discover the *Gosford*'s name and how she met her end. On subsequent dives, many different types of artifacts have been recovered: portholes; the ship's binnacle; compass and compass gimbal; melted portions of the ship's bell; 8-inch brass letters, which were probably part of the *Gosford*'s name or home port; capstan covers; ornate coathooks and drawer pulls; plus all manner of melted brass, some of it quite beautiful.

Conditions on the *Gosford*, because of her location within the protection of the anchorage, are never very bad, but large swells can reduce visibility to 5 feet or less. Usual visibility in the area is about 15 feet, though days of 30 or 40-foot visibility are common.

Because of the way she lies, depth around the wreck varies. In the bow, at the stem, the sand has been eroded to nearly 50 feet. At the stern, where there has been an accretion of sand, the depth can be as little as 28 feet.

For the photographer or hunter, the *Gosford* provides tangible satisfaction. The photographer will find all manner of subjects both macro and standard, from the picturesque bow of the wreck itself to colorful *Corynactis* and nudibranchs. For the hunter, large kelp bass are common all over the wreck, while the sand around the *Gosford* is a consistent producer of banquet-sized halibut. The reefs nearby are home to large succulent red abs. What more could any diver ask? The *Gosford* is one wreck that has something for every diver's interest.

P. S.

Humble SM-1

There was both good news and bad news on Thanksgiving Day 1961. The bad news was that the autumn storm pounding the southern California coast had claimed the oil-drilling vessel *Humble SM-1* off the northern Santa Barbara coast. The good news was that no lives were lost in the sinking—definitely a day for thanksgiving.

The *Humble SM-1* began her life as *LSM 251* (Medium Landing Ship) for the U. S. Navy. According to government records, she was built and launched by the Western Pipe and Steel Company of San Pedro, California. She was one of hundreds of Medium Landing Ships built by smaller shipyards for the navy throughout the course of World War II.

LSMs were self-propelled craft used extensively as amphibious troop and vehicle transports in the European, North African and Pacific theaters during World War II. These versatile vessels were primarily used to move men, vehicles, equipment, and supplies from navy transport ships to the beaches. LSMs are described in *Jane's Fighting Ships* as 203.5 by 34.5 feet, drawing 7.3 feet of water, and carrying a complement of 4 officers and 48 crew. It is also noted that to enhance their amphibious capabilities, LSMs, like submarines, were able to modify their displacement by pumping water into and out of ballasting compartments. *Jane's* gives tonnage figures for the maximum and minimum displacement capabilities of LSMs: 743 tons is listed as beaching displacement; and 1,095 tons, full displacement. Powered by twin 800-horsepower diesels, LSMs were only capable of 12 knots, but they had been designed primarily for capacity, not speed. In their open tank-well, they were able to accommodate 12 tanks or other vehicles, or the equivalent in equipment or troops. Standard armament was a pair of 40-mm anti-aircraft guns, but modifications and enhancements to LSM weaponry were commonplace.

Since the *LSM 251* was launched so early in the war, it is very likely that she saw some action. In 1950, like many other veterans, the *LSM 251* left the military for civilian life. Records show her being purchased by the Irwin Lyons Lumber Company of Coos Bay, Oregon for use as a coastal freighter. Along with her new career she received a new name: *North Bend*. Less than two years later, the *North Bend* changed owners and names again. Coming under the direction of the Oceanside Lumber Company of Astoria,

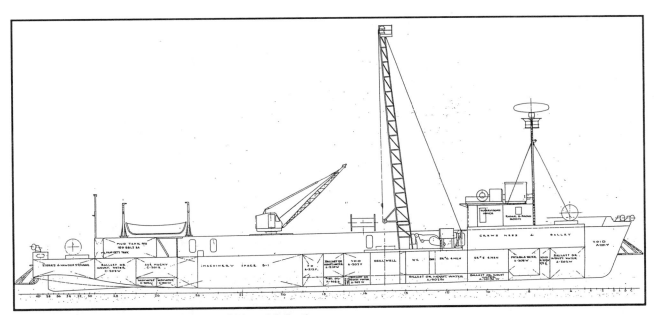

Yard drawing of drill ship SM-1. Courtesy of M. and J. Bastian.

Oregon, she continued service as a coastal freighter for the remainder of 1952 and then was laid-up, out of service. In 1956 she was sold once again, this time to the Humble Oil Company. Humble brought the old landing ship south to Todd Shipyards Corporation in San Pedro where plans were drawn up to convert the veteran navy ship/freighter to a state of the art, self-contained oil drilling rig.

Modifications to the ship included the creation of an on-board medical facility, a modern, expanded galley, diving locker, bunk areas for 24 crewmen, the addition of two 5-ton cranes, the removal of the ship's engines and their replacement with the compressors, mud and hydraulic pumps required for drilling, and perhaps most impressive, the addition of a drill well or moon pool. This was a nine-foot diameter opening from the main work deck completely through the hull and out the bottom of the ship. Through this well, with the 75 foot derrick-like draw works mounted nearby, workers could place or remove drill pipe or other equipment with ease and efficiency. On deck were mounted the enormous winches required for placing and holding the vessel in the multi-point moors required for underwater drilling operations. The modification also called for the removal of the landing ship's bow doors and their replacement with a more practical non-opening structure. In doing this, several feet were trimmed from the vessel's length giving her new dimensions of 192.6 by 34 feet with a 10.7 foot draft. Her gross tonnage in this new configuration was 735. By the time all the work was completed, the old *LSM 251* was virtually a new ship. When she appears in the records again in 1957, she again had a new name—*Humble SM-1*—and a new career to go with it.

In the 50s, the science of offshore drilling was in its infancy, and, with her modifications complete, the *SM-1* was the cutting edge of that technology. In fact, according to longtime commercial diver Woody Treen, the *SM-1* was the vessel that placed the first viable, underwater production well off Santa Barbara; it may have been the first well of its type in the world.

In November, 1961, the *SM-1* (then a unit of Global Marine Corporation and on lease to Texaco) was operating east of Government Point near the present location of Platform Herman. Anchored in a six-point moor, she had her bow to the northwest so as to face into the prevailing winds and seas. On the 25th, the crew was taken by surprise as a violent southeaster swept in with high winds and violent seas; the ship was in absolutely the worst possible position to face such a storm. The large seas inundated the exposed stern of the *SM-1*, and the solid six-point moor held her exposed to the onslaught. The sea found its way below through some usually protected hatches, and flooded out the ship's power systems. The loss of power was the beginning of the end for the *SM-1*.

On board at that time were 1,200 feet of 10 3/4" heavy-wall drill pipe along with many tons of drilling mud and bagged cement. As the waves flooded into the *SM-1* and she settled lower into the large seas, the crew attempted to dump some of the weighty cargo she carried. But without power to operate the cranes, it was a hopeless task. Without power they were helpless to drop their moorings as well; they were trapped, unable to fight or run. As the ship took on more and more water, her stability degenerated, and eventually her list was great enough to cause her cargo of pipe and cement to shift. The *SM-1* turned turtle and disappeared beneath the waves. Fortunately, all of those onboard the *SM-1* were quickly rescued by the oil company crewboat *Helen* and safely conveyed to Santa Barbara.

Woody Treen held the diving contract on board the *SM-1* but wasn't on board at the time of her

One of the galley-area portholes, deep inside the *SM-1*. Photo by M. and J. Bastian.

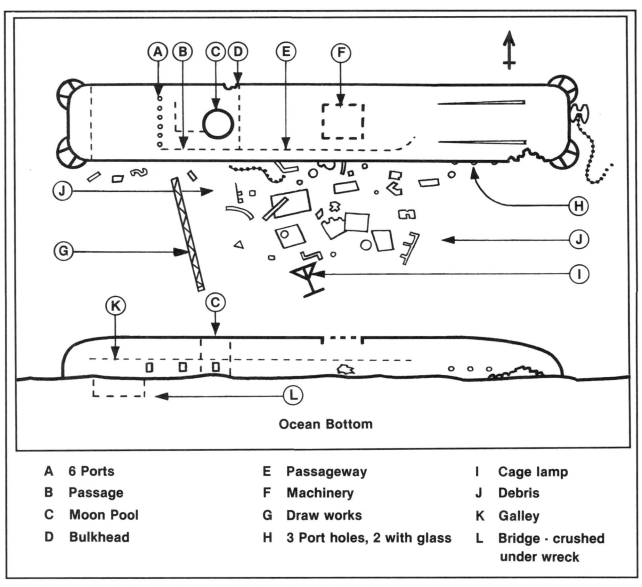

A	6 Ports	E	Passageway	I	Cage lamp
B	Passage	F	Machinery	J	Debris
C	Moon Pool	G	Draw works	K	Galley
D	Bulkhead	H	3 Port holes, 2 with glass	L	Bridge · crushed under wreck

Wreck diagram of SM-1. *Drawing by M. and J. Bastian, redrawn by Michael Brown.*

loss. Several days earlier, he had been injured when he was struck in the eye by a steel splinter. He was ashore recuperating when he received a call from his diving tender telling him of the sinking. When the *SM-1* made her plunge, she had taken two sets of Woody's hard-hat gear including compressors and miscellaneous tools and equipment to the bottom with her.

As soon as the weather allowed, Texaco sent commercial diver Pete Brumis down on the *SM-1* to recover some special, very expensive well-head equipment. In exchange for this recovery, Brumis was granted salvage rights to the rest of the ship. An attempt was made to recover the mud pumps and some of the other machinery on board by cutting into the machinery spaces through the bottom of the ship. How successful his effort was isn't known, but it certainly provided an excellent access for sport divers who would explore her later.

Interest waned in the drill ship until she was rediscovered by divers in the 70s. Though not widely known except by Santa Barbara locals, the *SM-1* is a popular but demanding wreck dive and a consistent producer of interesting artifacts.

Diving the Humble SM-1

Located just a short distance off Cojo Anchorage, the *Humble SM-1* is one of the prime coastal wreck dives in Santa Barbara County. She lies upside-down in 70 to 75 feet of water with her keel about 25 to 30 feet off the bottom. Visibility on the wreck ranges from 5 to 40 feet with 25 feet about average. The bottom in the area is sand and shale with many small kelp-covered reefs. Like most deeper water wrecks, the *SM-1* has become the focal point for most marine life in the area. The wreck is covered with a large living carpet of multi-hued *Corynactis* and all manner of invertebrates. Isolated clumps of the usually snowy-white *Metridiums* are stained reddish-brown from the rust they absorb from the *SM-1's* hull. The wreck also provides footing for a substantial amount of kelp (*Macrocystis*) which in turn provides shelter for vast numbers of kelp bass, rockfish and perch. The scattered wreckage on the bottom provides comfortable shelter for tasty lingcod and cabezon as well as some very shy lobster.

Because the *SM-1* is still relatively intact, penetration dives are possible, though not recommended. Access to the wreck's innards is not difficult thanks to the moon pool and the openings cut by salvager Pete Brumis. Some local divers who have studied blueprints of the ship have made penetration dives and recovered some very nice artifacts. Efforts by ex-

perienced divers in the mid-80s produced several beautiful, eighteen-inch, four loop-dog ports from the galley area on the wreck. Other divers have recovered large brass fire alarm stations. Amazingly, after being cleaned, soaked in fresh water and dried, these units worked when hooked to power after 25 years underwater. However, without the knowledge, experience and equipment, any attempt at entering the wreck is just foolhardy. The inverted hull with its maze of black, silt-laden passages could quickly become the last dive for one not prepared.

But a penetration of the *SM-1* isn't required to come up with an impressive recovery. Divers working around the collapsed draw works on the bottom off the starboard side of the ship have recovered beautiful, heavy brass lamps that are truly impressive when cleaned and polished.

Several years ago a local diver discovered one of Woody Treen's "light" commercial weightbelts on the wreck. The belt, which carried more than 60 pounds of lead, was recovered and returned to the surprised commercial diver. He was quite pleased to get it back after 20 years. The question remains, though: "What happened to the rest of the hard hat gear that was on board the *SM-1*?" The most likely answer is that it is still there, buried by equipment when the ship rolled over and covered by silt since. Perhaps the most exciting recovery a wreck diver could make would be one of the beautiful copper and brass helmets that were the commercial diver's mainstay for so many years. The *SM-1* is one of the few wrecks on the coast that might provide such an artifact.

P. S.

Santa Barbara to Point Dume

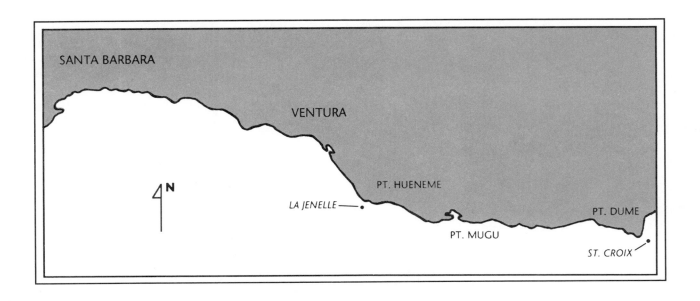

La Jenelle

Her career spanned four decades and during it she would be known by five different names. Built by the Bethlehem Shipbuilding Corporation, Ltd., in Quincy, Massachusetts, she was christened the *Borinquen* on September 24, 1930. She was 465 feet, 11 inches long with a beam of 59 feet, 10 inches. Her twin turbins, geared to a single screw, easily moved all 17,114 gross tons of her. From 1930 until 1949 she was a New York and Puerto Rico Steamship Company vessel, carrying passengers and freight between New York and South America with stops at Caribbean islands.

The Bull Steamship Company purchased the *Borinquen* in 1949 and renamed her *Puerto Rico.* As she had for the previous 19 years, she carried freight and passengers between the East Coast and South America, with stops in the Caribbean.

Arosa Lines bought the *Puerto Rico* in 1954 and renamed her *Arosa Star.* She was converted to a cruise ship and plied the waters of the Caribbean.

In 1960, the 30 year old ship was sold to the Eastern Shipping Corporation. Now named the *Bahama Star*, she carried passengers on three to five day Bahamas Islands cruises from a home port of Miami, Florida. The highlight of her career would occur just five years later, on November 13. On this date she and the S. S. *Finnpulp* rescued passengers and crew members from a holocaust aboard the *Yarmouth Castle.*

The 38-year-old *Yarmouth Castle* had left Miami for the Bahamas just a few hours before she caught fire. The label applied to her nearly three months earlier by California Congressman William S. Mailliard—he said she was a "shining example of a ship not in proper condition to engage in cruise trade"—proved to be all too true. Wood paneling in the staterooms and combustible furniture found throughout the ship fueled the flames. Many of the *Castle*'s lifeboats could not be launched. There were no life preservers in the cabins, nor were there life rings on the decks.

Lucky for most of those aboard the *Yarmouth Castle,* there were two other ships nearby. The *Bahama Star* and the *Finnpulp* raced to the rescue, arriving in time to launch their lifeboats and save 329 of the 489 passengers and crew.

Only four hours after the fire started, the *Yarmouth Castle* sank. The *Bahama Star* came so close to the

The end of the line for the ship La Jenelle. *Battered and broken on her beam ends, she's only a few months away from becoming a rock-filled jetty on the north side of Port Hueneme. Photo by Patrick Smith.*

blazing *Castle* that the paint on her stack blistered. Only a year younger that the *Castle*, she was similar in design.

The Geneva Conference of 1964 had outlawed the building of wooden superstructures such as those on the *Star* and the *Castle* and the *Star* needed very expensive alterations to bring her up to code. Instead of renovating the 36 year old cruiser, Eastern Shipping sold her to Sorenson and Bayles. Planning to convert her into a floating restaurant, her new owners renamed her *La Jenelle* and moved her to California. While they were searching for a suitable berth, Sorenson and Bayles anchored *La Jenelle* off Port Hueneme, California. On April 13, 1970, during a northwest gale, she dragged anchor and went aground just west of the Port Hueneme breakwater. A helicopter rescued her stranded crew, but there was no way to save her.

Close to shore, *La Jenelle* became another star—a star attraction. Unfortunately, she was a dangerous star. People removed whatever they could and a fire—apparently started by vandals—destroyed her interior. After one man fell off the wreck and drowned, providing fodder for a lawsuit, her owners disappeared. Eventually, the Navy was called in to dispose of her. Her superstructure was cut off, towed to 90 feet of water and sunk. Boulders filled what was left and *La Jenelle* became a new arm of the Port Hueneme breakwater. Later, the point on which the ship ran aground and the beach area on either side became La Jenelle Park.

The La Jenelle *wharfside in Port Hueneme, awaiting conversion to a floating restaurant—the beginning of the end. Photo by W. Bitters from the P. Smith collection.*

When it's really calm, snorkelers and scuba divers can visit the *La Jenelle*. Very little of the ship is visible. Because of the boulders, the area is said to be good lobster hunting territory. Because it's so close to shore, the visibility is usually poor. This is a shallow dive unless you venture away from the breakwater into deeper water (50 feet) to visit a reef that's nearby.

B. J. C.

St. Croix

Like so many others over the years, she was an East Coast transplant, brought to the Pacific Coast in the hopes of a brighter, more prosperous future. But, unfortunately for her owners, the result was much different. Almost seven months to the day after she arrived on the Pacific Coast, the wooden steamship *St. Croix* was swept by fire and destroyed—the brightest thing associated with her would be the glow cast by her fire-ravaged hull before she sank.

The 1,995-gross ton, wooden–hulled *St. Croix* was launched by the New England Shipbuilding Company of Bath, Maine, in 1895. The handsome 240-by-40-foot vessel had been designed and built for the International Steamship Company for passenger service between Boston and St. John, New Brunswick. She operated in the Northeast passenger trade for some 12 years—till 1906—when she was laid up. For nearly two years the *St. Croix* languished almost forgotten in a New York Harbor backwater.

Late in 1908 the *St. Croix* caught the attention of representatives of the Seattle-based Schubach & Hamilton Steamship Company. They were looking for a vessel to replace the aging steamer *Oregon* that they had been chartering from the White Star Line for their Seattle-Nome run. Negotiations resulted in the *St. Croix*'s sale to the West Coast company.

After some cleanup and refurbishing, the *St. Croix*, under the command of Captain Frederick Warner, departed New York Harbor for Port Townsend, Washington, on February 5, 1909.

The first part of her voyage, which took her around the tip of South America, was plagued by all types of electrical and machinery problems including breakdowns of her engines, steering gear, and wireless equipment.

Shortly after making the Pacific, Captain Warner took the *St. Croix* into Coronel, Chile, for further repairs. Apparently, all her serious problems were well taken care of there, for the old *St. Croix* made the 6,300-mile run from that port to Puget Sound in the very respectable time of 20 days.

Arriving at Port Townsend on April 21, 1909, the *St. Croix* once again was dry-docked for cleaning and repairs before taking her place on the lucrative Seattle-Nome run. During that summer the *St. Croix* established an excellent record for speed, comfort and reliability, soon becoming one of the most popular vessels on the Nome route.

In the fall of 1909 the *St. Croix* was moved south to the San Francisco–southern California route to compete with the Pacific Coast Steamship Company's vessels, *City of Topeka* and *Santa Rosa*. The *St. Croix*'s arrival on the Los Angeles–San Francisco run precipitated a rate war involving not only the Pacific Coast Steamship Company, but also the Alaska Pacific Steamship Company and every other line on the route, including the freelance passenger-carrying steam schooners. When the *St. Croix* burned, it was no secret that all those companies and individuals involved in maritime transport on the southern California coast heaved a collective sigh of relief at the demise of their fare-slashing competitor. There was contemporary speculation that perhaps the fire had been the work of an agent from one of the shipping lines involved in the rate war with Schubach & Hamilton, but this was never proven.

An incident that occurred just eight days before the *St. Croix* burned might, with the clarity of hindsight, seem like ominous foreshadowing of the liner's fiery end. On November 12, while the *St. Croix* was at sea off Santa Barbara, her chief engineer, Otis Doe, was scalded to death when the steam-whistle valve he was working on exploded. Chief Engineer Doe had been with the *St. Croix* since her purchase by Schubach & Hamilton. It had been his skill and knowledge that had overcome the numerous mechanical difficulties she experienced on her voyage to the Pacific from the East Coast.

On the morning of November 20, the *St. Croix* departed her San Pedro berth on schedule—10 A.M.—with 96 passengers and 78 crew members. As she cleared the breakwater, Captain Warner found that the sea conditions were fairly calm with just a slight chop, but visibility was hampered by extensive patchy fog, some of it very dense. About 12:30 P.M., with most of the passengers taking lunch in the saloon,

S.S. St. Croix, the floating pyre of Santa Monica Bay. Photo from the P. Smith collection.

Advertisement from the steamer St. Croix *when she began service to Nome, Alaska. Photo from P. Smith collection.*

the ship's alarm went off. At first there was no great concern by the passengers, most believing the alarm was just a drill. Yet moments later, when smoke was reported pouring from the aft second-class cabins, most passengers panicked and made a frenzied rush for the lifeboats. On deck the mob was met by ship's officers armed with revolvers, and with that sobering sight, the panic quickly died. On the bridge Captain Warner, also armed, ordered the crew to "Stand by your posts." And, to the passengers, "Stand by to abandon ship."

The calm, dignified demeanor of Captain Warner, his officers, and the crew had a calming effect on the passengers; the revolvers probably didn't hurt either. In a quick, yet orderly manner, the lifeboats were loaded. The first boat lowered away contained women and children. One of the pulley blocks gave way and dumped the lifeboat and its cargo of humanity into the chilly water. Suddenly, women and children were struggling in the choppy sea, fighting for their lives. Not all were winning.

One distraught young husband, seeing his wife and child fall into the sea, immediately sprang over the railing to go to their rescue. However, on hitting the water with a tremendous splash, he promptly disappeared below the surface; in the excitement of the moment he had forgotten he couldn't swim and had to be rescued by one of the *St. Croix's* sailors.

The crewmen who had been on board the lifeboat as oarsmen had been stunned by the fall but

recovered quickly and began helping the frightened women and children aboard another hastily launched lifeboat. One of the deck stewards who saw the lifeboat fall had also dived over the side to help those thrown from the boat. Unlike the excitable husband who had gone over, this unnamed hero managed to rescue three women and a baby before his arm was crushed between a bouncing lifeboat and the hull of the burning steamer. Amazingly enough, the hero seaman's injury and an injury suffered by what the papers described as a "heavy woman" as she was being pulled aboard a lifeboat by her leg, were the only ones suffered in the mishap. Crewmen righted the overturned boat, bailed it out, and began pulling soggy passengers aboard. To load the other boat that had been launched, crewmen on deck fastened a line around each passenger's waist and lowered them into the waiting boat. The other seven boats continued to be loaded normally.

Meanwhile, the fire was spreading rapidly. Shortly after it had been discovered, an ammonia tank, part of the *St. Croix's* refrigeration equipment, exploded. The fumes and intense flames made any attempts at fighting the fire impossible. This was amply shown when two of the assistant engineers, disregarding the danger, attempted to press close enough to fight the flames. They were both immediately overcome by the fumes, and it was only with great difficulty that they were recovered from the area. By 1 P.M., all the passengers had been removed from the *St. Croix* and by 2 P.M., since there appeared no chance at all of saving the ship, the crew too, had departed.

During the one-half-hour period it took to evacuate the burning steamer, the crew conducted itself according to the highest traditions of the sea. T. E. O'Neill, the ship's wireless officer, stayed at his post until almost the last possible moment, desperately attempting to jury-rig a power source to send a distress call; his valiant efforts were unfortunately unsuccessful.

Chief Engineer W. E. Towne stayed at his post in the engine room until the very end, he and Captain Warner being the last two to leave the ship. As they rowed away from the burning liner the ship's fuel oil tanks exploded, throwing large, burning pieces of deck and superstructure high into the foggy sky. Though they were only about 30 yards from the *St. Croix* when it exploded, they managed to escape unharmed from the concussion and rain of fiery debris.

The other eight lifeboats and two rafts that were waiting some 75 yards away heard the blast when the oil tanks went, but, because of the fog, were unable to see the explosion.

A short while later, Captain Warner's boat appeared through the fog and joined the others. The captain assigned officers and crew to each boat and ordered the group to stay close together, within sight, for the trip into the beach. Before they started, Captain Warner delivered a can of milk, which he had grabbed as he left the ship, to the lifeboat that contained the eight infants who had been on board the *St. Croix*. Once the youngster's food supply was laid in, the somber little flotilla of lifeboats began rowing slowly but steadily for the distant, fog-shrouded beach.

Almost three hours later, just about the time the *St. Croix* survivors were beaching their boats on the Malibu coast, the southbound Pacific Coast Steamship Company liner *City of Topeka*, Captain Hannah in command, came upon the still-blazing hulk of the abandoned liner. An excerpt from the *City of Topeka's* log describes the encounter:

> At 4:50 P.M. two and one-half miles south and east of Point Dume, sighted burning ship, which upon close examination proved to be the S. S. *St. Croix*. Ship was slowed and stopped, keeping a sharp lookout for boats and signs of life. Men were sent aloft but could not locate anything. Boats were cleared away ready to lower in case of need. Upon not finding anything, ship, under slow bell, circled around hulk.

The *St. Croix*, still burning, had been ravaged by fire and explosion. As Captain Hannah viewed the glowing hulk, he noted that the masts, large sections of the hull, and almost all of her superstructure were gone. The *City of Topeka* continued to circle the still-blazing liner for more than 30 minutes without sighting anything except an empty raft drifting nearby. The impression given by the drifting raft and the burning ship was one of total disaster—a fire so intense and sudden that all on board the doomed ship had perished. This was the dismal news that the community of Redondo Beach heard when the *City of Topeka* arrived at that port at 7 P.M. that evening.

As the news of the disaster quickly spread up and down the coast, vessels, including the revenue cutter *Perry*, and land parties departed from Long Beach, San Pedro, Redondo, and Santa Monica; they headed with all speed for the Point Dume area.

Meanwhile, Captain Warner had managed to get all his passengers and crew safely ashore on the Malibu beach below Point Dume. Once they were on the beach large fires were kindled to dry the clothes of those who had been thrown into the water in the lifeboat accident and provide warmth and light in the rapidly approaching dusk. Captain Warner sent several teams of crewmen to search the area nearby for habitation, but kept most of the crew working to make the passengers as comfortable as possible under the conditions. He dispatched the faithful Chief Engineer Towne and Purser J. S. Ford to proceed on foot the 15 or 16 miles to Santa Monica to report the situation. At 10 o'clock that evening, as they approached the gatekeeper's house at the Rindge's Malibu Ranch, the fog lifted. Standing on a low rise of hills, for a few moments they could see the diminishing glow of the *St. Croix* gleaming across the water.

After reporting the situation, Chief Engineer Towne and Purser Ford started back for the survivors' encampment on a "motor tricycle" that operated on the private railroad that crossed the ranch. The trio had nearly reached the spot where the survivors were camped when the tricycle jumped the track, severely spraining both of the chief engineer's ankles. Captain Warner was told that a message about their plight had been sent, and help would be forthcoming. Then the stalwart chief engineer was loaded back onto the righted "motor tricycle" and taken back to the gatehouse, where he was placed in a buggy and taken to Santa Monica for medical treatment. The Rindge Estate gatekeeper directed Captain Warner to some barns and outbuildings nearby where some of the passengers could take shelter for the night. For most of the passengers and crew, beds were made from straw. Others spent the night in front of the beach fires, huddled in blankets brought from the *St. Croix*.

In the wee hours of Sunday, November 21, the revenue cutter *Perry* arrived offshore from the survivors' beach camp. A short while later, some of the women, children, and injured were taken aboard the government vessel and transported to Redondo Beach. Later that day, as the *Perry* headed back to the Point Dume camp, she paused at the still-smoldering remains of the *St. Croix* long enough to fire two rounds into the hulk and send her to the bottom.

For the residents of Santa Monica Bay, the burning of the *St. Croix* provided an interesting interlude that neatly coincided with the Thanksgiving Day holiday. It was noted in several of the local papers that several ". . . parties will be formed to take the long jaunt up the beach . . . and look for any valuables that might have been cast ashore." There was never any statement in the papers as to how successful these searches were, but there was mention of charred timbers, oars, buckets, and other flotsam washing up on the beaches of the bay.

The cost of this marine misadventure was relatively small. No lives were lost, and there were only two serious injuries. Schubach & Hamilton Company lost some $50,000 since the vessel was valued at $225,000 and insured for only $175,000. The passengers lost everything they had had on board except for the clothes they were wearing when they abandoned the *St. Croix*. And, as a sorry prelude for the holiday season, the crew of the *St. Croix* had no compensation, no jobs and little chance of finding new ones. The situation could have been much worse, but there was a substantial toll paid.

Search for the St. Croix

Over the past two decades there have been many attempts to locate the remains of the *St. Croix*—none of them successful, to my knowledge. The major problem has been the discrepancies in stories about where the *St. Croix* finally did go down. Differences of as much as four miles occur in the official documents available to researchers; along this area of the coast, as little as one-quarter mile can make a tremendous difference. Beginning just 300 yards south of Point Dume is the edge of a moderate underwater drop-off called Dume Canyon. In one spot off the point, the 100-fathom curve is only about one-quarter mile off the beach. Though all the sinking reports on the *Croix* place her south and east of the point, no one so far has been able to determine exactly how far south and how far east. If, as some reports state, she were some six miles out when she went down she is lost to sport divers, being well beyond the 200-fathom curve.

If, however, she were only two miles off the beach and well east, as other reports state, then she could very well lie within the reach of sport divers.

Although it's not a confirmation of the latter position, in the mid 70's there was a rather interesting rumor that a game diver had discovered an incredible lobster hot spot off Malibu. The spot was supposed to be in about 100 feet of water consisting of piles of machinery and what might have been the bow of a large ship, complete with capstan. Despite considerable effort spent trying to track down the source of this rumor, I was never successful.

So, for the time being anyway, the final resting place of the *St. Croix* remains a mystery. But, with the availability of low-cost side scan sonar and magnetometers and the burgeoning interest in shipwrecks, she may not remain a mystery for much longer.

P. S.

Point Dume to Point Fermin

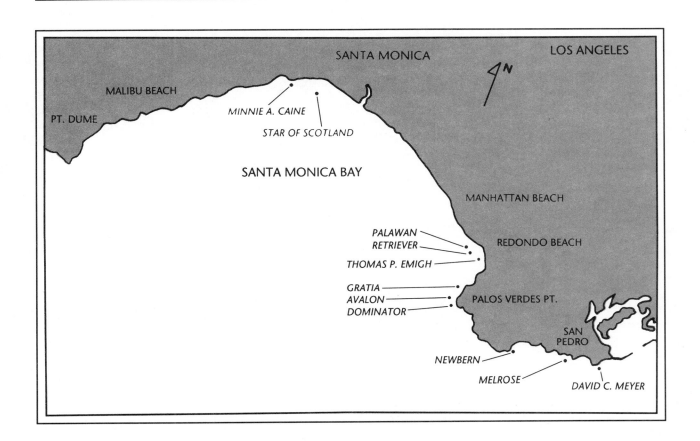

PT. DUME

MALIBU BEACH

SANTA MONICA

LOS ANGELES

N

MINNIE A. CAINE

STAR OF SCOTLAND

SANTA MONICA BAY

MANHATTAN BEACH

REDONDO BEACH

PALAWAN
RETRIEVER

THOMAS P. EMIGH

GRATIA
AVALON
DOMINATOR

PALOS VERDES PT.

SAN
PEDRO

NEWBERN

MELROSE

DAVID C. MEYER

Minnie A. Caine

It's not at all common for a ship to become famous because of things that *didn't* happen to her, but that's how the *Minnie A. Caine* became a celebrity. The year was 1929, the *Caine* was 29 years old and Jean Lowell's book, *The Cradle of the Deep*, had just been published. Claiming the book was her autobiography, Lowell wrote she had begun living aboard the *Caine* with her father when she was just 11 months old. Her mother hated the sea, she said, so for 16 years, little Joan was the only female aboard the boat. Her seafaring adventures, which were very dramatic, finally came to an end when the boat caught fire and sank off Australia. When this happened, Lowell claimed she swam to shore, a distance of three miles, carrying two kittens.

For a few weeks, Joan Lowell's book caused quite a stir and she was feted here and there. But then inconsistencies in the "autobiography" began to crop up. One of these involved the discovery of the *Minnie A. Caine*, afloat and "quite sound of spar and timber" in San Francisco Bay, according to the *San Francisco Chronicle*.

Although Miss Lowell would not admit her book was mostly, if not totally, fictional, newspaper articles of the time carefully pointed out the numerous deviations from fact. This was rather simple to do, as the log from the *Caine* still existed. It showed that Miss Lowell's father had been captain of the *Caine* for less than two years, seven months of which were spent in port. It also revealed that Joan Lowell had both a sister and a mother who had lived aboard the *Caine* while her father was captain.

The *Caine* was a four-masted, wooden schooner, built at the Moran Shipyard in Seattle and launched on October 6, 1900. She was 195.5 feet long, with a 41 foot beam. She was among the last of the sailing vessels built, as steam driven ships were coming into widespread use at that time.

Owned by the Charles Nelson Company, the *Caine* carried lumber from Seattle to Pacific coast ports as well as to Australia, Chile, Peru, and Hawaii. Until her final days, the most noteworthy event of her life was her grounding on Smith Island in Puget Sound, on Christmas day 1901. It took more than four

The schooner Minnie A. Caine, *circa 1905, at Commencement Bay, Washington, with a deckload of dimensional lumber for California ports. Photo from National Maritime Museum, San Francisco.*

months to free her. The cost of repairing the many holes in her bottom was estimated to be $25,000.

In 1926, the *Caine*'s lumber-carrying days ended, and she was consigned to a boneyard in San Francisco Bay. Like other sailing ships, she could not compete with the faster steamships. It was here that she was found after Joan Lowell's book was published.

In 1931, the *Minnie A. Caine* was bought by Olaf C. Olsen. He had turned other sailing ships into fishing barges and this is what he did to the *Caine*. Her masts were cut off at the deck. A cabin was built that functioned as a galley and a place where customers played slot machines when the weather or fishing were poor. The bowsprit was also cut off. Bait tanks and other items of necessity to fishermen were added.

The *Minnie A. Caine* served as a fishing barge in Santa Monica Bay for eight years. On September 24, 1939, she was anchored off the mouth of Topanga Canyon when a terrible storm came up. Late in the evening, the anchor chain parted and the ship was driven ashore, ending up at the foot of Sunset Boulevard. In the process, a rock broke her back. Sand built up around her before rescue efforts could be undertaken. By the time they were, the ship was stuck in place. Solidly entrenched, the *Caine* became

The Minnie A. Caine *cut down as a barge in the late 1930s. The platform built out on the bowsprit was called the jewfish platform and was reserved for anglers with heavy gear. Photo from the P. Smith collection.*

a minor celebrity once again, and people drove out Pacific Coast Highway (then known as the Roosevelt Highway) to gawk at her.

Unfortunately, the *Caine* had become a breakwater that caused unwanted land erosion elsewhere along the coast. In December, her owner, Captain Olsen, was ordered to "remove" her. On Christmas Eve he set her afire, watching her burn from a nearby bluff. Within a month, what remained of the *Minnie A. Caine* had disappeared from view.

Today, only divers can find any trace of the *Caine*, and that will be in the form of iron fastenings and charred timbers. These lie under the sand in 6-to-15 feet of water, just 50 yards offshore. This beach is popular with surfers, so daytime dives are not a good idea unless the ocean is flat clam. Large areas of the sandy bottom are covered with small boulders and cobbles, making it an excellent spot for lobsters.

B. J. C.

Star of Scotland

Compared to the East Coast of the United States, the Pacific Coast definitely comes in second with regard to the number and diversity of divable shipwrecks. This can be attributed to many reasons, a few of the more significant being the East Coast's wider continental shelf, more violent weather, and a longer history of maritime commerce with a much higher volume of traffic during the course of it. Despite this, the Pacific Coast—California in particular—has some truly unique wreck sites within reach of interested divers. One of the most interesting of these is the wreck of the *Star of Scotland* in Santa Monica Bay. Her diversified history and unique status as a living reef in the desert of Santa Monica Bay make her a popular destination for southern California wreck divers.

Commissioned into the Royal Navy on April 22, 1918, as HMS *Mistletoe*, she was one of a unique breed of warships developed specifically to counter the deadly effectiveness of German U-boats. Known formally as Convoy Sloops of War but eventually called Mystery Ships or Q-ships, the *Mistletoe* and her sisters were designed to look like an ordinary merchant ship. However, hidden behind special swing-away bulwarks and facade structures on deck were deadly guns, depth charge racks and throwers, and the trained British crews to handle them. The areas of the vessel that would usually carry cargo were often filled with wood and cork to provide extra buoyancy should the ship suffer serious torpedo or shelling damage. These areas also accommodated the gun crew or crews carried on board. The men who handled the weapons had to stay out of sight unless actually engaging the enemy. The crew of a Q-ship never knew when they might be scrutinized via the periscope of a cruising U-boat. The least little thing—like too many crewmen on deck—could alert a suspicious U-boat captain. Then, instead of surfacing and presenting herself as a target, the U-boat might just move off and fire torpedoes, never giving the British decoy ship a chance to duel it out. In the same vein, the visible crews on Q-ships, even though they were all the best of the Royal Navy, took great care to dress in mufti. Some crews grew so adept at portraying sloppy, unkempt, poorly disciplined civilian sailors, that in one case a Royal Navy

Captain in his Q-boat attire was denied entrance to a naval staff meeting because of his disreputable appearance.

One other trick the *Mistletoe* shared with her sisters was an ability to change her appearance. With the aid of canvas, wood and paint, her color and her basic bow, stern, and midships silhouette could be changed in a very short time. This was usually done under the cover of darkness while still at sea. Changing nationality and manipulating the number of masts, funnels, ventilators, and deckhouses, plus using different types of deck cargo and hull color, enabled a Q-ship to work an area for several days without arousing the suspicions of U-boat skippers.

Owing to the great need for these vessels to counter the U-boat threat, contracts for their construction were given to many different British shipyards. Because of this, there were more than a dozen different variations of Q-ships of *Mistletoe*'s class in the Royal Navy. Each builder was permitted to build to his own designs providing he maintained the prescribed dimensions for the class. The *Mistletoe* was built by Greenock & Grangemouth Dockyard Company and was built to the required Flower-class dimensions. She displaced 1,250 tons, had a length of 262.5 feet, and a beam of 35 feet. She was powered by a 2,500-horsepower, three-cylinder triple-expansion steam engine that would move her through the water at nearly

The Star of Scotland, *soon after World War I when she carried the name* Chiapas. *As a British warship, she bested several of the Kaiser's U-boats. Photo from the Allen Knight Museum.*

18 knots. She came basically armed with two four-inch guns, one three-pounder, light and heavy machine guns, and depth-charge throwers, along with a crack crew of 93 to run everything.

Even though she entered the war quite late, the following rather laconic excerpt from the *Mistletoe's* log testifies to her effective involvement in the war against the Kaiser's U-boats:

> 20 June. Sighted submarine on surface (3.30 a.m.), opened fire. Probably scored some hits. Submarine turned and opened fire on us. Submarine ceased fire and proceeded, throwing out black smoke from her engines. We ceased fire and proceeded to chase submarine. Overhauled him and opened fire, observed some hits scored. Submarine opened fire. We observed 5 direct hits round conning tower. (submarine's) Gun crew left guns fore of tower and proceeded with all haste down below. Submarine appeared to be in trouble. She turned and rolled over on her beam ends to port and sank.

This was just one of several engagements the *Mistletoe* was involved in during her abbreviated tenure in World War I.

After the armistice, the *Mistletoe* was converted to a survey vessel for the Royal Navy and served in this capacity for a short time before being decommissioned and sold to private interests in January 1921. She was purchased by the Clan Line, acting as agents for Cia. Naviera de Los Estados de Mexico, which changed her name to *Chiapas* and placed her as a general cargo carrier on the South American run between Panama and San Francisco. The facade she maintained during the war as a merchantman she now assumed for real.

A few years passed and the *Chiapas* was sold and renamed *La Playa de Ensenada*. Her job now consisted of hauling fruit from Mexico to U.S. Pacific coast ports. But with the close of the 1920s, times grew hard. The Depression forced many shippers out of business and caused their fleets to be laid up in the world's ports and backwaters. Fortunately for California divers this was not to be the fate of the *Star*.

She was sold again, this time to a rather sleazy entrepreneur who operated her as a floating speakeasy and gambling ship off Baja California under the new,

abbreviated name of *La Playa*. In 1933, with the added lure of prostitution to go with the gambling and gin, she appeared in Santa Monica bay. This time she was sporting the name *City of Panama*. Advertised as "Cruises to Nowhere," the ship and her vices were popular with Angelenos and were extremely lucrative for the owner. But the gay and glamorous facade presented by the gambling ship owners in their advertising was violently ripped away later that year when a 24-year-old passenger died as a result of a beating allegedly received on board the *City of Panama*. Though the first officer and master-at-arms were both tried and acquitted in federal court, the ensuing public outcry forced local law enforcement officials to shut down the *City of Panama*. The public was satisfied; justice had been served. After a brief hiatus—just about long enough for the paint of her new name to dry—she appeared once again off Santa Monica. This time called *Star of Hollywood*, she still supplied "dolls, drinks and dice" to L.A. locals, and large profits to her owners. Eventually, local opinion grew strong enough to force local politicians to once again shut the vessel down. Sometime during this period, for reasons as yet undiscovered, the *Star of Hollywood* had her propeller removed and her only means of propulsion came from tugs that chaperoned her from place to place. *The Star*, escorted by her tugs, was moved to the backwaters of San Pedro Harbor and laid up until she was sold once again in the late 30s.

The new owners had her towed back to Santa Monica Bay. Sporting her penultimate name—*Texas*—she was once again anchored offshore and operated as a gambling ship; profits for her owners were bigger than ever. She continued her shady career until 1939 when action by the state attorney general's office put all gambling ships on the California coast out of business once and for all.

In 1940 she was leased by Captain Charles S. Arnold who had her towed north and once again installed as a fixture in the waters offshore Santa Monica Pier. He renamed the ship *Star of Scotland* after a four-masted British sailing vessel he had previously owned and operated as a fishing barge in the Santa Monica area. Moving on board with his wife, Vesta, he operated the *Star* as a party boat and fishing barge. To entice eager fishermen, fishing stages were added to the sides of the ship, while the below-decks area

The Star of Scotland *operating as a barge off the Santa Monica coast shortly before her loss, January 23, 1942. Note the fishing platform mounted outside the hull. Photo courtesy of Vesta Arnold.*

was remodeled to provide a vast area for dining and dancing. Finally back in a respectable profession, the *Star of Scotland* provided exciting fishing and romantic dining and dancing for southern Californians just two miles off Santa Monica Pier.

By late 1941, the *Star* was due for a haul-out and repairs; the constant pounding of the shore boats against her hull had sprung some of her plates, and even the temporary cement patches that her crew had laid in were not very effective in slowing the leaks. Unfortunately, the only refit the *Star* received was at the violent whim of the not-so-Pacific Ocean. The Japanese attack on Pearl Harbor, which embroiled the United States in World War II, established military priority for all shipyard space and dry dock facilities. No time or effort could be wasted on a leaky fishing barge. The placing of additional pumps on board the *Star* was more than sufficient to handle the leaks until the early morning hours of January 23, 1942.

The seas in Santa Monica Bay had been quite violent for the previous few days. The *Star*'s already-strained hull began taking on water even more rapidly despite the extra pumps and the frantic efforts of the ship's owners, Captain Harry Wilson and Captain W. E. Monstad and a crew of three. Less than four hours into Friday morning—3:40 A.M. to be precise—the crew and owners realized that the battle was lost. As the distress flares burned red in the inky predawn darkness, one of the *Star*'s big lifeboats was prepared for launching.

Lifeguard Bill Papson, pulling graveyard shift on the end of Santa Monica Pier, responded immediately on

seeing the distress flares light up the sky. Quickly he recruited nearby fisherman Mel Edwards and Private Arthur Sherman, an Army Coastal Defense soldier guarding the pier, hustled them aboard the lifeguard boat *Pilikia*, and cast off for the beleaguered *Star*. Making their way from behind the shelter provided by the breakwater, they were violently tossed about by the heavy seas as they attempted to make the best possible time to the *Star*. When Papson, Edwards, and Sherman arrived on the scene, they found the *Star* very low in the stern and being severely battered by the huge swells. On board the *Star*, the crew was still trying unsuccessfully to get a lifeboat launched. As Papson maneuvered the *Pilikia* around the stricken *Star*, something suddenly gave way on the larger vessel. In less than two minutes the *Star of Scotland* disappeared beneath the huge swells in a swirl of oily debris.

On the *Pilikia*, Papson quickly moved in and plucked four of the crew from the water, cold and wet but otherwise in good shape. Skillfully maneuvering among the floating wreckage, Papson guided the little lifeguard boat through the debris in search of Bill Gillette, the missing crewman. Almost immediately they discovered Gillette floating face down. Edwards, who had already stripped off his excess clothing, dived in to retrieve the body. Once they were on board the *Pilikia*, artificial respiration was begun on Gillette and continued all the way back to the pier, where a medical examiner pronounced him dead. An examination disclosed

The snack bar on the forward deck of the Star of Scotland, *1941. Note the slot machines on the counter. Photo by Vesta Arnold.*

he had suffered a blow to the head that had probably killed him instantly.

The survivors of the *Star*'s crew were taken to lifeguard headquarters on Santa Monica Pier, where, after receiving dry clothers and hot coffee, they recounted their ordeal to waiting newspaper reporters. John Hughes, one of the crewmen attempting to launch the lifeboat, explained in the *Evening Outlook* what happened when the *Star* made her plunge: "I looked up and saw the whole mass of the ship rolling over toward me," he said. "I slipped into the water and went down as far as I could. All the time I was listening and expecting something to hit me. Nothing hit me and in another minute I was in the lifeguard boat."

Captain Wilson, one of the owners who was picked up clinging to a floating box after the sinking said in the same article, "It seemed to me it went down in about 10 seconds, but it may have been as much as two minutes. Something just let go all at once. I think possibly a swell got under the stage on the side and just lifted a whole row of plates at once. Otherwise I can't understand it, for the ship had many bulkheads." He went on to say that, although he valued the *Star of Scotland* at $100,000, and he and Captain Monstad had recently turned down an offer of $50,000 for the ship, unfortunately, there was no insurance on the vessel. He added that divers would be sent down to check the *Star* but he felt the chance of salvage was very slight. He concluded: "It is probable that we will have to destroy the hull as a menace to navigation."

His prediction proved to be exactly what happened. The following day the *Pilikia* transported Captains Monstad and Wilson, along with reporters, to the site of the sinking. Miraculously, the seas had subsided considerably in the hours since they had claimed the *Star*. With the mild weather and sea conditions the voyage was an interesting and pleasant change for most of the reporters; for the owners of the *Star* it was a much less pleasant trip.

Arriving at the site they found that the *Star* had marked her own grave; her masts, sticking some four feet out of the oil-calmed waters, marked her final resting place like twin tombstones.

Nothing could be done to save the *Star*. Within the week, wrecking charges were placed on her bridge and at the base of each mast and then detonated. This corrected the problem of her being a navigation hazard, and for the next two years she was left in peace.

Salvage divers Fred Hodge and Roy Basham examine the starboard running light they recovered from the Star of Scotland *in 1944. Photo by Emerson Gaze from the W. Beebe collection.*

In 1944, however, the need for scrap ferrous and nonferrous metals for the war effort awakened new interest in the *Star*. The salvage rights for the ship were sold to local salvage divers. Their plan was to rig the old Q-ship with explosives, blow her apart, and then gather the metal for the war effort and a profit.

The new owners made only one dive on the old ship before abandoning the project. When questioned by local reporters as to why they had given up their easy salvage project, the would-be salvors replied that they could not in good conscience blow up the ship, as it had become home to so many fish and lobsters. The sole item they removed from the wreck was her starboard running light, which they donated to the owner of the Galley, Santa Monica's oldest restaurant. To this day the light is still doing good service by providing illumination for the establishment's pay phone.

In the early 50s the *Star* began to draw sport divers. One of the first of these was Dick Anderson. This diving pioneer prowled the *Star*'s dark and spooky innards on an almost weekly basis during those early days of diving. A nearly intact virgin wreck with myriad artifacts, big lobster, and swarms of fish all form part of the tales he tells of those times. Since then the years have taken their toll on the *Star*; corrosion, anchors, and the passing years have lowered her superstructure but she still remains the most exciting wreck in Santa Monica Bay.

Diving the Star of Scotland

Immense and black, looming out of the blue-green mistiness, the wreck appears. Her perpendicular bow, betraying her World War I origins, is obscured periodically by great, darting silver clouds of juvenile fish that call the wreck home. Moving up to and over the bow, using our lights to probe the gloom, I realize the initial impression of the wreck being dark in color is merely a trick of the limited light in 70 feet of water. In the beams of our dive lights, the pinks, reds, oranges, purples, and yellows of the *Corynactis* anemones, which nearly obscure the long-unused steam anchor windlass, seem to glow with dazzling brilliance.

Moving aft, past the forepeak, I notice the entire character of the wreck changes. The softly blurred yet regular lines of the wreck's bow give way to a jumbled, twisted mass of steel beams and plates. In some places, as evidenced by exposed plumbing, lighting fixtures, and portholes, the vessel has literally been turned inside out. For the myriad large, tasty sand and calico bass that inhabit this part of the wreck, this disarray provides the piscatorial equivalent of the finest condo living.

Moving farther aft, just before the somewhat intact midships area, my light picks out several large lobster beneath some fallen plates. Their antennae quiver and point toward me, then they turn casually and disappear into the wreckage. I make a silent promise that their attitude won't be so blasé once lobster season opens.

Aft of the midships area, I find the remains of what was once the vessel's galley. Scattered about are platters, dishes, bowls and cups—nearly all are intact, some are still stacked; I scoop several into my goodie bag as souvenirs and swim on.

Moving toward the stern, I see the overgrown outline of a doghouse skylight through the blue haze some 25 feet away. Its glass panels are long broken away and the temptation to enter the dark opening is great, but common sense wins. The beam of my dive light is the only thing that probes the dimness within. Below, the light shines on a maze of pipes and catwalks, and, below those, the faint outline of the ship's three-cylinder steam engine can be seen.

But now air is low; it's time to leave. As I ascend I glance down at the wreck again and again till finally, just 20 feet from the surface, she fades from sight but remains indelibly in my mind.

I wrote the above description of the *Star* shortly after my first visit to her. She is still one of my favorite wrecks despite the vagaries of the conditions encountered while diving her.

Because she is only 1.9 miles off Santa Monica Pier, in 70 feet of water, one would imagine that conditions on the *Star* would not vary a great deal. That is not the case. Visibility on the wreck averages about 10 feet but ranges from zero (crash into the bottom and grope) to more than 100 feet. And days with visibility of 60-plus feet occur quite often during the winter offshore winds called Santa Anas. During these times one can truly get an idea of the rich resource the *Star* is. Since she is the only object of any size in several square miles, she attracts all manner of sea life. During the course of 15 years of diving the *Star*, I have seen or taken nearly every type of southern California food and sport fish on her. Black and white sea bass, Calico and sand bass, yellowtail, thresher shark, bluefin tuna, bonito, mackerel, barracuda, halibut, sculpin, lingcod, and cabezon have all been on the *Star,* though the populations change in size and makeup from year to year and season to season. About the only fish not seen out there are marlin, broadbill, and albacore, and if the cleanup in the bay is successful, who knows, those might show up, too.

You would expect the *Star* to be loaded with lobster, but that isn't the case these days. Though she is usually good for some, generally of good size, there is no large bug population on the wreck.

Over the years the *Star of Scotland* has produced many artifacts for the divers who visited her, but she still has some secrets to reveal. Recently, Mike Johnson, an avid *Star* diver, discovered a beautiful porthole just as he was getting low on air. Not wanting to leave the prize exposed and in plain view, he and his buddy dragged a nearby loose steel plate over the port to protect it until it could be recovered. The following weekend I went out with Mike to help him recover the port and take some pictures of the operation.

When we hit the bottom, we stirred up some sediment, reducing visibility, but could easily feel the porthole on the plate. Mike tied a lift bag on the port and floated it higher on the wreck where the water was cleaner and I could get some pictures. After we got the porthole on board our dive boat, Mike examined it closely for several minutes, then announced, "This isn't the port I found last week."

On our second dive we went back to the spot where Mike had found the port. Moving carefully this time so as to not stir up the bottom, we checked the area. Sure enough, there was Mike's original port lying on the bottom.

Apparently, when he'd covered his original porthole the week before, the plate he had grabbed from nearby also had had a porthole in it, but in the reduced visibility it had gone unnoticed! We floated the second porthole up, quite pleased with the day's work.

Little surprises like that are what make diving the *Star of Scotland* really special.

Other items recovered from the wreck include lights, gauges, coins, bottles, plates, valves, and other ship fittings.

Because the *Star* is also a popular spot for fishermen, divers should always fly the divers down flag when on the wreck. Also, for safety's sake, descents and ascents should be made via the anchor line.

The wreck contains many years' accumulation of monofilament fishing line, hooks, lures, and weights.

Mike Johnson with porthole recovered from the Star of Scotland. *Photo by Patrick Smith.*

For the most part, these pose no problem that can't be solved with a little caution and a sharp knife.

Even though there are still many areas that can be penetrated on the *Star*, the regular *Star* divers steadfastly refuse to do so. She was built well, but nearly a half-century of saline soaking has taken a toll on her structural integrity: the *Star of Scotland* is far too shaky for any penetration diving. On the bright side, new areas are constantly being opened up for exploration as her shakier sections give in to corrosion and gravity.

P. S.

Palawan

Named for an island in the Philippines, the *Palawan* was built by the Bethlehem-Fairfield Shipyard, Inc. in Baltimore, Maryland. The 441-foot-long, 57-foot-wide Liberty Ship was launched in August 1944. Liberty Ships were so named because they were paid for with money raised by Liberty Bonds, sold by the government. Before the 14,250-ton *Palawan* was commissioned in May 1945, she was converted to an internal-combustion-engine repair ship at Bethlehem's Key Highway plant. After her shakedown cruise in Chesapeake Bay, she took on am-munition and stores at Norfolk and, in June, sailed for Panama. She went through the canal, arriving in the Philippines in August. There she was a unit of ServDiv 101 and repaired small craft, with priority given to minesweepers.

In September the *Palawan* joined ServDiv 103 to support the ships of Task Force 52 during minesweep-ing operations in western Japan. She repaired ships at Sasebo, Japan, then Shanghai, China. At the end of April she left the Orient to return to the United States arriving in San Diego in June. There she was inactivated and finally decommissioned on January 15, 1947. Her active career with the U. S. Navy had lasted less than two years. Berthed in San Diego, she was with the Pacific Reserve Fleet until transferred to the Maritime Administration's National Defense Reserve Fleet in Suisun Bay, California, in 1962.

In 1977 the California Department of Fish and Game acquired the *Palawan*, at no charge, from the navy. (Public Law 92-402 offers coastal states surplus craft for use as artificial reefs. Although other states had taken advantage of this law, this was the first time California had.) The *Palawan* was to be the first of three Liberty Ships sunk off the coast as artificial reefs. A scrap-iron contractor paid $67,000 to strip her of her machinery and superstructure. All of her hatches and doors were removed to allow fish easy access to the inside, and she was cleansed of oil and grease. In September 1977 a U. S. Navy demolition team used 96 pounds of plastic explosives to send her to the bottom of the ocean, 120 feet deep, about a mile off the Redondo Beach jetty. The event was duly covered by the media, including both the *Los Angeles Times* and the *Los Angeles Herald Examiner*.

The plans to make artificial reefs out of two other Liberty Ships, the *Oahu* and the *Cheleb*, were aban-

The U.S.S. Palawan. *Photo from the U.S. Naval Institute.*

doned before the year was out. Fish and Game es-timated the cost of sinking them at $250,000 and decided to use considerably cheaper quarry rock in-stead.

Diving the Palawan

The *Palawan* and the remains of the vessel known as the *Retriever* lie only about 200 yards apart. The *Retriever* was found by divers seraching for the *Palawan*. Since the *Palawan* is four times as long as the *Retriever*, has a steel hull, and has been down only 11 years (compared to the *Retriever*'s 27), it is the easier to find of the two wrecks. Whereas the *Retriever* offers no more than 10 feet of relief, the *Palawan* rises almost 30 feet from the bottom. The ship sits intact and upright on the bottom and has deteriorated very little.

The *Palawan* is also easier to find because of the schools of fish that have made her home. Huge clouds of blacksmith, perch, and baitfish float above and around her. Sometimes, when metering the wreck, the schools of fish extend 20 to 30 feet above the vessel.

Diving conditions are the same on the *Palawan* and the *Retriever*. They are both 120 feet deep and visibility is rarely better than 20 feet. The presence of several dirty-water thermoclines reduces the light level considerably.

The two wrecks are good lobster-hunting sites be-cause they are the only shelters to be found on the sandy bottom other than a few small, scattered rock piles. Look for lobsters at the turn of the ship's bilge, where currents have scoured a narrow, tapered area between the sand and the bottom of the wreck. They sit at the very back and are almost impossible to reach.

The *Palawan's* location is well known to fishing boats, and there is a substantial amount of monofilament line snagged on it. Divers should always carry a knife when on this wreck. Since it is in the open ocean, descents and ascents should be made on the anchor line. Since it is deep, careful attention should be paid to bottom time.

B. J. C.

Retriever

It began inauspiciously, with one of Mike Curtis' infamous fathometer runs. Only three divers were on board the Deep Freak *(our 24 foot Wellcraft Airslot) that day, in foul weather off Redondo Beach. Mike was trying to find a favorite lobster reef, but haze was obscuring the lineups. After about 40 minutes of trolling back and forth in rolling swells, the instrument showed a promising blip. The anchor was dropped and the divers went down the line to see what was there. Descending 120 feet onto a sandy bottom, they spotted a few fish that might lead them to the reef in the murky 15 foot visibility. Finally, a dark shape materialized through the gloom. At first it looked like a stack of rotten wood. As the divers moved closer, it took on the form and substance of an old shipwreck.*

Mike and his buddies, Dave McCray and Mike Hisashima, were ecstatic. They set out to explore the find. Suddenly, Curtis noticed a round object, half buried in the sand--a porthole! McCray saw it at the same time and the race for the trophy was a dead heat. For a few seconds there was a frantic tug of war as greed won out over the buddy system.

The divers finally looked up and saw Hisashima about ten feet away. He was moving toward them, staggering under the weight of the portholes he carried under each arm. A quick look around revealed two more lying in the sand. Apparently the wooden hull had rotted away, leaving portholes scattered around for the taking—a diver's fantasy come true!

Excerpted from "Retrieving the *Retriever*," by Eric Hanauer, *Skin Diver* Magazine, April 1988.

Lying just 200 yards southeast of the *Palawan*, the *Retriever* was found in 1984. Her portholes weighed 45 pounds each and 11 of them were brought up over the next few months by Mike Curtis and eight of his friends. They also brought up a mast light, a hatch cover, a brass bilge pump, door knobs, and a number of other artifacts.

The wreck was tentatively identified as the *Retriever*, a sportfishing barge that sank during a violent storm on April 28, 1951. The 110-foot vessel had been used to transport houses to Catalina before being converted to a barge in 1946. Hanauer talked to the former owner of the *Retriever*, Gordon McRae, by phone. He learned that the barge had broken up and sank during a violent storm on April 28, 1951. According to

Hanauer's *Skin Diver* article, McRae told him the skipper of the vessel was taken off it when the storm warnings were broadcast. The article continues: "But he returned later, probably to safeguard his belongings on board. McRae watched from the pier as the *Retriever* left the water completely. 'She broke her back,' he recalls, 'and I knew she was going down.'" The skipper was thrown overboard and drowned; his body washed ashore the next day.

After their phone conversation, McRae sent Hanauer a brochure containing a picture of the *Retriever*. Looking at the photograph, Hanauer began to have doubts that the *Retriever* and the wreck he had dived were one and the same. It doesn't seem possible that this vessel could have had as many portholes as have been recovered. Is it the *Retriever*? We may never know.

Diving the Retriever

Since the vessel called the *Retriever* was wooden hulled and it has been down quite a few years, not much remains of it. In his April article, Hanauer describes her as looking "like little more than an underwater junk pile." Although the stern and bow are clearly identifiable, the wreckage rises no more than 10 feet from the bottom.

The *Retriever* lies about a mile off the Redondo Beach jetty, and visibility on the wreck averages about 20 feet. It is dark on the bottom because there are usually several layers of dirty water (thermoclines) between the surface and the 120-foot bottom. This is the open ocean, and descents and ascents should be made along the anchorline. Since this is a deep dive, careful attention must be paid to bottom time.

All that remains of the fishing barge Retriever. *Photo by Patrick Smith.*

The low-profile wreckage has proven to be a good site for lobster hunting. And, since it isn't dived all that much, the bugs seem to be less wary of human visitors than they are at other, more popular spots along the coast.

B. J. C.

Thomas P. Emigh

It was an ignominious end for a proud sailing vessel, but one that was suffered by many of the Pacific Coast wind ships. Shorn of masts and rigging, she was then heavily ballasted so as to provide a stable platform for the hordes of fishermen who swarmed aboard her. Her once-bright decks and brass were splattered with mackerel slime and blood: she had become a fishing barge.

This was the disgrace that the once fast and graceful windjammer *Thomas P. Emigh* was reduced to when she was purchased by H. C. Monstad in 1927.

The *Thomas P. Emigh* was built and launched by the Tacoma Shipbuilding Company in 1901. The *Emigh* was the epitome of the shipbuilder's art, yet she would be the last large vessel Tacoma Shipbuilding would turn out for 16 years, until the demand for ships grew during World War I. She was a handsome, four-masted, barkentine-rigged vessel, 211.5 by 42.4 feet and grossing 1,040 tons.

Like many other vessels constructed in the Pacific Northwest, she was designed primarily to carry the rich resource of that area: lumber. Her builders created in her not only a grace of form that belied her tremendous capacity—she could carry just over one million board feet of lumber—but speed as well. This she amply proved, not as a newly launched vessel, but some eight years after her launching in March 1909. Under the command of Captain M. A. Ipsen, the *Emigh* flew home—Honolulu to Port Townsend, Washington—in just seven days, 22 hours, smashing the previous record set in 1881 by the *Klikitat* by almost two days.

In 1923, as part of the Charles Nelson Company fleet, she was kept active both with coastal work and long-distance voyages to Mexico and Hawaii. Oftentimes on the coastal trips she and her fleet sister, the *Minnie A. Caine*, would suffer the ignominity of being loaded to the gunwales and then towed to their destinations by a company steam schooner. Fortunately, they were allowed to unfurl their sails and run with the wind on their Mexico and Hawaii schedules.

The end was rapidly approaching for sailing ships, however, and in 1929, the Charles Nelson Company—now the Nelson Steamship Company—was selling its sailing vessels in favor of steamers. When the *Emigh* was sold to H. C. Monstad, its metamorphosis from working barkentine to fishing barge was fairly extensive. It entailed the removal of her masts and rigging and the addition of enough ballast to move her deeper into the water, making it easier for the fishermen to swing their catch on board. The extra ballast also served to stabilize and steady her movement at anchor so as to ride easily and reduce her ability to afflict her passengers with *mal de mer*. The addition of an auxiliary generator, pumps, bait tanks, and free-for-use bamboo poles almost completed the change. With the remodeling of the ship's galley into a snack bar and lunchroom, and perhaps a few unadvertised slot machines, she was ready to go.

For the next five years the *Emigh* was operated off Redondo Beach where thousands flocked to her decks in pursuit of fish and fun, in that order. During the Depression, visits to the local fishing barge were primarily for the purpose of acquiring substantial amounts of protein for the inexpensive cost of a boarding pass and shore-boat ride. There was no need for expensive tackle, because handlines or the free cane jack-poles supplied on board were more than adequate and quite effective.

Often during the depths of the Depression, a fortunate fisherman could provide fish for his family and

With her deckload stacked as high as her booms, the barkentine Thomas P. Emigh *heads south with a full load of lumber. Photo from the National Maritime Museum, San Francisco.*

Thomas P. Emigh *ashore at Redondo Beach, April, 1932. Photo from the P. Smith collection.*

much of his neighborhood, with enough left over to sell and cover the cost of the fishing trip. Any enjoyment that might occur in the course of the day's fishing was a bonus of secondary importance.

On April 20, 1932, Los Angeles was struck by a violent storm that severely crippled all forms of transport in the area. Of the maritime casualties, the local fishing barge fleet probably suffered the heaviest damage and the greatest number of losses. In the aftermath of the storm, the area between Redondo Beach and San Pedro saw numerous small craft lost, plus the *Emigh*, along with the barges *Melrose* and *Gratia*, grounded or stranded on the beach.

For the curious, the *Emigh* was the most accessible of the three, having come ashore just south of the piers at Redondo. By the second day after the storm, the unusual sight of a large vessel ashore had drawn huge crowds to Redondo Beach. The *Emigh* had become an overnight tourist attraction that provided a much-welcomed influx of visitors and their wallets. The *Emigh's* owner, H. C. Monstad, received a request

from Redondo city officials that he leave the ship beached, at least until after the summer season. Since the vessel was badly strained, and there was no likelihood she could be repaired, he consented. It was an agreement the Redondo city fathers would soon come to regret.

Redondo Mayor John M. Clarke was quoted in the *Redondo Reflex* saying that he anticipated that the *Emigh* would draw "a goodly number of summer visitors to Redondo." In addition, plans were made to end the old barkentine's days in a spectacular manner. Come the fall, she was to be torched as a fiery end to both her existence and the summer season.

The bonhomie with which Redondo Beach looked upon the *Emigh's* wrecking ended less than one month later.

Because of the way she lay stranded, the *Emigh* was causing serious disruption to the normal ebb and flow of the tides along that section of beach. By the end of May, the *Reflex* reported that she ". . . causes a loss

The battered Thomas P. Emigh *shortly after she was pulled from the beach at Redondo. Photo from the P. Smith collection.*

of approximately five feet of shoreline each high tide." The newspaper went on to say that more than 200 feet of concrete beachfront walk and the base of the public stairs in that area had also been destroyed, and no respite was in sight. But perhaps the worst and most dangerous part of the situation was the sewer pipe that had been exposed, undercut and broken at the foot of Ainsworth Court. Raw sewage in substantial quantities was fouling the beach. This presented a very serious and immediate health hazard, for despite the broken sewer pipe, the *Emigh* continue to draw tourists like a magnet.

To compound the deteriorating situation, a conflict was emerging between Redondo Beach and the county as to which one had responsibility for the tourist attraction that was destroying one of southern California's most popular beaches. The discussion over jurisdiction concerning county beach and city tidelands was a thorny one producing endless debate, little consensus and no results. There was one thing the officials in both groups agreed on however: Nothing would be done till responsibility was assigned.

In the first few days of June, a chlorination unit was installed at the site of the sewer pipe break. Though the noxious discharge continued, the threat of disease was somewhat mitigated.

Just into the second week in June, the county signed a contract with Robinson-Roberts Marine Construction Company for the removal and destruction of the *Thomas P. Emigh*. The county contract gave the company 15 days to remove the ship from the beach and float her out. If they were successful to this point, then arrangements would be made to move the ship to deep water and sink her.

On Saturday June 22, three days ahead of their contracted due date, Robinson-Roberts was successful in refloating the battered *Emigh*. The entire operation had been a struggle for the salvage crew to the very end. Disaster loomed in the final moments of the enterprise when, to quote the *Reflex*, a large "tidal wave" struck the *Emigh* just as she was being pulled free of the beach. In offering proof of the size and power of that exceptional wave, it was reported that it "grabbed a five ton tractor and carried it to sea." During the course of this inundation, the supervisor of the project, Larry Roberts, was caught in the maelstrom and very nearly carried away with the tractor. As it was, it was fortunate that the effort to float the *Emigh* was pretty much complete at that point, for the injuries he suffered from his unforeseen dip put him in the hospital for the better part of a week.

As in everything else she had thus far encountered in her career, the *Emigh* survived. She was towed several hundred yards offshore and anchored. She was to be fitted with a tow bridle within a few days, then taken out and disposed of in deep water. The first part of Robinson-Roberts' job was done; Redondo's erosion problem was solved.

Hardly had her hook been set when County Supervisor John R. Quinn offered the *Emigh* to the Navy

An excellent shot of the erosion created by the Thomas P. Emigh *when she came ashore at Redondo Beach in April, 1932. Photo by C. Doyle from the P. Smith collection.*

as a target for the battleship fleet then based in nearby San Pedro. The Navy declined, with thanks.

Less than three weeks later the *Emigh* was back in the headlines: "Barge *Emigh* Breaking Up," greeted readers the morning of August 22. The accompanying story described how, after weeks of neglect, the ship was awash and broken into three sections that were barely hanging together. Some timbers and debris had already begun to drift ashore, and residents were expressing concern that the derelict would fall to pieces and wash up onto the beach once again.

A sidebar story revealed that the 300 feet of beach walk and stairs had been repaired, and a concrete bulkhead was installed to stabilize the beach damage the *Emigh* had caused.

Supervisor Quinn pronounced that, since the *Emigh* was now on the "high seas," she had become the responsibility of the federal government. This being the case, the county and Robinson-Roberts happily washed their hands of the whole affair. No response or action of any kind was forthcoming from the government, and meanwhile, the ship continued to fall to pieces.

An attempt was made to tow the *Emigh* to Catalina Island, but she was entirely too flimsy to make it even as far as Rocky Point. The attempt was abandoned almost before it began.

Some effort was made to slow her "suicidal disintegration" by tying her together with steel cables. This ploy was only moderately successful. The *Emigh* continued to hazard the boats and bathers along Redondo Beach as pieces of her were slowly but inevitably torn free by the passing Pacific swells.

The debate as to who was responsible for what in disposing of the *Emigh* carried on. Meanwhile, waterlogged and forlorn, she continued to go to pieces.

Then one day the problem was solved. Much to everyone's relief, the *Thomas P. Emigh* quietly sank where she had been moored, just a few hundred yards off Redondo Beach.

Diving the Thomas P. Emigh

The site of the *Thomas P. Emigh* is one of the most difficult to locate for divers, despite widespread documentation as to where she sank.

When she settled to the bottom in 1932, her hull was already falling to pieces from her stranding and salvage, plus the pounding she took when she was refloated and anchored offshore. When she hit the bottom the disintegration continued at an accelerated pace. Her destruction became a race among the marine borers consuming the wooden portions of the ship, the speed with which the sand buried the wreck, and the constant influence of the surge, currents, and tides to scatter the wreck asunder. From what remains today, it looks like the marine borers won, hands down.

What remains of the *Emigh* is primarily her fastenings and metal fittings: hinges, portholes, pipes and plumbing, a capstan, kerosene and electric lamps, and fastenings of all types. The problem is that most of the time all this equipment lies beneath 60 feet of water and from 2 to 6 feet of sand. Most of the time there are a few pieces—usually pipes or steel fastenings—protruding above the sandy sea floor. In several years of visits to the site, I have only found it completely exposed on two occasions.

Because of its location near the head of the Redondo undersea canyon, visibility on the *Emigh* is usually excellent. Apparently, upwellings keep the area clear, with the visibility rarely less than 25 feet.

Since the site is quite close to the area where several of the old Redondo commercial wharfs were located, divers often come across old bottles, crockery with steamship company logos, and other debris from these structures. In one case, a diver who had spent an unsuccessful dive looking for pier debris wandered across the *Emigh*. He located her by a large, brass masthead lamp sticking out of the bottom. As he pulled his find from the sand, a second matching lamp was revealed just below the first. Both lamps were intact and in excellent shape. When he brought them up and examined them, the smell of kerosene was still noticeable in their fuel reservoirs.

Even though the *Thomas P. Emigh* is fairly close to the beach, there is a moderate amount of boat traffic in the area. Observe the standard precautions of using a float and divers down flag if diving off the beach, or of descending and ascending via the anchor line if off a boat.

P. S.

Gratia

Though not the largest nor most violent storm to strike the southern California coast, the fierce nor'wester that slammed ashore April 20, 1932, packed a punch that staggered the Southland. It also caused the destruction of a score of vessels; the three-masted bark *Gratia* was one unfortunate victim.

Built by Russell & Co. and launched in November 1891 at Port Glasgow for A/S Excelsior, the *Gratia* was a handsome vessel some 250 feet in length, 38 feet in beam, and displacing 1,583 gross tons. That she was built by the most expert craftsmen and of the finest materials was demonstrated by the fact that nearly 25 years after her launching she was still receiving the highest rating—100A1—from Lloyd's of London on her surveys. Throughout her lifetime she served her owners well, ranging the oceans of the world to deliver her general cargoes to such exotic ports as Hamburg, Callao, Rangoon, and Perth.

Though her globe-girdling career spanned some 36 years, they were not always smooth sailing, as is evidenced by an excerpt from the log kept for her voyages of 1891 and 1892. A three-page section, written in Norwegian, describes an incident in which the crew mutinied after the ship's cook reported sick. The captain apparently suggested that, until the cook's recovery, the crew provide for themselves from the ship's galley. The crew not only rejected this plan, but as a measure of their displeasure, refused to stand watch or carry out any other ship's work as well. The situation came to a climax with the crew charging the captain on the poop deck. Apparently, the captain became glib at this point, not only talking the crew out of doing him bodily harm, but convincing them to carry on with their seamanly duties as well. Though not documented in the log, some who knew the captain, and his rather laconic manner of speaking, suggested it was more likely the persuasiveness of one of Mr. Colt's inventions rather than the skipper's golden tongue that encouraged the *Gratia's* crew back to the straight and narrow.

Finally, in 1927, the *Gratia* was purchased by a Redondo Beach group, which brought her to the southern end of Santa Monica Bay and anchored her there to serve as a deep-sea fishing barge. With two of her masts and nearly all of her rigging removed, she soon became one of the more popular of the numerous offshore barges.

Lying several miles off the popular resort town of Redondo Beach and served by a flotilla of swift shore boats, the *Gratia* provided not only fishing but also dining, dancing, and, it was rumored, gambling and alcoholic refreshment for her numerous guests. She continued in this vein until the evening of April 20, 1932, when a fierce nor'wester slammed into the southern California coast.

Though all her passengers were removed prior to the storm, a crew of six remained on board to oversee the vessel through the forthcoming tempest. For the first seven hours of the turmoil, things went pretty well. The crew was comfortable enough except when one of them had to go out to check the anchor lights and the ground tackle that held the ship.

Despite her age, the *Gratia* required no pumping, the skill of her Scottish builders still evident after her many rigorous years at sea. She rode the mountainous seas well, owing to the foresight of her owners, who left a substantial amount of her last cargo—coal—aboard as ballast. Though this had been done to ease the *Gratia's* rolling at anchor and reduce any discomfort afforded to the less hearty of her customers, it now served to steady the vessel in the violence of the storm.

Sometime in the early-morning hours of the 21st, as the gale was reaching new heights of fury, tragedy struck. The shank of the *Gratia's* anchor snapped from the tremendous forces generated by the storm, and, in a matter of moments, she and her crew of six were being swept toward the rocky reefs that fringe the cliffs of the Palos Verdes Peninsula.

Though the crew did manage to drop a second anchor, it was for naught. In a short time the huge waves drove the *Gratia* heavily onto the razor-sharp offshore reefs. Probably because of the large amount of ballast she carried, she remained upright and on an even keel, wedged tight.

Though their position was much better than any of them could have hoped for, the *Gratia's* crew still had big problems. Even though only 200 yards separated the men from the narrow rocky beach, the white frothing maelstrom would surely destroy anyone foolish enough to attempt the passage. And, even if someone did manage to reach the beach and rig a line for the others to follow, once there they would be exposed to the full force of the elements with little chance of making it up the nearly vertical 100-foot high cliffs. So they did the only sensible thing they could under the circumstances: they stayed on board the battered *Gratia*, firing distress rockets and praying help would arrive before the raging surf pounded the ship to pieces.

Almost before the *Gratia* hit the reefs, the Coast Guard was aware of her plight and had dispatched guardsmen to the area at which she was expected to come ashore. Because of the poor visibility, several powerful searchlights were borrowed from the Sixty-third Coast Artillery and placed on the cliffs just above where the *Gratia* grounded. With the illumination provided by the powerful lights, the coastguardsmen lowered the heavy lifesaving gear down the precipitous cliffs to the narrow surf-washed rock beach, then descended themselves and proceeded to set up their equipment.

The guardsmen, using a Lyle gun, fired a light line out to the *Gratia*, whose crew speedily used it to pull out a tail block with an endless line rove through it, which they made fast as high as they could on the vessel's one remaining mast. A breeches buoy was soon in operation, and, without any mishap, the crewmen were quickly brought to shore, thoroughly soaked but none the worse for their experience. By 3 A.M., with the gale starting to lessen in intensity, the *Gratia*'s crew and the coastguardsmen with all their equipment were back on top of the cliffs; the *Gratia*'s crew were more than ready for some hot food and much-needed sleep, while the coasties carried on with their life- and property-saving duties elsewhere along the ravaged coast.

And so the *Gratia* sat on the offshore reefs, alone and abandoned with the huge swells of the weakening storm pounding her stout Scottish steel hull, just an old sailing ship that had outlived her usefulness and run out of luck. Or so it would appear to most people. But in the gloomy gray of the dawn, there appeared on the cliffs a man with a little more vision and tenacity than most, Hugh Nabors.

Nabors was a carpenter by trade, who like most working-class Americans, had been hard hit by that economic cataclysm called the Great Depression. For him, looking down from the cliffs, the *Gratia* wasn't a worthless hulk but his lucky ship and she'd just come in.

The Gratia *after many months of salvage. Nearly everything above the main deck has been removed and scrapped. Photo from the National Maritime Museum, San Francisco.*

Wasting little time, he managed to get to the bottom of the cliffs and then swim the 200 yards out to the ship through the boiling surf. He clambered aboard, then made himself at home. He got a fire going in a fo'c'sle stove using some of the 500 tons of coal that were aboard as ballast. Then, after he was warmed and his clothes dried, he whipped himself up a rather sumptuous repast from the supplies he'd found on board and settled in on his prize for the duration.

As for the *Gratia*, that her bottom looked something like a Swiss cheese really didn't matter because she was jammed so tightly on the reef that she didn't move at all, and her mid and upper decks and cabins were as solid and tight as they'd ever been.

For the next 16 months, "Captain" Nabors refused all the offers and threats made to get him to relinquish his occupancy of the *Gratia*. As a result of his tenacity his rights to a claim on the vessel were upheld, and he ultimately entered into an agreement with the salvage company of Ellis & Spitzer, which had purchased the vessel to salvage what metal and coal they could.

When the ownership issue was settled and the salvage begun, yet another controversy arose when it was decided to auction the steel salvaged from the *Gratia* by lots to the highest bidder. There was a considerable amount of hard feelings when the majority of the metal was purchased by Japanese agents. The *L. A. Times* prophetically reported the local concern that the metal going to Japan would soon be turned into "shot and shell," whereas, had the local companies vying for the metal been the high bidders, the steel would probably have gone into the superstructure of the Golden Gate Bridge.

When all the easily accessible metal had been removed, a considerable portion of the *Gratia* still remained. To remove what was above the surface, huge charges of dynamite were exploded within her hull, razing what was left of the old wind-ship to below the ocean's surface.

Diving the *Gratia*

Today, even after the extensive salvage and her destruction by explosives, large portions of the *Gratia* yet remain. Ranging in depth from 15 to 25 feet, her plates and fittings are strewn over a wide area of rocky bottom.

Though the visibility is usually better in the winter months, ranging from 15 to 30 feet, the shallowness of the wreck makes it mandatory that conditions be flat calm before diving the site. The heavy kelp that grows in the area is oftentimes scoured away after the heavy swells of winter storms sweep through, revealing areas previously hidden by the dense growth.

Those winter storms also have a tendency to uncover artifacts, and most divers feel that the best time to dive the *Gratia* is during a Santa Ana condition as soon after a big storm as possible.

I recall one instance diving the *Gratia* under just those conditions. A storm ten days before had "mowed" all the kelp in the area and really turned the bottom over. For the last several days warm Santa Anas had raised temperatures into the 80's and flattened the ocean to mill-pond smoothness.

On the bottom the visibility was about 20 feet and the lobster were thick among the wreckage. With several in my bag, I was checking another likely looking spot under a plate when I caught a glimpse of a unique shape in the dimness. It was the ornately cast hanger that once held the ship's bell. Needless to say, I tore up the bottom and searched the surrounding area thoroughly, but without any luck—there was no bell to go with the hanger.

It's amazing the amount of articles that still can be found on a ship that has been professionally salvaged. Among the plates, and in the sandy pockets of the bottom, one can find large brass hinges, door locks, keys, china, and all types of fastenings and fittings. And enough history for anyone.

P. S.

Avalon

The *Avalon*, a triple-deck, twin-screw vessel, was built at the Globe Iron Works in Cleveland, Ohio, in May 1891. Christened the S. S. *Virginia*, she carried passengers from Chicago to Milwaukee and back for the Goodrich Steamship Company of St. Joseph-Benton Harbor, Michigan. In April of 1918, the U. S. Navy requisitioned the ship for use in World War I. She was to carry troops to Europe, departing from the East Coast. To get there, however, she would have to pass through the St. Lawrence River locks. The 1,985 gross ton, 269-foot-long vessel with her 38-foot beam could not do so whole. The Manitowoc Shipbuilding Company cut off her bow forward of the collision bulkhead, plus 6 feet of stern overhang. This was completed on October 17. Starting November 15, both sections of the boat were towed to Boston Navy Yard, arriving December 28. Once the stern and bow were rejoined, the steel-hulled ship was nearly 4 feet shorter.

When the *Virginia* arrived in Boston, she was renamed the U. S. S. *Blue Ridge*. The Navy never did use her and she sat out the war in Boston harbor. She was decommissioned in March of 1919 and struck from the Naval Register that July. In August she was declared war surplus and purchased by Thomas J. Farley, acting as an agent for Wilmington Transportation Company, which was owned by William Wrigley Jr., founder of the chewing gum company bearing his name. Wrigley also owned the Chicago Cubs and

A trail-board, half-hull model and wheelhouse bell that were removed from the Avalon *when she was taken out of service. These are on display at the Catalina Island Museum, Avalon. Photo by Patrick Smith.*

the entire island of Santa Catalina. He bought the *Blue Ridge* to ferry tourists between San Pedro, California and the city of Avalon on the island. Extensive alterations were made to the ship, and it was renamed the *Avalon*.

Both the town and the ship were named after the paradise of Avilion in Alfred Lord Tennyson's *Idylls of the King*. According to this story, King Arthur convalesced in Avilion after being wounded in battle. Promotional brochures for Wrigley's "Island Paradise" once claimed, "Visitors to Avalon and Catalina escape worries, cares, smog and complicated living patterns of the mainland and are renewed in body and spirit."

The *Avalon* and the *Catalina*, Wrigley's other passenger ferry, were known as the Great White Steamers. During World War II, the *Avalon* was taken over by the U. S. Maritime Service and carried cadets to and from the Maritime Training Station in *Avalon*. She was returned to her owners after the war. In 1951, the *Avalon* was permanently retired from her passenger-carrying duties; her binnacle, engine-room telegraph, wheelhouse bell, and steering wheel were removed. They are on display at the Catalina Island Museum along with other mementoes from her days as a Great White Steamer.

The *Avalon* sat at a dock in Wilmington until 1960, when she was sold to Everett J. Stotts for scrapping. When he finished removing her machinery and superstructure he sold her to Al Kidman, who made her

The Avalon *in later years with the Catalina Lines logo on her stack. Photo from the Los Angeles Maritime Museum.*

Exploring the stern compartment on the steamer Avalon.
Photo by Jack McKenney.

into a salvage barge. Her decks were cut down and a crane positioned on her stern. Twice during this process the *Avalon* caught fire.

The once-proud Great White Steamer-turned-salvage barge was being used to salvage the *Dominator* off Palos Verdes on July 18, 1960, when the weather turned foul. Torn from her anchorage when her anchor chain snapped, her decks awash, the *Avalon* sank in 70 feet of water.

Diving the Avalon

The *Avalon* broke in two when she settled on the bottom. The bow lies 40 to 50 feet from the rest of the wreck. Visibility averages about 15 feet, with 25 to 50 not uncommon. Care should be taken to avoid monofilament line snagged on the wreck; the *Avalon* is a popular fishing spot.

Although the stern is still recognizable, midships has no discernible structure. It is a confused mass of steel deck plates and hull ribs. A boxlike cabin lies off the port side. Also off the port side is the crane. Its derrick, encrusted with sea life, lies alongside the stern.

Divers were on the *Avalon* just days after she sank, and the big artifacts and pieces of brass are long gone. Small items, such as keys, coins, coat hooks, and cage lamps, however, still turn up occasionally. Since things salvaged from the *Dominator* were on the *Avalon* when she went down, not everything found on this site is from the *Avalon*.

The wreck lies about three-quarters of a mile off the beach, and because visibility is usually poor, it is not the best spot for wide-angle photography. Macro life abounds, however. *Corynactis californica*, plumeworms, starfish, and hermit crabs are among the colorful close-up subjects to be found here. Fish are plentiful, with yellowtail and bluefin tuna, bonito, barracuda, and kelpbass commonly seen. The wreck is said to be a good lobster spot in season.

Since the *Avalon* lies between ridges that run parallel to shore it can be difficult to locate.

B. J. C.

Dominator

Like most bad news, the intruder showed up just before dinner time, and, like "The Man Who Came to Dinner," lingered on. The patience and nerves of Palos Verdes Police and residents, the U. S. Coast Guard, Marine Underwriters, a lonely Greek captain, and many other participants would be sorely tried by the stranding of the S. S. *Dominator.* The excitement began shortly before 6 P.M., March 13, 1961. The S. S. *Dominator,* en route from Vancouver, B. C., and Portland to Los Angeles, was groping her way south in dense fog looking for the entrance to Los Angeles Harbor. She was scheduled to top off fuel bunkers for the final leg of her journey to Algeria with a cargo of 9,000 tons of wheat and beef.

For the *Dominator*'s master, Captain Charitos Papanikolpulos, who was visiting the Pacific Coast for

the first time in his 22-year maritime career, the journey had been easy and uneventful until he entered the Santa Barbara Channel. Shortly after taking a position fix in clear weather near Santa Barbara, heavy fog had set in and navigation had become difficult. Although the *Dominator* was fitted with a radio direction finder (RDF) and an echo sounding device, the World War II vintage ship did not have radar and so in bad weather was navigated by what is known as dead reckoning. This is done by keeping careful track of the ship's speed and direction from a known point. This, along with periodic Radio Direction Finder and depth-sounder checks, was the standard means of navigation in bad weather prior to the advent of such devices as radar, Loran, and satnav. However, with dead reckoning, such variables as wind, currents, and swell all can have considerable effect on a vessel, with the degree and direction of such effects sometimes

Despite this kind of pounding, when this picture was taken there was still hope that the Dominator *might be saved. She still had steam up, while offshore salvage vessels kept a steady pull on the unfortunate Greek freighter. Photo from the Southwest Instrument Company.*

A Los Angeles sheriff on sea patrol around the battered freighter Dominator *off Palos Verdes. Photo from the P. Smith collection.*

difficult to gauge. On a transoceanic voyage a ship's master can wait out the bad weather and take a sun or star fix to re-establish his position, then continue his voyage secure in the knowledge of his vessel's location. On a coastwise voyage with such things as headlands, islands, and reefs nearby, the uncompensated effects of wind and current can put a vessel in jeopardy in a very short time.

This was the fate that befell the *Dominator* and her crew. Despite careful navigation and slow speed she apparently was caught in a current which, unbeknownst to Captain Papanikolpulos, pushed her inshore and off her course.

At about 5:45 P.M. the residents along Rocky Point Road in Palos Verdes (an exclusive seaside suburb of Los Angeles) became front-row spectators at the opening curtain of the Decline and Fall of the S. S. *Dominator.*

The *Dominator* was a Liberty Ship built in 1944 at the Walsh Kaiser Company yard in Providence, Rhode Island. Launched as the *Melville Jacoby*, she was 441 feet long, 57 feet wide, drew nearly 28 feet of water, and was 7,176 gross tons.

Surviving the war, she changed owners and names (ex *Victoria*, ex *North Queen*) several times before coming under the ownership of the Compania Naviera S. A. of Panama, which renamed her *Dominator*. In the mid 50s she was sold once again, this time to Greek owners represented by the Transmarine Nagivation Company.

A shipwreck is an event that, circumstances allowing, always draws a crowd. In the case of the *Dominator*, two things combined to generate even more interest than usual in such a stranding. First, it had been a slow news period. The media was looking for a story to splash across the front pages, and what could be more exciting and newsworthy than a shipwreck? Second, the event was literally in the backyard of one of the largest urban areas in the country; for a large part of Los Angeles's residents the stranding of the *Dominator* seemed to rouse the sea dog that resides within us all.

By the morning of the 14th, crowds numbering in the hundreds began to gather along the cliffs overlooking the stranded ship. The pea-soup fog of the previous day had cleared away to bright sun and clear skies. To the spectators, the moderate swell that slapped at the *Dominator*'s hull seemed incapable of doing any real damage.

News teams converged on Rocky Point by air, land, and sea, and while TV crews began live coverage of the event, newspaper reporters began interviewing anyone who didn't interview them first.

It must have been somewhat frustating for the media and disappointing for the spectators as they arrived on the scene and first glimpsed the wreck. Aside from the fact that she was only a long stone's throw off the beach and obviously stranded on the rocky point, she appeared well and whole, totally intact. Her crew of 29 dawdled about the deck, some even fishing from the fantail, as a trickle of smoke rose from her single midships funnel.

The Coast Guard cutters *Heather* and *Dexter* hovered nearby protectively as did two large commercial tugs. They had lines on board the *Dominator* from the unsuccessful attempt to drag her off the reef during high tide the previous evening.

As the day wore on, the moderate swells of the morning began to increase in size and power. As they crashed against the side of the stranded vessel sending foam and spray higher than her masts, the size of the crowds watching the spectacular display also increased. Lured by TV updates they came by the thousands to watch the event unfold. Throughout the day Captain Papanikolpulos would periodically attempt to power his way off the rocks, but all the attempts were fruitless.

With the increasing swells, concern was mounting over the very real possibility of puncturing one of the *Dominator*'s cargo holds and allowing the grain cargo to become water soaked. If that happened the grain would swell, quite probably splitting the hull apart and eliminating any possibility of a successful salvage. As it was, the outer hull of her double bottom had already been punctured by the rocky reefs where she lay; and as the swells grew larger the outlook for her surviving this ordeal grew bleaker.

By the morning of the 15th a super-derrick barge from the Smith, Rice Co. had arrived on the scene, hooked up her cables, and begun her effort at freeing the stricken freighter. Throughout the night the weather had steadily grown worse, with the *Dominator* now rolling under the onslaught of huge ground swells and wind in excess of 40 knots. Some salvors felt that such conditions could actually help with the salvage attempts, and as the Smith, Rice Co. barge began exerting a pull equal to that of 25 tugboats, hopes were still high that the *Dominator* would be freed. After several major pulls the attempt was abandoned until later in the day to coincide with a high tide. The total gain for this attempt; a mere 10 feet.

At this point the crowd of spectators on the cliffs overlooking the site numbered, by police estimates, in the 7,000-to-10,000 range. As might be expected, the residents in the area were more than a little irate about the situation, but the Palos Verdes Police were simply not able to handle the massive tide of curious onlookers. Street closures and barricades had no discernible effect on the influx, and finally, Palos Verdes Police were forced to call for reinforcements from Redondo Beach and Los Angeles. The additional police on the scene didn't seem to matter much at all. The sightseers still came. Driving if they could and parking anywhere, they were indifferent to the $10 parking tickets the police passed out with impartial enthusiasm. Walking if they had to, many carried umbrellas, picnic baskets, lawn chairs, and small children. They staked out spots along the cliffs like squatters establishing homesteads and, in nearly a carnival mood, began vigil over the stranded ship. For those who came with no supplies, there appeared hot dog and soda-pop vendors who contributed to the festival-like atmosphere. A feeling of camaraderie was in the air as the spectators viewed the disaster on their doorsteps.

It should be pointed out that the area residents were not participants in this feeling of bonhomie that flowed through the visiting crowds. On the contrary, fisticuffs broke out between irate home owners and free-ranging spectators on several occasions, as the sightseers flagrantly trespassed around the fine homes. In one extreme case the lady of the house found nearly a dozen strangers casually floating in her backyard swimming pool, which happened to have an excellent view of the stranded *Dominator*.

Despite several more attempts by the Smith, Rice Co. barge, the *Dominator* remained fast on the rocks. Her only movement was her rolling back and forth on the reefs under the constant pounding of the heavy waves. It was decided to make no further attempts until the following day when the effort would begin anew with daylight and a high tide. But during the night the situation took a change for the worse.

At about midnight of the 15th, Coast Guard Radio, Long Beach, received a terse distress call from the beleaguered ship requesting immediate assistance: "*Dominator* breaking up. Master requests assistance. Can you evacuate crew?"

The Coast Guard dispatched another cutter to the scene but because of the heavy seas and winds of 40 knots, no attempt was made to rescue the crew until the following morning. At that time the Coast Guard maneuvered a shallow draft LCM into the *Dominator*'s lee and prepared to take the crew to safety.

Lt. Commander Eugene McCrory of the cutter *Heather*, who was viewing the rescue via binoculars, was surprised when the crewmen began appearing on deck with duffel bags and suitcases. Angrily, he radioed the rescue boat: "Tell them to forget that baggage," he ordered. The response came back from the *Dominator*'s crew, "No luggage, no go."

The Coast Guard gave in and began loading 22 of the crew and their gear. One Greek sailor even brought a bag of toys, which included a small bicycle for his child.

As this was going on, Captain Papanikolpulos was in radio contact with the owner's agent stating, "The master definitely is going to stay aboard regardless of who says what."

The reply came back, "Owner approves, but wants it known it wasn't an order." The captain then inquired if he must remain aboard alone. "Indeed, he must," came the reply from the agent. The captain, aware that there was no danger of outside salvage claims to his vessel as long as the tugs hired by the owners had lines on his ship, thought the situation over for a bit, then replied.

"The master is of the opinion," he radioed, "He doesn't want to stay aboard alone."

Captain Papanikolpulos—personal gear in hand—was waiting when the LCM made a second trip to pick up the remainder of the *Dominator*'s crew.

With the crew safely off, it appeared that the major part of the drama of the *Dominator* stranding was over, but that wasn't to be the case.

The removal of the crew seemed to be the signal for every young swashbuckler in L.A. to try to get aboard the Greek freighter, under the misapprehension that he could claim the vessel, or perhaps just for the adventure of it. Despite the best attempts of the police on shore and the lifeguards and Coast Guard offshore, a group of about a dozen young men launched themselves through the heavy surf and made for the wreck. Several were eliminated by cuts and bruises incurred by the surge on the rocky beach. A few more were rescued from riptides by alert lifeguards, but several managed to climb aboard and roam the wreck at will.

Apparently uneasy about spending the night aboard, they jumped into the surf surrounding the ship and struck out for shore when darkness fell. The surf, which hadn't diminished during the day, proved too much for the adventurers. Guided by lifeguards who called instructions from shore via bulhorns, they managed to make it back to the *Dominator* and get aboard.

At this point, a Marine helicopter was dispatched from El Toro Air Station to perform an aerial rescue of the would-be swashbucklers.

Illuminated by searchlights from shore, the chopper lowered a rescue basket and began hauling the young men up, one at a time. Everything was going smoothly until the last adventurer was being lifted

Bow of the Dominator *on the beach at Palos Verdes, circa 1970. Photo by Bonnie J. Cardone.*

from the deck in the basket. Just as the basket left the deck, the helicopter was struck by a huge comber.

The pilot, Captain Bernard Pautach, a skilled professional, managed to maintain control. Throwing the chopper into a rapid climb, he escaped with his last passenger dangling below the craft, drenched but safe.

After landing, all three young men were arrested and booked: bail $263.

Swashbuckling ain't what it used to be!

The following morning, agents for the *Dominator*'s owners recommended that the ship be turned over to the insurance underwriters. During the night the sea had taken a tremendous toll on the freighter, and it was obvious she would never leave those reefs in one piece.

The sea around the ship was becoming a foul-smelling gruel as the cargo of grain washed into the sea through cracks in her hull. On her port side above the waterline, the hull visibly bulged as the water-soaked cargo swelled and strained the ship even further. On deck, the after deckhouse had been torn to pieces by the still-pounding surf, and the ship's bridge and superstructure on the starboard side were nothing more than twisted junk.

The *Dominator* was dead. The only thing that remained to be done was the sale of the salvage rights to the highest bidder, who would pick what value he could from her bones. The ultimate winner of those salvage rights was a burly six-footer named Al Kidman. What looked, initially, like a real financial windfall for him ended up being the means to Kidman's bankruptcy. During the course of his salvage attempts he lost three barges, two with cranes. One of these barges was the cut-down hull of the *Avalon*, the Great White Steamer of Catalina Island fame.

For those who lived on the cliffs overlooking the *Dominator's* final resting place, it was many months before life returned to anything like normal. Sightseers continued to swarm into the area while the

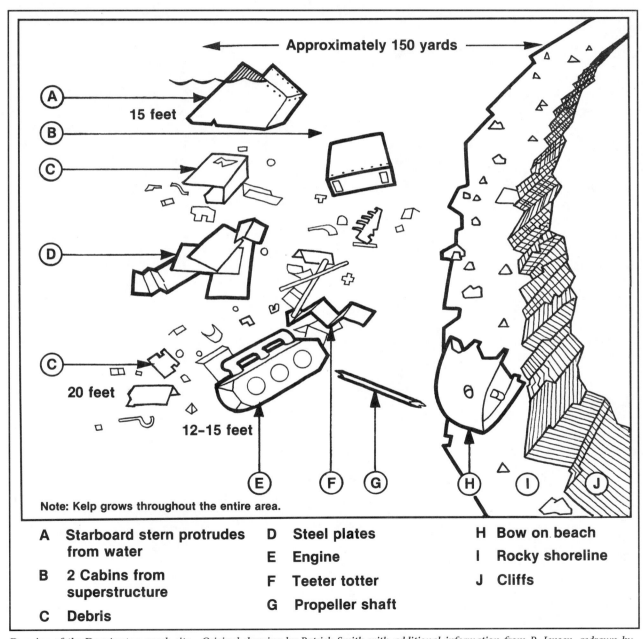

Approximately 150 yards

15 feet

20 feet

12–15 feet

Note: Kelp grows throughout the entire area.

A	**Starboard stern protrudes from water**	**D**	**Steel plates**	**H**	**Bow on beach**
		E	**Engine**	**I**	**Rocky shoreline**
B	**2 Cabins from superstructure**	**F**	**Teeter totter**	**J**	**Cliffs**
		G	**Propeller shaft**		
C	**Debris**				

Drawing of the Dominator *wreck site. Original drawing by Patrick Smith with additional information from P. Jensen, redrawn by Michael Brown.*

Palos Verdes Police continued to pass out citations for everything from trespassing and littering to illegal parking, at a rate never equaled before or since. And those gentle onshore breezes, which in the summer make Palos Verdes an oasis while the rest of L.A. swelters, that year brought the yeasty stench of rotting grain and great clouds of flies, which were breeding in the spoiled wheat.

Finally, the salvors gave up, and the sea claimed the *Dominator*. Today, a large rusty section of her bow that the waves have cast up on the beach is about all that remains above water, but among the reefs just offshore lie major sections of hull and engine. For a cautious diver, the *Dominator* can be an interesting dive.

Diving the Dominator

Some 28 years after stranding, the *Dominator* has become a vital part of the offshore ecosystem in the Rocky Point area. The wreck provides shelter and footing for all types of marine flora and fauna. Perhaps because of its proximity to Redondo Canyon, an area of considerable deep-sea upwelling, the diversity and size of fish found around the wreck are greater than that at most other coastal dive spots. Yellowtail, bonito, barracuda, bass, and bluefin tuna are seen fairly often along with such uncommon visitors as squid up to three feet in length and triggerfish. During lobster season, when conditions allow, the area is a lobster hot spot.

Peter Jensen is a local diver with several years of experience on the *Dominator*. "It can be a dangerous area if you don't use common sense and watch conditions carefully," he says. "But using those prerequisites, it can be a heck of a dive with something new almost every time."

Peter divides the wreck into four main areas, though wreckage is scattered everywhere: the stern, the compartments, the teeter-totter, and the engine.

The stern of the ship is an intact structure made up of two or three compartments. It sits in about 20 feet of water at about a 45-degree angle. This piece is found easily since a triangular-shaped corner of it breaks the surface just north of the point.

Moving south, the next major piece of the wreck is known as the compartments. This appears to be an intact section of superstructure made up of several compartments. Over the years, several portholes have been recovered in this area. It sits in about 15 feet of water and is a good bet during lobster season.

Just beyond the compartments is the area Peter calls the teeter-totter. This is a large section of decking, about 20 by 40 feet, that balances on top of reef and other wreckage. During moderate swell, the whole piece reportedly teeters back and forth. It goes without saying that caution and common sense should be used generously in this area. However, its location adjacent to the engine makes it a good and productive area for brass artifacts.

The southernmost piece of large underwater wreckage on the *Dominator* is her engine. This monstrous piece of machinery stands upright in about 15 feet of water and breaks the surface at low tide. The engine and the areas immediately surrounding it are probably the choicest spots for artifact hunting. Oilers, valves, gauges, brass handles, and all types of brass are scattered around the bottom, waiting for the sharp-eyed diver.

Several things should be pointed out if one plans to dive the *Dominator*.

First, because the area is an exposed point and quite shallow, conditions must be very calm before even thinking about diving the site. As with any steel wreck there are sharp edges to consider, and one doesn't go into such an area when there is any surge sweeping the bottom.

Second, since the preferred method of diving the *Dominator* is by boat, you should keep in mind that over the years more than a dozen small boats have been lost in the area. Most of them involved sightseers trying to get just a little closer, then suddenly finding themselves stranded or without a propeller after getting a little too close. Bear this in mind when anchoring here.

Lastly, the area goes through periodic change with relation to the density of the kelp found in that section of the coast. During the warm summer months, with long daylight hours and mild sea conditions, the kelp can become quite dense. During these times it's better to find another dive spot—wait for a periodic storm or big swell to thin out the kelp before attempting a visit to the *Dominator*'s final resting place.

P. S.

Newbern

There is an old seaman's superstition that any voyage that begins on the 13th day of the month will be an unlucky one. In the case of the Pacific Mail Steamship Company vessel *Newbern* this was to prove, unfortunately, all too true.

On October 13, 1895, the *Newbern*, under the command of Captain John Von Helm, with 25 passengers and 10 crewmen, departed its penultimate stop, Ensenada, Mexico, on its regular voyage from Guaymas, Mexico, to San Francisco. The final leg of the voyage was proceeding uneventfully until the *Newbern* reached the vicinity of the Coronado Islands, just south of San Diego. An unscheduled stop on the rocky reefs of South Island was avoided only by luck and good visibility. The near-stranding precipitated an investigation, and it was discovered that the vessel's compass had a serious deviation problem. After the captain made some adjustments to the balky instrument, the *Newbern* continued north at her standard cruising speed of ten knots.

At 3:12 A.M. the following morning, the passengers were rudely awakened by a violent, grinding shock, and then were thrown from their berths as the *Newbern* careened over onto her port side. Rushing quickly on deck, they found their worst fears realized. A dense fog blanketed the area reducing visibility to practically zero, but jagged black rocks could be seen through the eddies of the heavy sea-mist within 50 feet of the doomed vessel. Minutes after grounding, the *Newbern* rolled even farther onto her port side and then stabilized, as the sea flooded her aft sections.

The *Newbern*'s crew and captain calmed and reassured the frightened passengers, while as a precaution, the vessel's five lifeboats were lowered. Thus satisfied, some passengers who had come on deck in their nightclothes as the *Newbern* first struck, returned below to dress properly. Despite the lateness of the year, the weather was mild and the night was warm, and the passengers experienced little discomfort as they waited for daybreak so the lifeboats might be used.

During this time, Captain Von Helm, who had given up any attempt to extricate his vessel in the

Though the Newbern *met her end by stranding at Palos Verdes on October, 14, 1893, that wasn't the first time she'd had problems—as shown by this 1882 photo of her on her beam ends at Folsom Street Wharf, San Francisco. Photo from the National Maritime Museum, San Francisco.*

darkness, had kept the crew busy removing the $250,000 in silver bars that made up the most valuable portion of the *Newbern*'s varied cargo. All the treasure, save two of the 25-pound ingots, was recovered before seawater flooded the compartment and placed it beyond the crew's reach. The remainder of the cargo, which was made up of cochineal (a type of red dye), tanbark, hides and oranges, ultimately became a total loss.

One other part of the cargo was pretty much of a total loss, too . . . because it escaped. As part of the deck cargo was a consignment of 80 live sea turtles, headed north to provide exotic fare for San Francisco gourmets. Apparently during the confusion of the wreck, 76 of them took the opportunity to make their escape as the *Newbern* listed over. The four that remained were ultimately rescued and taken to Redondo Beach, where they were involved in a celebration banquet—as the main course.

As daylight broke, the fog lifted slightly and the passengers, baggage, mails, and crew were all safely transported the 50 feet that separated the *Newbern* from the rocky beach. On his arrival on shore, the vessel's purser, H. A. Childs, began an overland trek to Redondo Beach, the closest help, some eight miles to the north. Meanwhile, after placing the first officer in charge, Captain Von Helm took the second officer and seven of the crew, loaded the recovered silver into one of the ship's boats, and sailed to San Pedro, where the treasure was placed in railroad company vaults.

With the arrival of Purser Childs at Redondo and Captain Von Helm and the treasure at San Pedro, the world was made aware of the *Newbern*'s plight. Rescue and salvage ships were immediately dispatched from both ports for the scene of the wreck, where eventually some four commercial vessels, the *Falcon*, *Pelican*, *Coos Bay*, and *Warrior* arrived.

Despite the fact that the wind and seas remained calm, the *Newbern* had been beyond saving as a vessel nearly from the moment she struck the rocky shore. By the time salvage vessels arrived on the scene, she had broken in two and begun going to pieces; there was nothing left to do but try to salvage whatever of the cargo, equipment, and machinery they could. According to contemporary reports, divers were sent into the wreckage to try to recover the remaining silver bars, but apparently were not successful. Other

Bronze and brass fittings recovered from the Newbern: *a hinge skylight brace, brass spikes, a melted T-hinge, a large lag bolt, and an ornate drawer pull. Photo by Bonnie J. Cardone.*

problems plagued the salvors. Some three days after the *Newbern* went aground, her bow section, really the only part of the vessel above water at that point, caught fire and burned so fiercely that no portion of the vessel remained to be seen except for the smaller pieces of wreckage and debris strewn along the beach.

The Court of Inquiry investigating the *Newbern*'s loss ultimately decided that Captain Von Helm shouldn't be held responsible for the vessel's loss. Even with this vindication, Captain Von Helm was forced to retire from the sea; the *Newbern* was the third vessel lost under his command, and ship owners were not willing to place a jinxed commander on their ships.

After the fire and inquiry, the *Newbern* passed from sight and thought until April 1974, when two ardent wreck divers, Bob Crowther and Glen de St. Jean, chose the shore adjacent to Marineland of the Pacific for a Saturday morning dive. Ironically, it was not a wreck dive they had planned, but a game dive to the rocky offshore reefs in search of the rock scallops found there.

They were nearly through their dive, with limits of scallops in their bags, when Glen spotted a flash of green among the rocks and sand of the bottom. Signaling Bob over, Glen dropped to the bottom and began fanning sand. In the few moments it took Bob to reach the spot, Glen had uncovered several verdigris-covered brass spikes, a handful of square-shanked brass nails, a small piece of copper sheeting, and a large brass hinge. They both realized that hardware like this could mean only one thing: a wreck!

The following morning found Glen and Bob once again slipping and sliding down the rocky cliff trail—this time with twin 72s, marker floats, lines, and determination whetted by the finds of the day before. Conditions for the search were excellent—glassy seas, two-foot-surf—and, when they got in the water, visibility in excess of 30 feet.

They began their search in the general area where they had found the pieces the day before, and began a parallel search pattern down the coast. Within a few minutes they began swimming over iron beams and plates scattered across the bottom. Poking out among the rocks, sand, and decomposing iron was the tell-tale green verdigris of brass and copper artifacts strewn through the area as well.

Almost immediately Glen found an intact octagonal wood-hull-type porthole. He quickly tied it to his lift bag and started to move on, when his eye was caught by a six-inch in diameter, half-circle of brass protruding from a decomposed iron matrix. When he dropped down to inspect it more closely, he could see a design of some type on the edge of the piece. Glen quickly but carefully went to work with his rock pick, chipping the piece from its place in the iron.

A hasp and melted brass padlock recovered from the Pacific Coast Steamship Company vessel Newbern. *Photo by Bonnie J. Cardone.*

Bob, too, had discovered a complete wood-hull porthole, but his was also partially embedded in iron, and it needed some careful chipping with his rock pick to facilitate its removal. It took only a few minutes before it popped free of the bottom in a black cloud of iron oxide.

By this time, Glen had managed to remove his piece from the iron and discovered that he had recovered a small, ornate, gimballed bracket for an oil lamp. On the support he could see a finely carved foliate design: a vine and leaf motif of delicate complexity. After carefully placing it in his goody bag, he joined Bob, and together they continued to survey the area.

A short distance away they came across shards of broken porcelain scattered along the bottom. Nearby was a marble doorknob and a large "T"-hinge poking out of a big mound of decomposed iron. In an area of exposed bedrock with sand-filled cracks and potholes, they settled down for a moment to do a little fanning. Careful but steady fanning soon removed the light overburden of sand, revealing the bottom of the holes to be carpeted with all manner of small ship's fastenings and hardware; brass sheeting nails and spikes, ornate brass drawer pulls, locks, keys, handles, and hooks. The area was an underwater hardware store.

Between their enthusiasm and their exertion, both Glen and Bob were running low on air. Quickly gathering together their finds, they headed back to the beach. Even though they had full tanks in the car, they decided to forego another dive that day in favor of beginning research into discovering what vessel they had found.

Initially, they had several helpful clues to guide them. From the remains, they knew they had a steam-powered, wooden-hulled vessel of medium size. The lack of any major pieces of machinery indicated that extensive salvage had been carried out at one time, and clues that the vessel had burned were evident on some of the melted brass artifacts they had recovered. If she had been salvaged, that meant, somewhere, records existed. Among the pieces they had recovered, they found a broken plate with a maker's mark on the bottom and a date of 1879. This gave them at least a beginning date to work from in their hunt for the vessel's name.

Their search went through century-old shipping loss lists, newspapers, and books on California maritime history. One of their early candidates was the double-ended San Francisco ferry, *Saucelito*. This 692-ton side-wheeler had been launched in 1878 for the North Pacific Coast Railway Company, then lost, burned to the waterline in a conflagration at the Port San Quentin wharf. There had been some speculation that she was to be sold to new owners in southern California, her burned hulk towed south to be converted to a barge. But further research eliminated this possibility; *Saucelito* never left San Francisco after she burned.

Continued effort finally turned up the *Newbern* and the story of her abrupt end on the reefs of Palos Verdes. It also revealed her history, which if anything, was more exciting than her loss.

Built in 1862 at Brooklyn, New York, by C & R Poillon for Wakeman, Dimon & Company, she was launched as the *United States*. She displaced 948 tons, had a length of 198 feet and a beam and depth of 29.8 and 17.8 feet, respectively. On June 27, 1863, she was purchased by the Navy, and on August 15, 1863, she was commissioned as the U. S. S. *New Berne* at the New York Navy Yard. She was a trim and staunch vessel, propeller-driven, with strapping supports of iron, two masts, and a single, tall, thin funnel set slightly aft. She was designated a supply ship and was assigned to the North Atlantic Blockading Squadron during the Civil War. Her duty was the essential but tedious job of transporting mail, supplies, officers, and seamen from northern ports to and from the ships and stations of her squadron. On several occasions, however, the tedium was enlivened by the ship's pursuit of a Confederate blockade runner. In at least two instances, she was successful in either capturing or destroying the enemy vessels. The *New Berne* was decommissioned in March 1868, and transferred from the Navy to the War Department in December of that year.

Shortly thereafter, the *New Berne* was sold to Hartehan & Wilson, and brought to the West Coast by way of Cape Horn. When she reached San Francisco, her name was shortened to *Newbern* and she began general trade and passenger runs to and from Mexican ports in the Gulf of California. In 1871, the *Newbern* was purchased by the Colorado Steam Navigation Company, which continued to run the vessel on the San Francisco–Sea of Cortez route. In 1878, she came up for sale once again, and was bought by the Oregon

Firebox plaque recovered from the steamer Newbern. *Photo by Patrick Smith.*

Improvement Company of Portland, Oregon. At the time she was sold, the *Newbern* underwent an extensive overhaul at the Risdon Iron Works in San Francisco, and was refitted with new engines and boilers. The *Newbern* was almost immediately leased to the Pacific Coast Steamship Company, where she covered the same Mexico-San Francisco route. It was during this arrangement, under the command of Captain Von Helm, that she stranded and was lost.

Diving the Newbern

The *Newbern* lies in depths ranging from 6 to 25 feet, with visibility averaging 20 feet, and on occasion surpassing 40 feet. The area has a fairly rugged, rocky bottom, scattered with many boulders 3 to 5 feet in diameter. Patches of bottom between the reefs and boulders contain sand pockets that have trapped many small artifacts from the *Newbern*, plus numerous lead fishing sinkers lost over the years by anglers fishing from the shore.

There can be great variations in the amount of kelp growth encountered on the site. During the late summer and fall, diving the *Newbern* is most difficult, because the higher water temperatures and the greater hours of sunlight encourage rapid, dense kelp growth throughout the area. Occasionally the growth is so dense that it precludes any safe, enjoyable diving on the wreck. However, in the winter, spring, and early summer, the kelp in the area is periodically thinned or totally removed by storm-generated large surf.

Such storms also tend to turn over the bottom and expose previously covered areas of the wreck; diving the *Newbern* after one of these storms can be very interesting and productive.

Because most of the *Newbern* lies in very shallow water, surge, to a greater or lesser extent, is nearly always present on the wreck, but rarely presents problems for divers. Other consequences of the *Newbern*'s shallow location are the usually warm water temperatures and the tremendous amount of bottom time available. On several occasions while working quietly on some project, I have managed three and a quarter hours bottom time with twin 72s.

With the sale and demolition of Marineland of the Pacific during the winter of 1987–88, all beach access to the *Newbern* site was eliminated. This was really a great loss, since there are so few interesting wrecks that are available to divers as beach dives. Now, with access restricted to boats only, the number of divers able to enjoy this unique wreck will be greatly limited.

P. S.

Melrose

The double-ended, paddle-wheel, auto-transport ferry *Melrose* holds several maritime distinctions along the Pacific Coast.

When the Southern Pacific opened its new, large, modern shipyard in west Oakland in 1902, the main purpose of the facility was the maintenance and repair of its fleet of vessels. With its heavy equipment, machine shop, and the marine railway, there were few jobs it couldn't handle. For six years, maintenance and repairs, along with minor rebuilds, were the mainstays of the yard. But in April 1908, the first vessel to be completely constructed at the facility was launched— the *Melrose*. She was an experiment in ferry construction, designed primarily to accommodate that new development in transportation technology, the automobile. The *Melrose* became the first of more than 30 San Francisco Bay vessels to be built that were devoted exclusively to the auto-transport trade.

The *Melrose* was a handsome vessel, 274 by 43 feet, with a gross tonnage of 2,662. She was powered by two inclined compound steam engines, which gave her a total horsepower of 1,040. She went into service January 11, 1909, on the Creek Route, the passage between San Francisco and Alameda. The name of the route came from the eastern portion of the trip, which involved travel along Oakland Creek.

For the most part, her 21-year career hauling passengers and autos across the bay was relatively tranquil. But in any harbor as heavily trafficked and subject to periods of dense, heavy fog as San Francisco, incidents are bound to occur. Several of the *Melrose*'s most notable ones included the destruction of her terminal when she overshot her landing in July 1910. In 1917, she lost a crewman, and in 1926, she became stranded for a time on the Oakland mud flats. Yet considering the thousands of crossings she made over the years, her career could almost be called uneventful.

In 1931, after over 20 years of service, she was sold to southern California owners who wished to convert her into the queen of the local fishing barges. Their plan was to restore her original fine fittings and add equipment to her interior areas, so as to offer posh dining and dancing, along with fishing, for her customers. Even before her conversion was complete, she was being called by the contemporary press the

The ferry Melrose *began her career as the first ferry specifically designed to carry automobiles. She ended her life as "the most palatial" of the local fishing barges. She is shown here early in her career on San Francisco Bay. Photo from the National Maritime Museum, San Francisco.*

". . . most palatial of all the scores of fishing barges in the Southland . . . ."

On the evening of April 20, 1932, just prior to her completion, she was caught in a violent, 50-knot gale while anchored off Whites Point. Though she and her five-man crew weathered the first 24 hours of the storm, by the morning of the second day, the *Melrose* was dragging her anchors and there was nothing her crew could do to stop the drift toward destruction on the jagged coastal reefs. Throughout the night, coastguardsmen vainly attempted to remove the *Melrose*'s crew. At each attempt, they were thwarted by the furious winds and seas. After several unsuccessful tries, they could only watch helplessly as the ferry and her crew slowly drifted closer to their doom.

With dawn on the third morning, the wind dropped and the seas began to calm. The crew of the *Melrose* was able to row ashore at Whites Point, arriving safe and sound. The *Melrose* hadn't been so fortunate. The wind and seas had driven her broadside on the coastal reefs. The huge seas quickly broke her

back and began tearing her superstructure asunder. Within hours, her stack had been swept over the side and her hull was twisted and breaking up from the pounding she was taking. By the time the storm had passed, the ". . . most palatial of all the fishing barges . . ." was nothing but a twisted pile of wreckage off the Palos Verdes shore.

Even though her owners claimed the Melrose's value to be nearly $20,000, no attempt was made at salvage. The *Melrose* remained where she struck, exposed to the prevailing westerly wind and swell which quickly removed her from sight at least above water. Under the influence of the wind and waves, the *Melrose* was broken apart and scattered across several acres of bottom.

Diving the Melrose

Because Whites Point is within Royal Palm Park, access to the *Melrose* is quite easy, with parking adjacent to the area where she's located.

After the storm. The Melrose *ashore at Whites Point, April 23, 1932. Photo from the P. Smith collection.*

Though the remains of the *Melrose* lie mainly up-coast and offshore from the rocky point on the south side of the beach, entry is better from the point, rather than directly from the beach inshore from the site. There are three reasons for this: First, by entering from the point, one avoids the difficult rock and cobble entry through the surf. Second, by entering from the point, it is a shorter, easier swim to the site. And finally, when a swell is running, surfers often use the northern side of the point for wave-sliding.

Fifty years of storms and waves have scattered the remains of the *Melrose* over probably three acres of the sea bed. The bottom mainly consists of rocky outcroppings and scattered cobbles and boulders, with pockets of sand. Visibility on the site can range to 25 feet, but 6 to 10 feet is more usual. Wreckage can be found scattered and buried nearly everywhere, in depths ranging from 6 to 20 feet. The interesting thing about the artifacts recovered from the *Melrose* is the excellent condition of some of the pieces. In one case, right next to a six-inch copper steam pipe twisted like a pretzel, I found a perfectly intact china plate with nary a scratch on it. This diversity in the condition of the pieces found on the *Melrose* makes it a truly interesting dive spot.

Items recovered from the *Melrose* include pumps and valves, coins, eating utensils—cups, plates, forks, and spoons—along with hinges, gauges, and other ship's fittings.

P. S.

David C. Meyer

It was just a little shortcut, less than one-quarter mile on a voyage of more than 1,000 miles. Hardly worth the effort, it meant perhaps five minutes saved over the duration of a passage of many days. Just the same, Second Officer J. W. Erickson, of the steam lumber schooner *David C. Meyer*, took that fateful shortcut in the waning hours of March 9, 1926.

The *David C. Meyer*, of the McCormick Steamship Company, had departed Saint Helens, Oregon, some five days earlier with a cargo of 1,500,000 board-feet of lumber on board. In the darkness of the final hours of March 9, she was approaching her destination, San Pedro, California, with Second Officer Erickson on watch. The *Meyer* was just southwest of Point Fermin and less than two and a half miles from Angel's Gate and Los Angeles Light, the entrance to San Pedro Harbor, when Erickson decided to alter course, and cut between the Point Fermin whistle buoy and the reefs just a short distance inshore. It had been a long voyage, and he took the opportunity to save a few minutes despite the direct orders of the *Meyer*'s captain, Hajalmar Danskanen, not to change course.

The error of the second officer's decision became apparent within a few minutes of the course change. The *David C. Meyer* came to a loud and abrupt stop, firmly aground on an outlying finger reef just below Point Fermin Lighthouse. The top of the reef was just 3 feet below the surface—the *Meyer* was drawing 18 feet forward when she struck.

After several fruitless attempts to back the *Meyer* out of her predicament, Captain Danskanen began radioing for help. His SOS calls were picked up by most every ship in L.A. and San Pedro Harbors, with the Red Stack tug *Pilot* the first vessel to arrive on the scene. But by the time the *Pilot* had arrived, the *Meyer* had nearly 12 feet of water in her hull.

In the interest of safety, 18 crewmen and the captain's wife were transferred to the tug at first light. Captain Danskanen and 11 crewmen (including Second Officer Erickson) remained on board to work with salvage crews to try to save the *Meyer*.

Arriving shortly after the *Pilot*, was the Merritt, Chapman & Scott salvage vessel *Peacock*. Work was immediately begun to lighten the *Meyer* by jettisoning the lumber that made up her forward-deck cargo.

The amount of water in the *Meyer* had extinguished her fires, making it impossible to use the ship's cargo-handling equipment for offloading the lumber. A heavy ground swell prevented the use of the derrick-equipped salvage barge *Sampson*, leaving the salvors only the option of unloading the immense cargo by hand. As the lumber was jettisoned, it was gathered into large rafts and then towed into San Pedro.

While the work of lightening the *Meyer* continued, tugs made periodic efforts to drag her from her rocky perch, but to no avail. Eventually, as she settled lower, the weight of her cargo and the pounding she was taking from the heavy ground swell broke her back. All efforts to save the *Meyer* had to be abandoned. Salvors then turned their energies to rescuing her cargo of lumber. After several weeks of heavy work, the majority of the cargo had been saved.

Further salvage efforts later in the year managed to recover part of her hull, her engines and most of her pumps, winches, and other gear. The remains of the *Meyer*, lightened by the removal of her equipment, drifted over the shallowest part of the Point Fermin reef, and settled into a deeper area closer to shore. There she remained, out of sight and out of mind, until divers discovered her resting place in the early '70s.

The *David C. Meyer* began her career as a Hough-type hull in the Astoria, Oregon, yard of the McEachren Shipbuilding Company. While still on the ways, she was named *Areturus*, but with her completion in 1920, she was launched as the *Anson S. Brooks*, for the Brooks-Scanlon Corporation of Jacksonville, Florida.

The vessel was 272 by 46 feet, 2,510 gross tons, and was powered by twin 700-horsepower, triple-expansion steam engines built by the Builders Iron Foundry. At the completion of her fitting-out, the *Brooks* was taken to Cuban waters, where she operated until mid-1922. At that time, she returned to the Pacific Coast, where she was operated as a coastwise lumber carrier until 1924. In March of that year, Brooks-Scanlon Corporation sold the *Anson S. Brooks* to the Wiggins-Meyer Steamship Company of Portland, Oregon. After Wiggins-Meyer changed her name to *David C.*

The David C. Meyer *early in her career when she operated for the Brooks Scanlon Corporation. Her rather unusual rig was required because she had to unload her lumber cargoes inside covered wharves. Photo from the National Maritime Museum, San Francisco.*

The cost of a shortcut—the wooden steam schooner David C. Meyer *impaled on the Point Fermin reefs. Note the deck—loaded lumber cargo going overboard. Photo from P. Smith collection.*

Meyer, she continued working in the coastal lumber trade.

Although documentation is unclear, contemporary sources suggest that Wiggins-Meyer either sold or chartered the *Meyer* to the McCormick Steamship Company just before her loss in March 1926.

Diving the David C. Meyer

Though the *Meyer* is less than two and a half miles from Los Angeles Light and San Pedro Harbor, it receives very little diver traffic. She lies in the middle of a very nice kelp bed in about 25 feet of water. Because of her location, a boat is the only reasonable way to dive the wreck. But, when coming in by boat from the south, considerable caution is required to avoid the reefs the *Meyer* hit. On the site, visibility can range from 10 to 30 feet, with 15 feet being about average. Aside from the periods when heavy winter storms denude the area, the site usually has a good covering of kelp. This has never been a problem, but of course, experience in diving around kelp should be mandatory for anyone wishing to dive the area.

The most noticeable object on the *Meyer* is her concrete collision bulkhead. It is doing a much better job as a home for sea life and as an addition to the local reef than it ever did in preventing collision damage. It stands upright, wedged into the bottom. At its base is an immense pile of chain, welded by time and rust into one solid mass. The remainder of the wreck—though difficult to pick out of the heavy bottom growth—is scattered around the area. Valves, lights, and fittings of many types have been recovered from the *Meyer*.

It's usually wise to plan dives on the *Meyer* for the morning hours, since the prevailing westerlies can cause an afternoon wind chop that can get pretty rough.

Though not a spectacular dive, the *David C. Meyer* is backyard-close and interesting, with the potential for artifacts for the sharp-eyed diver.

P. S.

Los Angeles Harbor to Long Beach

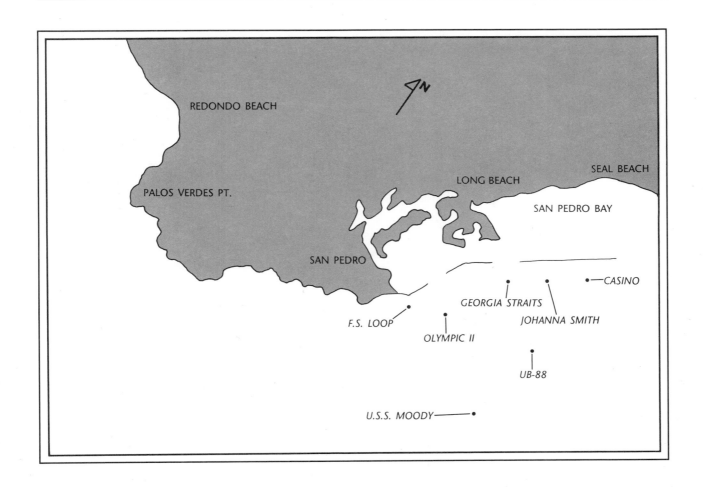

F. S. Loop

For Captain Gus Anderson of the steam schooner *F. S. Loop*, the early September trip had begun as just another cargo run from Portland, Oregon, to Los Angeles. In Portland, he had thoroughly checked the stowage, lashings, and cable hold-downs on his capacity cargo of dimensional lumber. Everything about the vessel had been neat, secure, and shipshape at departure, but now, a day later and after several hours of mauling by the fierce nor'wester that was pounding the northern California coast, the *Loop* could hardly be identified as the same vessel. As the Coast Guard cutters *Shawnee* and *Tahoe* approached to offer assistance, she presented a most disheartening sight; her hull, obviously waterlogged and terribly battered, rolled drunkenly in the huge white-capped swells. A substantial portion of her deck-load of lumber had been swept away along with sections of the bridge, house, and both her boats. The captains of all three vessels knew it was only because the *Loop*'s cargo was buoyant and supporting her weight that she had not plunged beneath the cold, gray seas off Cape Mendocino.

The *Loop*, or what was left of her, survived the 50-mile tow to the shelter of Humboldt Bay where she was safely anchored near the main wharf at Eureka.

Notice of her pounding went out to her owners, who in turn notified the marine underwriters who insured the vessel. Arriving at Eureka three days later, the underwriters' representatives estimated the cost of repairing the *Loop*'s house, engine (which had been knocked from its base), masts, rudder, loading gear, and boats at $20,000. The hull, which could be seen to be strained and twisted, was not even inspected. The underwriters, who felt that repair of the 29-year-old vessel could run as much as $50,000, declared the *Loop* a total constructive loss and recommended she be junked. Even the cargo of flooring and planed lumber that had saved her and her crew's lives was too damaged by water to be useful for anything other than firewood.

For most vessels, this would have seemed to be the end of the line, and in most times it would have been. But the year was 1936, and the country was in the middle of the Depression. Tough little vessels like the *Loop*, even severely damaged ones, wouldn't be cast aside quite so casually.

The *F. S. Loop* was a member of a class of vessel known as steam schooners—designed, built, and unique to the Pacific Coast. Known in the trade as a single-ender, and designed primarily to carry huge cargoes of lumber from the vast, rich forests of the Pacific Northwest to the cities and towns of central and southern California, she served this function exceedingly well. Not only did she provide a means for lumber resources to move south, but on her return trips she supplied towns and mills along the northern coast with foodstuffs, machinery, and manufactured goods that would be otherwise unavailable. Some of the steam schooners were even set up to accommodate a few passengers on these coastwise voyages, though apparently the *Loop* never did.

Built in 1907 at Marshfield (Coos Bay), Oregon, by the Kruse & Banks Shipbuilding Company, she was a stout vessel that cost nearly $120,000. Displacing 794 gross tons, her hull was constructed of local wood—Douglas fir—while her 500-horsepower, triple-expansion, oil-fueled steam engine was obtained from the United Engineering Works of San Francisco. Measuring only 193 feet in length, 39 feet in beam, and drawing 13.6 feet of water, she was not impressive in size. But she had a cargo capacity of more than 800,000 board feet of lumber, nearly enough to build a small town. This was because all her cargo holds and her midships deck were used to full advantage. Midships was an area of massive proportions, 140 by

"Wood floats, so the more lumber aboard, the less likely the vessel is to sink," was the creed that many steam schooner operators used when loading their ships. Here the F.S. Loop *is shown in San Pedro preparing to discharge a deck cargo of dimensional lumber stacked nearly 20 feet high. Photo from the National Maritime Museum, San Francisco.*

39 feet. On nearly every southbound trip this area was stacked 15 or 16 feet high with cargo, either planed lumber or creosoted poles and piles. Nearly every cubic foot of cargo space available both within and without the hull was used. For the crews of steam schooners such as the _Loop_, this meant that in fair weather or foul, to get from the foc'sle to the stern of the vessel, they had to scramble across the top of the deck load, a hazardous trip in heavy weather.

After suffering major damage in the September 1936 storm, the _F. S. Loop_ sat idle only two months before she was purchased by Dr. W. J. Ross, owner of the Dr. Ross Pet Food Company, and towed south to Los Angeles for extensive repairs. After several months of work, which included strengthening her hull, rebuilding her superstructure, and replacing her damaged steam engine with a 1917 model, 12-cylinder gasoline engine of 750-brake horsepower, the _Loop_ sailed south to Mexican waters to begin a new career as a floating fish reduction plant. Operating under a concession from the Mexican government, the _Loop_ captured and processed sea lions into dog food. It was said that the smell generated by this type of work could knock a strong man senseless several miles leeward. The _Loop_ continued in this malodorous work until January 1939, when she arrived at Los Angeles and was laid up.

During the next seven years of her career it seems the only thing that changed for the _Loop_ was her owners. For although she was sold four times and maintained her registry as either a freighter or a fishing vessel, she apparently never left her berth in L. A.'s Watchhorn Basin after January 1939.

Contemporary local papers reported that the _Loop_ sank at her berth in mid-1945, with just her superstructure protruding above the water. During the following months several attempts were made to refloat her, but they were unsuccessful.

Late in 1946 a more experienced salvage crew did manage to get the _Loop_ pumped out and floating. To celebrate their success they took an early lunch and lifted a few "cool ones." On returning to the site, they found the recalcitrant _Loop_ back on the bottom.

The U. S. Army Corps of Engineers, the government body responsible for harbors and shipwrecks within navigable waterways, declared the _Loop_, along with two other harbor derelicts, the _Storm King_ and the _Golden State_, hazards to navigation. So another attempt was made to remove the _Loop_ in 1947—this time for permanent disposal in 100 fathoms of water. On this attempt, the salvage company placed huge pontoons within the _Loop_'s hull to provide some flotation to get her off the muddy harbor bottom. Then, heavy, two-inch steel cables were run beneath her hull, and, at low tide, attached to two navy surplus landing crafts. As the tide rose, the _Loop_ was lifted clear of the bottom and was ready for towing.

The salvage crew had estimated it would take about four hours to make the nine-mile tow to the disposal area off Point Fermin; everyone figured to be home in time for dinner. Unfortunately, no one had figured on the capriciousness of the sea. Eight hours into the tow the _Loop_ was only some 2,000 yards off Angel's Gate Light, just one-third of the way to deep water, when the cables supporting her hull began to break. The strain of the wind and the waves, which had been building since the tow began, proved too much for the equipment; the _Loop_ plunged to the bottom in 83 feet of water with only 48 feet over her fo'c'sle and poop deck.

Despite intensive efforts over the next 12 months, the salvage company was unable to refloat the _Loop_.

With its working capital almost totally expended, the salvage company was ready to call it quits, but the bonding company on the project, looking at the very real possibility of having to forfeit its $35,000 bond on the incompleted job, suggested one last-ditch effort. Instead of trying to raise the _Loop_, why not blow her up? Down, that is, below the 60-foot depth the Corps of Engineers required for harbor approaches. Everyone involved agreed, but it was decided to bring in an expert in underwater demolition to do the job. That expert was E. R. Cross, modestly described by one local newspaper as "the greatest deep-sea diver on the West Coast."

Since no drawings or blueprints existed for the _Loop_, Cross, a thorough and seasoned professional, made several dives on the sunken hulk, crawling through every compartment, making notes on the size and placement of the various structural members that had held her hull together for 48 years. From this information he estimated that it would take about 2,500 pounds of blasting gelatin to complete the job successfully. Cross found that lots of people really got excited when they learned he wanted to move a ton and a quarter of high explosives down to L. A. Harbor. To move that amount of explosives required permits or permission from the Los Angeles Police Department, Port Security office, City and Harbor Fire departments, the Harbor Police, Coast Guard, California Department of Fish and Game, Harbor Department, and the Army Corps of Engineers. It took five days to secure the permits and only four days to place the explosives and do the job.

Once the explosives were placed on board the work barge and towed to the site, the job of placing the hundreds of ten-pound sticks of blasting gelatin began. Naturally, the weather refused to cooperate; rough seas, large swells, and inky black water plagued the divers. On several occasions the divers were swept off the wreck to the bottom 20 feet below while clinging to a 50-pound box of high explosives. In an article in *Water World* magazine, Cross wryly commented that although blasting gelatin was reasonably safe to handle, "There is a thrill in dropping through black water with 50 pounds of high explosives pressed against your belly."

On the third day of the operation, the tender vessel they were working from, the *Ruby A*, parted her anchor line while Cross and another diver were working. As the boat began to drift rapidly downwind, it dragged the one diver off the *Loop*'s deck, while Cross, who was working below decks, felt the sudden strain on his air hose and lifeline. He shouted to his tender to pay out all 400 feet of his lines to give him the slack and the time needed to work his way out of the hull. Even after he managed to get into the open, there was still a problem. There was no other anchor on board, and both divers required decompression. This could be done in the water, as the *Ruby A* drifted. But with divers over the side, the engines couldn't be run and the vessel couldn't be maneuvered; the rocks of the breakwater were less than 2,000 yards away.

It was close, but both divers were decompressed and brought aboard; the foam-washed rocks of the breakwater were but a short distance away when the *Ruby A* powered up and ran for safety. They had been within a few minutes of having to salvage their own boat.

By the next day the job was done. The 2,500 pounds of explosives were tied together with 3,000 feet of primacord, which ran to a buoy wired to a detonator on board the *Ruby A*. She had been posi-

tioned on the choppy waters some 2,000 feet from the buoy that marked the *Loop*'s final resting place.

Nearby, but well clear of the blast site, were vessels carrying representatives of the Coast Guard, Corps of Engineers, Fish and Game Department, and local press. Private boats and fishing craft also hovered nearby, ready to move in when allowed, to scoop up any fish killed by the detonation.

A final check was made and the signal to detonate given by Cross. At the buoy, the sea boiled up in two humps, like an oceanic camel, then subsided. The harbor approach was cleared; the *F. S. Loop* was no longer a hazard to navigation.

Diving the F. S. Loop

Since the intent of the dynamiting of the *Loop* was just to cut her superstructure down to acceptable depths, a considerable portion of her still remains.

A gear-driven, wood-bodied winch drum recovered from the old steam schooner F.S. Loop. *Photo by Patrick Smith.*

Sitting in about 75–80 feet of water, her engine and her hull ribs rise some 10 to 12 feet off the bottom. The seafloor in the area is made up of sand and cobble, and since it doesn't provide a lot of shelter, the remains of the *Loop* have become the focal point for most of the sea life in the area. On clear days, when visibility gets up to 25 feet or more, a startling amount and variety of sea life can be found on the wreck.

One particular trip to the *Loop* will stay with me forever. At the site, the water had the murky-green color that's common with coastal dive spots. At the anchor line, my buddy and I paused for a moment to adjust our gear, then we headed down. The visibility was a hazy 8 feet. At about 30 feet we got some good news and some bad news: The good was that the visibility increased to a dim but crystal-clear 40-plus feet, and the bad was that the water temperature felt as though it had just arrived, express, from Antarctica—it was cold! The *Loop* was spread out below us, so we dropped from the anchor line and swam to the bottom. The ribs sticking out of the sand and the clear, dim water gave the feeling of being in an immense cathedral; we both stopped on the bottom and savored the feeling. Then we became aware of the fish. Scuttling across the bottom from hiding place to hiding place were large, fat, gray-and-black-striped sand bass, while above the wreck silver clouds of six-inch mackerel skittered about in perfect unison. At the edge of the wreck a large male sheepshead hovered like a stately tricolored submersible.

Above the wreck, in the clear water, patrolled perhaps the most exciting members of this piscatorial parade, yellowtail. A school of perhaps two dozen of the graceful creatures cruised back and forth along the perimeter of the wreck, their silvery color muted in the dimness.

Years ago yellowtail were common along the southern California coast but the disappearance of the kelp beds, increased pollution, and heavy fishing pressure have all but removed them from the coastal areas. Their last bastions along southern California are the offshore islands and banks such as Tanner and Cortes. To find a school of 25-pounders practically in L. A. Harbor was almost unbelievable. But we had come to look for artifacts, not game, so each of us picked an area and began digging. By the end of our dive we had recovered T-hinges, valves, oilers, handles, a silver quarter dated 1924, and an interesting assortment of bottles and crockery.

I have encountered similar conditions several times on the *Loop*. But for the most part, visibility ranges from about 5 to 15 feet. Though this curtails the aesthetic enjoyment of the wreck, it isn't much of a hindrance in searching out artifacts on the old girl. Because she's close, I dive the *Loop* whenever I'm in the area, and I am rarely disappointed. But periodically, when the clear water moves in, I get the rare pleasure of experiencing a fascinating dive right in my own front yard.

P. S.

Olympic II

Not all accidents that send ships to the bottom of the sea are dramatic. The *Olympic II*, however, died as dramatically as she lived. It happened about 7 A.M. September 4, 1940. The *Olympic II* was a fishing barge, permanently moored three and a half miles off the San Pedro light, Los Angeles Harbor.

The morning was foggy and the night watchman, L. R. Ohiser, had been ringing the ship's bell at brief intervals as a warning to other vessels that might be in the area. Twenty-four men, boys, and girls were aboard the *Olympic*, seven of them did not survive.

Although the *Olympic's* survivors all recalled hearing the ship's bell being rung, Captain Shunji Sato of the *Sakito Maru* said neither he nor any of his crew did. He also claimed the *Sakito's* fog horn was being sounded at regular intervals, something no one from the *Olympic* remembered hearing.

The first intimation those aboard the *Olympic* had about the ship's impending doom was when the *Sakito* suddenly appeared out of the fog about 100 yards off her port side. Seeing the *Sakito*, Ohiser began frantically ringing his bell. Captain Sato, when informed there was a boat dead ahead, ordered his helm hard a-starboard. According to *Olympic* survivors, this headed the *Sakito* directly at them.

The 9,400 ton *Sakito* struck the much smaller *Olympic* amidships. The crash knocked most of the *Olympic's* passengers off their feet. The Japanese captain then made his biggest error: He ordered the *Sakito's* engines full astern. When the ship pulled back, water rushed in the huge hole left in the *Olympic* and she sank within two minutes.

Ten survivors were picked up by Captain L. H. Smith, who was operating *Water Taxi No. 17*. Seven more were rescued by the *Lillian L*, the *Olympic's* tender. Two bodies were recovered immediately. The body of the captain, Jack Greenwood, wasn't found for 13 days. By December 6, the bodies of all but one of those lost in the tragedy had been found.

The *Sakito Maru*, owned by the N. Y. K. Line, sustained only minor damage, which was quickly repaired. The day after the collision, Hermosa Amusement Corp., owners of the *Olympic*, filed a $200,000 suit against the N. Y. K. Line, the *Sakito Maru* and Captain Sato. A United States District Court issued an attachment against the ship and placed a deputy marshal on board to prevent its departure.

A Federal Board of Inquiry was convened the next day, September 6, to fix responsibility for the accident. As the inquiry was being held, divers examining the *Olympic II* and trying to find the bodies of the missing victims, found the *Sakito Maru* had cut more than 27 feet into the hull of the fishing barge.

By the morning of September 7, the amount of liens against the *Sakito*, her captain, and her owners totaled $650,000. By the end of that day the total had reached $787,000. However, agents for the *Sakito* posted a $203,000 cash bond with U. S. District Judge Ben Harrison, and the vessel was allowed to depart for Japan on September 8. Whether there was further legal action taken or more money collected from the N. Y. K. Line is unknown.

The Star of France

Although she went to her grave with another name, the *Olympic* was christened the *Star of France*. An iron-hulled, three-masted ship, she was built in Belfast, Ireland in 1877 by Harland & Wolff. She was a square-rigged bark of 1,644 gross tons, 258 feet long and 38 feet wide. Her owners were James Porter Corry, Robert William Corry, and John Corry.

The *Star of France* was one of five ships known as "Corry's Irish Stars." She sailed between England and India transporting jute. (Jute is a plant fiber used for burlap and twine.)

The *Star of France, her masts cut to the crosstrees, just before she was renamed the* Olympic II. *Photo courtesy of the National Maritime Museum, San Francisco.*

The heavy brass cover of the deck washdown pump recovered from the Olympic II. *The cover shows her original name, home port, the house flag of Cory & Company, the pump maker's name and district, and the ship's year of launch. Photo by Patrick Smith.*

In 1898, the *France* was sold to the Puget Sound Commercial Company, managed by J. J. Moore. According to Steve Lawson, writing in the California Wreck Divers' *Porthole* (June 1988), certain restrictions, still in effect today, prohibited the use of foreign hulls for coastal trading. Thus, the *Star of France* could not be placed under American registry. Instead, she was registered in the new American territory of Hawaii.

The *Star of France* was sent to Port Townsend, Washington, in the early 1900s and for a short time, her cargo was lumber. In 1902, Pacific Colonial Company bought the ship, chartering her to Alaska Packers Association. Three years later, the company bought the vessel. Fitted with the company's distinctive porthole storm covers, the *Star of France* was sent to Alaska each spring, where she functioned as a salmon packer until 1925.

From 1925 to 1934, the *France* sat idle in San Francisco Bay, her sailing career over. Faster, more reliable steamships had forced her into retirement. In 1934, she was purchased by Captain J. M. Anderson. He converted her into a fishing barge, which included cutting her masts to the first crosstrees. He also gave her a new name, *Olympic II*, and permanently anchored her in Horseshoe Kelp area off San Pedro.

Discovery in 1963

For more than two decades, the *Olympic* lay forgotten on the ocean floor. Fishermen found her to be a productive area, but memories faded as to exactly what was attracting so much marine life. Then, in 1963, Rusty Shields of the Commercial Diving Center buoyed the site and sent two divers down to verify it was a shipwreck. One of the divers was George Edwards, the other was a high school student named Roy Hauser. Hauser was a deckhand on the *Rio Rita*, a charter dive boat. He is now co-owner of Truth Aquatics, which has three dive boats operating out of Santa Barbara.

After diving the wreck, the three did some research, uncovering the ship's identity and her history. They salvaged large amounts of chain from the vessel, then began running charter trips to her. One of the divers on the first trip, in 1965, was Dan Chambers. He had never been on a wreck before, nor had he ever been as deep as 100 feet. While sightseeing on the *Olympic*'s deck, Dan found an object covered with marine growth. It was the ship's bell, the very one the night watchman had rung so diligently.

Bronze plate recovered from the Olympic II. *Photo by Patrick Smith.*

Approaching the bow section of the Olympic II. *Notice the fishing nets. A small anchor has snagged on the top, under some nets. Unable to retrieve it, the boat's crew cut the line and left the anchor, chain, and line below. Many anchors have been found on this wreck. Photo by Bonnie J. Cardone.*

Dan knew what is was immediately. Scratching off some of the growth with his knife, he confirmed the object was brass. However, since he did not have a lift bag he was unable to bring the heavy bell up with him. He made a second, bounce dive, and tied a line from the bell's twisted and bent bracket to the anchor. When this had been raised, Dan pulled the line up hand-over-hand. It was incredible that a first time wreck diver should find the ship's bell, but Dan's

luck continued. As he was lowering the bell to the deck of the boat, the bracket fell off. It had been attached to the bell by a steel bolt that had rusted through. With luck like that, it is no wonder Dan became an avid wreck diver and one of the founders of the California Wreck Divers.

The bell was just one of many artifacts brought up by some of the *Olympic*'s first divers. Especially prized were her portholes with their unique Alaska Packers storm covers. Roy Hauser, who salvaged a lot of chain and no brass, has since regretted his choice of objects! In 1972, the California Wreck Divers salvaged the ship's capstan, which was donated to the Los Angeles Maritime Museum in San Pedro.

Diving the Olympic II *Today*

The *Olympic II* lies in 100 feet of water. Visibility can range anywhere from two inches to 75 feet. Even if it's limited, macro photography on her is still good. She is covered with *Corynactis californica*, also known as strawberry anemones. These tiny little animals come in shades of red, pink and lavender. Nudibranchs and scallops, as well as featherduster worms, can be found in among the *Corynactis*.

The highest part of the bow, which is on its starboard side, is about 70 feet below the surface. It is draped with fishing nets. Anchors are frequently found here, left by boats after they become fouled. The bowsprit, covered by marine growth, extends out over the sand. When the visibility is good it makes an impressive photograph.

The midships was dynamited to eliminate structures that were a navigational hazard. What remains is parallel to the sand and rises no more than five feet above it.

The stern also lies on its starboard side and the top is just 60 feet below the surface. This part of the wreck is about 40 feet long.

B. J. C.

U.S.S. *Moody*

The first officer of the American sub painfully straightened up, wiped the sweat from his eyes, then, once again, bent back to the periscope before him. He automatically resumed the same slow shuffle as he continued to search for the enemy from forty feet below the sea.

To the crew in the control room, the first officer seemed preoccupied. But who wouldn't be, with the responsibility of ship and crew on one's shoulders? However, it wasn't worries of ship and crew that caused the first officer's preoccupation, but the memory of the death of his good friend, the young lieutenant, just the day before.

The lieutenant and a volunteer crew were rowing the sub's small boat out to pick up survivors from a sinking vessel, when suddenly, an enemy aircraft came diving out of the sun with machine guns blazing. The first few seconds had done the job for the lieutenant and his small crew. The plane's second attack, this time on the sub, eliminated the chance of recovery of any of the men in the small boat. "Crash dive! Take 'er down fast!" had been the orders.

The sub's operating orders has been nearly as hard to live with as the orders to leave the bodies of their shipmates after the attack: "Do not, repeat, do not engage the enemy under any circumstances. Observe size, direction and speed of any enemy vessels encountered."

Thoughts of the young lieutenant's death kept running through the first officer's mind. "It just isn't fair," he thought. Suddenly he paused in his periscope sweep of the horizon; far to the west, something had appeared to change the vast empty expanse of sea and sky. Several smudges of smoke were barely visible on the razor edge of the horizon.

"Come right to 265 degrees, all ahead full." The first officer spoke calmly, but inside, his nerves were jumping. While it was his watch, the sub was his ship. Perhaps there was a way to avenge his friend, the young lieutenant. . . .

When they had gotten close enough, the first officer could see it was a perfect situation: two enemy ships laying mines, and one destroyer as an escort vessel. He couldn't get all three, but there was a good chance for two. It would cost him his commission, but he never hesitated. "Stand by all forward torpedo tubes."

The answer came quickly, "All forward torpedo tubes loaded and ready, sir." The first officer jockeyed the sub into her final firing position, then gave the order: "Fire one, fire two!" A quick course change and the crosshairs of the scope were set on the second ship. "Fire three, fire four!" He watched the second two torpedoes for a moment as they streaked away, then he quickly swung back to view the first target. As he watched, the entire midsection of the ship disappeared in a sheet of flame. The vessel slowed and began to settle into the water. The concussions from torpedoes three and four announced their accuracy even before the first officer could swing back to view their effect, which was awesome; the vessel has been blown in half and both sections were beginning their final plunge.

The cheers of the sub's crew quickly died as the captain entered the control room and roared, "What goes on here?" He shoved the first officer aside and grabbed the handles of the periscope. A brief glance told the story; two mortally wounded vessels and an irate destroyer headed their way at flank speed!

The captain responded swiftly. "Down scope—crash dive—take 'er down emergency!" As the sub headed down, the captain turned to the first officer. "You're relieved of command and confined to quarters."

As the first officer was making his way to his cabin, the first of the depth charges exploded.

Even though the above scenario is merely a portion of the action-filled script of the 1933 movie *Hell Below*, it is far more than just entertaining fiction, particularly for California wreck divers. Though the story, characters and incidents were fiction, the destruction of the "enemy" vessels was quite real and diving the remains of one of those vessels has become the "E Ticket" for southern California divers.

The film, which starred actors Walter Houston, Robert Montgomery, Robert Young, William Bendix, Sterling Holloway, and Jimmy Durante, was called "very well-made and entertaining" by critics of the era. But unlike the other cast members who went on to cinema fame, the vessels destroyed for *Hell Below*, after their brief but dramatic debut on the silver screen, slipped into obscurity; names, location, and history all forgotten, until November 1973. At that time a group of local divers had been searching the area southeast of Angel's Gate (Los Angeles Light), for the wreck of a freighter rumored to have sunk out there in the 50s. The charts for the area did show an unidentified obstruction of some type in 22 fathoms of water. They wanted to find out what it was.

The quest had gone on sporadically for many weekends. The searching had expended many yards of fathometer graph paper, but except for the discovery of several productive deep-water lobster reefs, the effort had produced nothing in the way of a shipwreck. Their enthusiasm for the search had begun to wane.

Doing any kind of organized search of an area that far offshore (nearly eight miles) without Loran was practically impossible. Only by taking bearings from prominent coastal structures were they even able to maintain any semblance of order in their search, and this was crude at best. A day with a little haze or fog eliminated any chance of locating the wreck. But suddenly, as quickly as a stylus can zip across a fathometer graph, all the excitement and anticipation were back. The flat never-changing line that represented the bottom on the fatho's graph suddenly jumped up 20 feet, maintained that height for a considerable distance, then plunged back to the bottom at 130 feet. Markers went over the side, followed quickly by the anchor. The divers followed shortly after.

It took them but a few seconds after they reached the bottom to realize several things: first, this wreck, whatever it was, was not the freighter they had been looking for. Second, they really didn't care.

The group had been diving the wreck for several weeks before I was invited to take a look at her and try to figure out exactly what had been found.

The next weekend we left the Long Beach launch ramp at 7 A.M. under slightly overcast skies. After passing Angel's Gate, we found the sea flat and glassy with hardly any swell. Some 40 minutes later, just after the water color changed from the murky green of the inshore waters to the deep indigo blue of open ocean, we spotted the marker buoy that had been left the weekend before. We made several fathometer runs over the site before we dropped anchor and began gearing-up for the first dive of the day. Soon after, we were over the side and beginning our descent to the wreck below.

As I pulled myself down the anchor line, I thought about some of the information the divers had mentioned about the wreck. They were sure that it was some type of military vessel because some of the

bronze valve handles they had brought up were marked U.S.N. Also, the ship was broken in half, the two pieces separated by some 50 or 60 yards. This seemed to indicate she had either been involved in a collision or accident, or been used as a target vessel. The problem with these hypotheses was that all of us had been doing research on local shipwrecks for quite some time, and an accident or collision involving a ship of the size they described would certainly have been noted. That the location was only about eight miles off the harbor seemed to refute the idea the vessel had been used as a target. The fact that the ship was sunk for a Hollywood feature was still many fruitless hours of research in the future, with the real key to her identity coming not from that effort, but from the vessel herself.

The visibility from the surface had been a respectable 40-plus feet, but as I passed through a numbing thermocline at about 75 feet, the visibility improved perceptibly; following the curve of the anchor line down through the pristine dimness I could make out the lighter and darker areas of the wreck spread below me. The lighter areas, white actually, were clumps of huge white *Metridium* anemones. There were thousands of them everywhere and as the beam of the dive-light swept over them, their snow-whiteness was almost startling. Almost as breathtaking were the amount and colors and their variations—pinks, scarlets, crimsons, magentas, lavenders, and blood-reds—of the colonial *Corynactis* anemones, which blanketed nearly every surface not already claimed by the cauliflower-like *Metridiums*. The degree and intensity of the colors were truly amazing. It took me a few moments to assimilate everything and realize what else I was seeing; the canoe-like stern, twin screws, stern house, davits and torpedo tubes midships—there was only one type of vessel this could be—a World War I vintage four-stack destroyer.

As I moved forward along the starboard side of the ship, the beam of my dive-light reflected in the slightly overgrown but still unbroken lenses of a row of portholes. Running along the edge of the deck were immense brass stanchions, their bronze life-line cables still semi-taut, and now festooned with all manner of sea life. Great swarms of bocaccio and vermilion rockfish hung over and around the wreck and drifted about in living clouds.

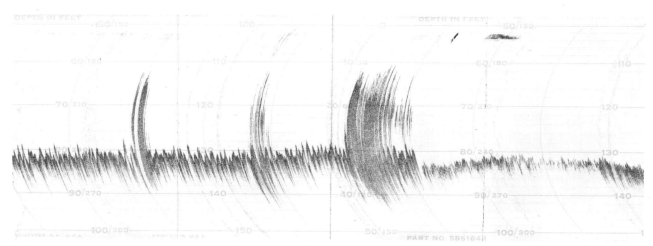

Fathometer tracings of the wreck of the U.S.S. Moody. *Photo from the P. Smith collection.*

Moving farther forward, and now swimming up across the slightly listing deck, I passed the remains of the midships spotlight tower, whaleboat davits and the clusters of once-deadly torpedo tubes. Just beyond these fairly well-preserved weapons, the hull came to an abrupt and jagged end. Dropping down to the sand I checked my depth gauge; it read 132 feet.

Glancing down I noticed two small, intact portholes, loose at my feet. Quickly I gathered them into a goodie-bag, and after hooking it to a lift bag, I added enough air to get the load slightly positive, swam it up to the main deck and tied if off near where our anchor was hooked in some twisted wreckage.

Probably because of narcosis, my mind wandered. Instead of going back to look at the exposed compartments at the hull break, my attention was caught by the torpedo tubes and how remarkably intact they appeared. Swimming closer I noticed the large, bronze traversing wheels and the brass speaking tubes nearby, all of it carpeted with either *Metridium* or *Corynactis*.

By now my bottom time was getting limited, even if it seemed as though I had just arrived moments before. I snapped the lift bag on to a ring on the anchor line, put in a little more air, and let it go. It began moving slowly up the line, then accelerated as it moved higher, finally disappearing into the brightness above. My buddy and I started up but at a slower, safer pace.

That was the first of many dives to the then-unidentified *Moody*. Because of her excellent condition and

abundance of artifacts, she became the favorite wreck for many local divers. The late cinematographer Jack McKenney declared the wreck "one of the prettiest" he'd ever seen after his first dive to the *Moody*.

During this period, considerable time was being expended in searching for the identity of the wreck, but despite this effort, nothing was turning up. Finally, on one dive several months after her discovery, one of the local divers recovered a bronze bearing block hand-stamped #277. Experience had taught that often, especially on naval vessels, the ship's I.D. number was stamped on various machinery parts. In this case also, it proved to be true. A quick check through navy records produced a name and a history to go with the number.

The U.S.S. *Moody* was a Clemson-class destroyer built by the Bethlehem Ship Building Corporation, Squantum, Massachusetts, and was commissioned September 14, 1919. She was named for William Henry Moody, who served as a U. S. congressman, was appointed Secretary of the Navy by Theodore Roosevelt in 1902, and then Attorney General in 1904. He became an associate justice of the Supreme Court in 1906, and after a prolonged illness, was retired by a special act of Congress in 1910.

The *Moody*, DD-277, displaced 1,308 tons, was 314 feet in length with a beam of almost 31 feet. She was powered by two 13,000-s.h.p.-geared turbines, and along with her sister ships was one of the fastest vessel types in the Navy, with a speed of 34.7 knots. As for armament, the *Moody* was well endowed in that department, too. She carried four 4-inch guns, one 3-inch gun, and twelve 21-inch torpedo tubes, clustered in four groups of three.

Though launched too late to participate in World War I, the *Moody* had an active career that included operations and training exercises in the Atlantic and Caribbean, as well as a substantial number of operations carried out in various areas of the Pacific, including Alaska, Hawaii, Panama, and New Zealand. She was decommissioned at San Diego in June 1930, in accordance with the London Treaty Limiting Naval Armaments, and then towed to Mare Island Navy Yard, San Francisco, for scrapping. At this point, however, fate, in the form of MGM, stepped in. The film company purchased the *Moody* for the movie *Hell Below* and immediately set about restoring the *Moody's* weaponry, this time in wood and canvas rather than steel. The strange part of the restoration was that during her "scrapping" by the Navy, her four clusters of torpedo tubes were never removed, so when she made her screen debut, her "makeup" consisted of "prop" weapons, except for her torpedo tubes, which were the real thing.

In *Hell Below*, the *Moody* played the part of one of the "enemy" minelayers and in preparation for this, her hull was cut in half, then "stitched" back together with steel cable. For the scene where she's torpedoed, a spectacular explosion was set off to simulate the torpedo hit while smaller, structural explosions severed the binding cables. So on cue, the *Moody* takes the hit, breaks in half, the two halves drift apart while slowly sinking (this was managed by use of water-tight compartments set to flood at a calculated rate), then, still on cue, she dramatically slides beneath the waves amid suitable flotsam and debris.

On film, this scene was so dramatic and played so well, that it was used not only in *Hell Below,* but it was also borrowed by the documentary series *Victory at Sea* in several of their episodes to portray various vessels sinking.

Diving the Moody

Even after diving the *Moody* for nearly 15 years, I am still dazzled by every visit I make to her. She is so unique and offers such diverse aspects that to describe her in complete detail would be almost impossible.

Cinematographer Jack McKenney examines a small non-opening porthole from the Moody. *Photo by Patrick Smith.*

On one recent dive we found the wreck to be nearly covered by gelatinous fingers of squid eggs. Almost every horizontal surface of the wreck, plus the seafloor for a considerable distance surrounding it, was piled high with dead squid and their embryonic offspring. This unusual bonanza was being taken advantage of by nearly every inhabitant of the wreck. The schools of rockfish that usually hovered around the wreck were so stuffed on squid that they were just lolling on the wreck, too bloated even to swim. The anemones were also partaking, many of them with squid or squid eggs protruding from their maws.

For photographers, subjects abound on either half of the *Moody*. On the forward half, the knife-like bow sweeping up from the bottom is a dramatic shot. On the stern, the unusual thin-bladed props, the torpedo tubes, plus myriad types of sea life are guaranteed to drive any photographer crazy with their limitless options.

Because of her depth, the *Moody* hasn't been picked over as much as some other local wrecks, and artifacts are still plentiful. Handles, gauges, railings, portholes, junction boxes and lights are still to be found by a sharp-eyed relic hunter.

Because of her offshore location, conditions on the *Moody* can be extreme. Visibility ranges from 2 to well over 100 feet, with the average running 15 to

U.S.S. Moody *with her crew at muster on the foredeck. Photo from the National Archives.*

30. Currents, too, can be a problem, with those from the surface to 30 feet sometimes running in excess of two knots. Obviously, no diving is done during the extremes, but even afternoon westerly winds can make decompression stops difficult.

Though the required decompression stops are lengthy, boredom rarely occurs. Aside from looking at recovered artifacts, this spot, appearing no different from any other spot in the ocean, is in fact the Times Square of the Catalina Channel. While soaking out, it's not uncommon to encounter ocean sunfish, squid, seals, porpoise, sharks, pilot whales and comb and medusa jellyfish.

Obviously, a visit to the *Moody* should be limited only to very experienced open-water divers.

P. S.

UB-88

The entry in the log of the United States destroyer *Wickes* is brief and to the point:

> At 4:00 made stn'd speed 15 knots. At 4:08 commenced firing on *UB-88* with number 1, 2, 4 guns. At 4:12 ceased firing and stopped. At 4:16 *UB-88* sank bow first. At 4:20 standing in for San Pedro . . . Captain at the conn— Navigator on bridge. Approved: W. F. Halsey, Commander, U.S.N., Commanding.

Though this action was an insignificant footnote in W. F. (Bull) Halsey's naval career, it marked the end of a long voyage for one of Kaiser Wilhelm's very successful *unterseebootes.*

At the outbreak of World War I on August 1, 1914, there was a belief among both German and British admirals that submarines were primarily defensive weapons. They were considered of little value when compared to the mighty battleships and cruisers that were the major units of both fleets. This mind set was not so strongly held by the Germans as it was by the British, and early in the war German U-boats were sent on patrols up and down the English Channel. Despite early losses, the Germans provided two dramatic examples of how effective an offensive weapon the submarine could be.

On September 5, 1914, Korvettenkapitan Otto Hersing, commanding the *U-21,* sank the British light cruiser *Pathfinder* with a single torpedo; 259 members of her crew were lost with her.

High-ranking naval officers on both sides believed that the sinking was a fluke and still were not convinced of the submarine's potential. But on September 22, 1914, doubt was put to rest for all time. A spectacularly successful attack was carried out by the *U-9*—one of Germany's oldest and least sophisticated U-boats—on three of Britain's armored cruisers.

In less than one hour the *U-9,* skippered by Kapitanleutnant Otto Weddigen, sank the British cruisers *Aboukir, Hogue,* and *Cressy,* warships totaling more than 36,000 tons. The attack also claimed the lives of 1,460 British sailors and officers. The submarine's place as a modern weapon of war was firmly established. Fortunately, in both world wars, Germany didn't provide enough support for the powerful and effective U-boats it fielded. In each war changes in

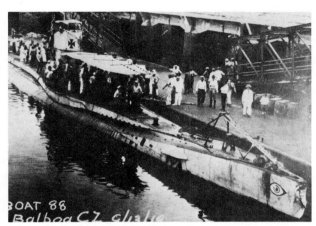

The Kaiser's U-boat, UB-88 *at Balboa, Canal Zone, August 13, 1919. Photo from the National Archives.*

technologies and tactics, along with the industrial contributions of the United States, managed to thwart the German attempts at controlling the sea lanes.

Despite the crudeness of her technology by today's standards, the *UB-88* was a frighteningly effective weapon. In less than four months, on three war patrols, she sank 13 Allied vessels—totaling 32,141 tons—and severely damaged two others.

Built by Aktiengesellschaft Vulcan shipyard of Hamburg, Germany, the *UB-88* was launched December 11, 1917. Classified as a small coastal operations U-boat, she displaced 510 tons surfaced, 640 tons submerged and carried a crew of 34. Within her 182-by-19-foot hull she mounted five 20-inch torpedo tubes and on deck, a single 4.1-inch (105 mm) gun.

She was commissioned into the Imperial German Navy on January 26, 1918, and placed under the command of Oberleutnant zur See (lieutenant j.g.) Johannes Ries. After running the *UB-88* through nearly five months of shakedown in the North and Baltic seas, Captain Ries received orders for his vessel. *UB-88* was assigned to the I U-Flotille, Flandern (1st Submarine Flotilla, Flanders) at Zeebrugge, Belgium.

She departed Kiel on June 4, 1918, via the eastern route around Denmark and by June 10, she was off the east coast of England. Late in the day she encountered a convoy of five freighters and six trawlers, escorted by two destroyers and several aircraft. Captain Ries began his attack immediately. After gaining a good firing position without being detected, he fired

one torpedo. The aim was good. It struck and sank the 1,555-ton Swedish steamer *Dora.* The escorting destroyers immediately saturated the area with depth charges, but the *UB-88* escaped with minor damage. She arrived safely in Zeebrugge on June 12 and reported for duty with I U-Flotille, Flandern.

During the next three and one-half months, the *UB-88* conducted three war patrols. The first began on June 20 and was concluded on the 29th of that same month. During this nine-day period the *UB-88* was rammed once, losing her main periscope but carrying on with her secondary scope. She also survived two depth-charge attacks by Allied escort vessels. Her score for her first patrol: Nine vessels sunk. In two instances Captain Ries and his crew managed to sink two ships in one day.

The *UB-88* departed on her second war patrol on July 29, 1918. This cruise, though somewhat longer than her first, proved to be far more dangerous and far less productive. While cruising the area between Le Havre and the Isle of Wight in the English Channel, the *UB-88* encountered a French destroyer escorting two steamers. Captain Ries attacked immediately and fired two torpedoes at the Allied ships. One struck the British steamer *Bayronto*, while the other missed. Though heavily damaged, the *Bayronto* was able to make it to port; an aggressive attack by the French destroyer prevented the *UB-88* from finishing off the crippled steamer. During the course of the attack the U-boat was mauled by more than 40 depth charges dropped by the destroyer. But, amazingly, the sub suffered little damage. Two days later Captain Ries attacked one of four cruisers that had been escorting a convoy into the French port of Brest. The torpedo missed and the only thing that Captain Ries received for his brazen attempt was another severe depth-charge pounding. This time the *UB-88* suffered extensive concussion damage to her electrical system, but effective damage control efforts allowed her to continue the patrol.

The following day, in attacks on two separate convoys, two more Allied steamers were sent to the bottom by Captain Ries and the *UB-88*. Both vessels—the American freighter *Lake Portage* and the Norwegian steamer *Hundvaago*—were destroyed by single torpedo hits. The final attack of this cruise was carried out on August 9 while the *UB-88* was returning to Zeebrugge. She caught the British ship *Anselma de*

Larringa near the mouth of the Seine River and pumped one torpedo into her hull. Even though she was damaged, the British ship managed to escape a second torpedo and reach the shelter of Le Havre. Two days later, on August 11, the *UB-88* entered Zeebrugge harbor and concluded her second patrol.

Nearly a month later, on September 7, the *UB-88* departed for her final war patrol. Captain Ries headed north up the east coast of England and Scotland, turning west above the Orkney Islands, then sailed south down the west coast of Ireland. He had circumnavigated the British Isles in search of targets but found none.

On September 14, *UB-88* finally reached her area of operations, a roughly triangular area at the mouth of the English Channel marked by Cherbourg, Brest, and Falmouth. Two days later in a submerged attack, she sank the 3,050-ton British steamer *Philomel* with a single torpedo. Continuing her cruise, the *UB-88* struck again two days later, sinking the Swedish freighter *Fanny*. However, with the sinking of the *Fanny*, hunter's luck seemed to abandon the sub. For the next six days she found no other targets. With supplies running low, Captain Ries began the homeward trek to Zeebrugge. Shortly after midnight on September 22, the *UB-88* found her last target. Firing a single torpedo in a surface attack, the U-boat sank the 4,221-ton British steamer *Polesley* just off the Cornwall coast.

Arriving at Zeebrugge seven days later, *UB-88* stayed only long enough to refuel, then she departed for Germany. She arrived at Heligoland, on October 3, and was reassigned to the II U-Flotille, Hocseeflotte (2nd Submarine Flotilla, High Seas Fleet). Inactive, she remained with this flotilla until the war's end.

On November 26, 1918, the *UB-88*, along with the other vessels of the High Seas Fleet, were surrendered and interned at Harwich, England. At this time the U. S. Navy requested the use of several German U-boats to study German technology and, secondarily, to display them in conjunction with the current Victory Bond drive. The *U-111*, *U-117*, *U-140*, *UB-88*, *UB-148*, and the *UC-97* were consigned to the U. S. Navy with the condition that they be destroyed at the conclusion of the bond drive.

Late in March of 1919, navy crews arrived and took command of the allocated U-boats. Shortly afterward, the *UB-88* and her five sisters were placed in special commission in the U. S. Navy. After less than two weeks of familiarization and shakedown, four of the U-boats and their American crews were ready for the transatlantic voyage. Two of the subs, the *U-111* and the *U-140* could not be readied in time, owing to sabotage.

On April 3, the *UB-88*, *U-117*, *UB-148*, and the *UC-97*, along with the submarine tender *Bushnell*, departed Harwich en route to New York via the Azores and Bermuda. The official designation of this flotilla was the Ex-German Submarine Expeditionary Force.

The fleet arrived at New York on April 27, and immediately became the focus of interest for what seemed to be the majority of New York City's population. After being examined by naval designers, marine engineers, and thousands of tourists, orders came through listing the U-boats' itineraries. The *UB-88* was assigned the longest schedule, with ports on the East Coast south of Savannah, Georgia, ports on the Gulf Coast, the Mississippi River as far north as Memphis, Tennessee, and the Pacific Coast.

Beginning her tour on May 5, 1919, she made appearances at more than 25 East Coast ports. She was placed in dry dock on July 1 in New Orleans for repairs to her port tail shaft. With repairs completed on July 22, the *UB-88* headed south to continue her tour. After passing through the Panama Canal, she headed north, working her way up the coast with stops in Mexico, California, Oregon, and Washington. After making her last port of call—Bremerton, Washington—she headed south, arriving at the submarine base at San Pedro, California, on November 7. The *UB-88* was laid up there until November 1, 1920, when she was placed out of commission. The following January, the *UB-88* departed San Pedro on her final voyage.

On January 3, 1921, the U. S. Navy minesweeper *Pocomoke* stood out from Sub Base, San Pedro, with the *UB-88* in tow. Now rust-stained and shabby from several months of neglect, the once trim U-boat—awarded the Iron Cross for "valorous sea duty"—appeared as a mere shadow of her former self. Shortly afterward, the battleship U.S.S. *New Mexico*, flagship of the Pacific Fleet and observation ship for the destruction of the *UB-88*, left harbor and made her way out to sea. On board was Admiral Hugh Rodman, Commander-in-Chief of the Pacific Fleet. His guests included such military and civilian notables as

Admiral W. Twining, Chief of Staff; Rear Admiral J. L. Jayne, Commander of Training, Pacific Fleet; and Los Angeles Mayor Meredith P. Snyder. Also on board to document the event were numerous reporters and photographers along with several film crews.

By 3:15 P.M. all the participants had arrived at the designated site, an area some eight miles south-southeast of the Los Angeles Harbor Light. The *Wickes* carried out 57 minutes of sighting and maneuvering, then commenced firing at 4:08. Four minutes and 20 four-inch shells later, it was over; the *UB-88*, mortally wounded, went the way of her war-time victims. She slipped beneath the choppy waters of the gray Pacific at 4:16.

Though the U-boat had been rigged with 25 pounds of TNT, to be used to sink her if the *Wickes*'s gunfire proved insufficient, it was never used. The second shell fired by the *Wickes* severed the tow and firing cables between the *Pocomoke* and the sub, and the gunfire proved to be more than adequate.

Search for the UB-88

Though she has been the goal of many searches over the past years, the *UB-88* has yet to be located. Log records from all the ships involved in the U-boat's destruction are, unfortunately, vague or conflicting concerning an exact location of the sinking. Depending on which source is used, there is as much as a two-mile difference in the location given as the *UB-88*'s grave.

There are at least three groups actively searching for the U-boat. It appears that each has picked what

One of the posters used to promote the postwar Victory Bond Drive in which the UB-88 *participated. Photo from the National Archives.*

UB-88 *and* UB-148 *alongside the USS* Bushnell *at New York Navy Yard during the Victory Bond Drive in the spring of 1919. Photo from the National Archives.*

it feels is the most likely area and is running fathometer (and in one case, magnetometer) sweeps through them. One team has been involved, on a weekend basis, for several years, but without results. However, with the continuing interest and ongoing search efforts to locate her, it's a good bet the shattered hulk of southern California's U-boat will be found, sooner or later.

    P. S.

Georgia Straits

Like so many summer mornings in southern California, August 7, 1965 found heavy fog blanketing the coastal areas.

For King Frey, owner and licensed skipper of the tug *Georgia Straits*, the fog was a minor inconvenience as he slowly and skillfully guided the vessel out of L. A. Harbor. On board he had 13 friends and family members all ready and eager for a day of fishing on the broad blue briny; a little early morning fog was not going to delay the good times. Some 30 minutes out of the breakwater with the *Straits'* foghorns sounding as prescribed by the International Rules of the Road, the mournful bellow of another vessel's foghorn was heard through the mist. While he continued to sound the *Georgia's* twin foghorns, Captain Frey had his crew keep a sharp lookout for the nearby ship. The fog signals from the unseen ship continued to get closer, but because of the way the fog seemed to distort the sound, it was difficult to pinpoint an exact location of the vessel.

Suddenly, there it was. Bearing down on the *Georgia Straits'* port bow was the immense bow of the Mexican tanker *Reynosa*, outbound for Manzanilla, Mexico, with a partial load of diesel fuel.

According to Chris Barclay, on board the *Straits* that fateful morning, "The tanker was lightly loaded and standing high out of the water. Seeing her bow coming through the fog, she looked as tall as a building bearing down on us."

As soon as he saw the other ship, Captain Frey knew a collision was inevitable. Despite his best efforts in the few moments he had, the *Straits* was impaled some 15 feet abaft her stem by the large tanker.

Almost at the moment of impact the captain of the *Reynosa* reversed his engines, but it was too little, far too late. The impact was violent. It rolled the *Georgia Straits* nearly 20 degrees to starboard and hurled all of those on her to the deck. Fortunately, none was hurt.

After the momentum of the *Reynosa* was dissipated by its impact with the smaller vessel, there was a moment of near absolute silence. Both vessels were locked together and save for the lap of the waves, all sounds seemed muffled or absorbed by the fog.

Al Rowe, another member of the *Straits* crew, scrambled to the tug's bow. He quickly noted that the Mexican tanker had penetrated nearly six feet through the tough, double-planked oak hull of the tug and that the port lifeboat had been crushed. He called to the lookout on the *Reynosa*, who was staring down, wide-eyed, from nearly 30 feet above him, "Launch a lifeboat! We have women and children on board." The reply to his request came floating down through the fog: "*No comprende.*"

Just then, the tearing and grinding began again as the *Reynosa*, leaving a gaping wound in the smaller vessel, pulled away. Within moments, nearly as quickly as she had appeared and without offering any aid at all, the undamaged *Reynosa* backed into the dense fog and disappeared.

Captain Frey checked his crew, then made for the radio. His pleas for assistance were crackling across the airways within a few minutes of the collision. Luck was with the crew of the *George Straits* that day. Even though they were within five miles of the Coast Guard facilities at San Pedro and Long Beach, help was even closer at hand. Two Coast Guard cutters returning from patrol, the *Morris* and the *Minnetonka*, were nearby and intercepted the Mayday calls. They immediately altered course and made for the crippled tug, but because of the fog it took them nearly an hour to arrive on the scene.

Meanwhile, the *Georgia Straits'* crew was fighting for survival—the vessel's and their own. The undamaged starboard lifeboat had been launched and moved around to the impact area on the port bow of the tug. Mattresses pulled from the numerous bunks on board were dropped down to the lifeboat, where Captain Frey's 16-year-old son, David, wedged

them into the shattered V-shaped wound in the *Georgia*'s hull. Water pressure held the mattresses in place while they served to reduce substantially the amount of Pacific Ocean rushing into the hull. In addition to the *Straits'* own pumps, a bucket brigade was formed in an attempt to at least hold their own against the still steadily rising water. It was a futile effort. Within a short time the water had risen over the batteries and there was no more power for the pumps. The tug now began to settle rapidly.

Jack Zimmerman, a test pilot for Hughes Helicopter Company who was on board that day, was heard to mutter, "This is going to be a hell of a way for a test pilot to die."

Just then the Coast Guard cutter *Morris* appeared through the fog and quickly maneuvered alongside the stricken tug. As the crew of the *Morris* was placing portable high-volume, gasoline-powered pumps on board, the *Minnetonka* arrived and came in on the other side of the *Georgia Straits*. The *Minnetonka* immediately began removing the crew from the tug. With great efficiency, the guardsmen even managed to rescue most of the fishing gear and the picnic lunch the *Straits'* crew had packed for the day as well.

The *Georgia Straits* was in bad shape. Even with the addition of two more portable, high-volume pumps, she was settling lower into the water each moment.

There were nearly four inches of water on the main deck when Captain Frey, true to the traditions of the sea, finally left the doomed *Georgia Straits*. A few minutes after he had gone aboard the cutter *Minnetonka*, the stern of the tug slipped below and the bow reared toward the foggy sky. Moments later, the *Georgia Straits* plunged beneath the glassy, gray waters some three miles off the Long Beach breakwater.

There was an interesting finale to the sinking of the *Straits*. Several minutes after the tug had disappeared, the damaged port lifeboat, apparently torn free when the tug hit bottom, burst to the surface and rocketed some 15 feet into the air before crashing back into the sea and slowly sinking—a last salute to the departed vessel.

It was then, as the survivors of the *Georgia Straits* were watching the lifeboat sink, that they became aware of another aspect of the collision and sinking: the water around the Coast Guard cutter was supporting an impressive population of good-sized blue sharks.

The tug Georgia Straits. *Photo by A. Rowe.*

The *Georgia Straits'* career had been a long and varied one. It began in Vancouver, British Columbia, in 1905, when she was launched as the tug *Belle* for the Hastings Mill Stevedoring Company. The *Belle* was not a big vessel, only 92 by 18.7 feet and some 89 tons, but she was tough. With her double oak-planked hull she was a staunch craft and over the years carried out many difficult towing assignments for her owners. One of the more exciting incidents of her career occurred in 1925 when she came across the freighter *Wakena* in mortal distress.

In the Northwest, it was common knowledge that the *Wakena* was a bad luck vessel. In her ten-year career, the twin-screwed gasoline freighter had encountered more than her share of mishaps. Perhaps the worst incident was the asphyxiation deaths of her first mate and quartermaster because of a carbon monoxide build-up in November 1915. But in early 1925, at the time of her sale by the Border Line Transportation Company to the Latouche Packing Company, all thoughts were on her bright future in Alaskan waters, not on her past problems. Unfortunately, the change of owners didn't change her luck.

On May 27, 1925, while en route to her new Alaskan home, the *Wakena* caught fire off Nanaimo, British Columbia, and was completely destroyed. The potential was there for the loss of the officers and crew as well as the ship, but thanks to the timely appearance of the doughty tug *Belle*, the *Wakena* took no one with her when she made her final plunge.

In 1932, under the ownership of the Preston-Mann Towing Company Limited, Vancouver, the *Belle* was dry docked, and her original steam engine removed and replaced with a 400-horsepower Union diesel. Even though she was 27 years old, the refit and repower made her as capable as nearly any tug available in the area.

In 1942, Preston-Mann's entire fleet of ten vessels, including the tug *Belle*, was purchased by the Straits Towing & Salvage Company of Vancouver. For the next seven years the *Belle* continued excellent towing work for her new owners. In 1949, in accordance with a new company policy to name all Straits Towing vessels after famous straits, the *Belle* received a new name: *Georgia Straits*.

In 1964, Straits Towing Company sold the *Georgia Straits* to West Coast Salvage & Contracting Company

The ship's wheel, recovered from the tug Georgia Straits. *Photo by Patrick Smith.*

who almost immediately resold her to Max Walden of San Francisco. Walden set about converting the drab but efficient little tug into a cruising yacht.

The plan was to use the best equipment and materials to install luxurious amenities and the finest appointments on board, while keeping as much original equipment (such as the wood-burning stove in the deckhouse) and character of the vessel as possible. But the work had hardly begun when illness forced the sale of the *Straits* for the last time. Her new owner this time was King Frey of Los Angeles. He owned the tug just about a year before she was sunk by the *Reynosa*.

Diving the Georgia Straits

The *Georgia Straits* lies in 80 feet of water some three miles off the Long Beach breakwater. Although she was totally intact (except for the collision damage) when she went down in 1965, the *Straits*, made of wood, has deteriorated a great deal since then. The highest relief on the site now is the engine, which stands about 10 feet above the bottom. Most of the hull and structures have been ravaged by marine borers and reduced nearly level with the bottom. Since she went down, not more than a half dozen divers have visited the site; it is difficult to find and not widely known. Because she is so seldom visited, there still are numerous artifacts to be found. Items recovered so far include the ship's wheel (a beautiful piece made of teak and brass), the binnacle and telegraph, propeller, lights, her fog horns, and various pieces of china.

The *Georgia Straits* is usually a difficult dive; visibility is seldom more than about 15 feet, and the bottom is very silty and easily stirred up. But the potential for an unusual or interesting artifact makes this a worthwhile dive for the experienced diver.

P. S.

Johanna Smith

This is a tale of two vessels, both with the same name, both in the same business, and both having the same fate. This is the story of the ships called *Johanna Smith*.

Though the second vessel of that name has a history of less interest to divers, she should be mentioned; she was the old Ward Line vessel *Yumuri*. She was a steel ship built for passenger service by the Delaware River Company, Chester, Pennsylvania, in 1890. Her tonnage was 3,648 and her dimensions were 336.2 by 43.2 feet. She was set up to accommodate 80 first-class and 30 second-class passengers. She first operated on the East Coast—till 1908—and then on the Pacific Coast until the late 1920s. During her career, she had numerous names. Sequentially they were: *Yumuri, U. S. Lawton, Badger, Rose City, Rose Isle* and finally, *Johanna Smith II*.

During the late 20s and early 30s, she operated off the coast of Long Beach as the gambling ship *Rose Isle*. It was under this name that she gained some notoriety owing to the gangland style murder of Charles Bozeman, a dealer on the vessel. In 1932, after the destruction of the first *Johanna Smith* by fire, the *Rose Isle* was sold, and re-named *Johanna Smith II*. She continued operating as a gambling ship until 1935, when she, too, caught fire, burned, and sank like her namesake. Shortly after her sinking, salvage efforts were successful in raising her in her entirety. She was floated into Long Beach where she was broken up for scrap. Of the *Johanna Smith II*, nothing remains for divers but her memory and her name.

The first *Johanna Smith* was designed by Edward S. Hough and built by Captain W. A. Magee at Kruse & Banks, North Bend, Oregon, in 1917. She and her sister ship, *C. A. Smith*, were the largest wooden ships built on the Pacific Coast (1,921 and 1,878 tons respectively) prior to shipbuilding carried out by the U. S. Shipping Board after America's entry into World War I.

More than 257 feet in length and 50 feet in width, these two ships were the design forerunners of the standardized wooden cargo steamer—the Hough-type steamship—that was mass produced for the U. S. Shipping Board in World War I.

Due to wartime shortages, it was impossible to obtain engines for the *Johanna Smith* and her sister, so

Burdened with a massive load of dimensional lumber, the Johanna Smith *is shown here being operated as a barge. Note the diminutive smokestack she supports for cooking and heating on board. Photo from the Victor C. West collection.*

they were operated as barges. Consequently, the vessels built originally for the Inter-Ocean Transportation Company, a subsidiary of the Smith Lumber Company, were sold to the Coos Bay Lumber Company, in February 1918. Coos Bay Lumber continued to operate them as barges until 1921. At that time, both vessels were outfitted with deLaval steam turbines and twin screws, the only Pacific Coast wooden steam schooners to be powered that way.

In March, 1922 the *Johanna Smith* was sold again. For the next six years she plied the waters of the Pacific Coast carrying lumber and supplies for the Pacific States Lumber Company. Then, in 1928, there came a series of new owners for the ten-year-old vessel, and a controversial new career—she became the first gambling ship on the Pacific Coast.

She was sold to Albert Howard in February, 1928, who by May, had converted her into what the *L. A. Times* described as "a palatial gambling ship." She was moored about 12 miles off Long Beach, and in short order she became a big money-maker. Though she was popular with some of the local citizenry, to law enforcement she was anathema. The district attorney's office and the local police made numerous attempts to shut the *Johanna Smith* down, but to no avail; legally, she was beyond the jurisdiction of state and local governments, and she appeared in compliance with all federal laws, too. Finally, two months after she opened, it was discovered that the *Smith* had violated an obscure 136 year-old Federal

statute. A federal marshal, along with the help of two Coast Guard cutters, seized the ship and towed her into San Pedro. Despite skillful legal maneuverings, the *Smith* was declared forfeit, and auctioned off in December 1928.

By May 1929, the *Johanna Smith* was back: new owners, same business. She moved up and down the coast, and was harried at every port. From Long Beach to Ventura and back again, the *Smith* kept moving, looking for a port without harassment so she could operate. Periodically, when she tripped up legally and was seized, she would be sold by the government, and within a few months be right back in business. This was the manner in which the *Johanna Smith* passed the next three years. She continued in this line of endeavor until July 22, 1932, when at 6:30 in the evening, she was swept by an intense fire.

In spite of the speed with which the flames consumed the *Smith*, all 50 passengers and 40 crew members were safely removed. Those on board the burning gambler were preparing to leap into the sea and use the craps and blackjack tables for floats when the timely appearance of four Coast Guard cutters and three Navy shore boats prevented that desperate measure. The only injuries noted in the *San Pedro News-Pilot* article on the disaster were several broken ribs suffered by the ship's carpenter when he was caught in the crush of the crowd to abandon ship. Coast Guard documentation of the incident noted that two safes containing a total of $18,000 were rescued from the burning ship as well.

The fire continued to ravage the ex-lumber carrier until a great portion of superstructure and most of the hull down to the waterline had been consumed. At this point instead of sinking as expected, the *Johanna Smith* rolled over and, still attached to her anchor chains, floated upside down.

There was some contemporary speculation in the "extra" editions of the local papers that perhaps the fire hadn't been accidental. Competition between the various gambling ships had erupted into violence on occasion. Perhaps the most notable incident occurred in the early morning hours of July 8, 1935 when the gambling ship *Monte Carlo* was raided by a group described by the *L. A. Times* as "persons unknown." A contemporary rumor that was given much credence by law enforcement was that the raid was carried out by the crew of a rival gambling ship. In the foggy dawn, a band of eleven armed men surprised the watch, boarded the ship, and chained the entire ship's company. Then, after ransacking the ship and robbing the passengers and crew, the armed raiders reboarded their own boat and escaped into the fog with $40,000 in cash and jewelry.

In newspapers the day following the *Smith's* conflagration, however, Blazer and Turner, the *Smith's* owners, vehemently denied the fire was anything but an accident and requested there be no inquiry held. They further stated that they were already in the process of purchasing another vessel (the *Rose Isle*) to replace their incinerated investment. Though the owners' request against an inquest was overruled, and an investigation was carried out, it was inconclusive and no cause for the fire was ever determined.

Meanwhile, the Coast Guard cutter *Shoshone* had made the three mile trip from San Pedro to inspect and destroy the remains of the *Smith*. The plan was to sink the hull with explosive charges or break it up so the pieces could be towed away. A Coast Guard crew clambered aboard the overturned hull of the charred gambler and proceeded to chop a hole through her bottom, close to the keel. After penetrating the bottom, they placed a wrecking charge (a 25 pound block of waterproofed explosive used by the Coast Guard, Navy and Army Corps of Engineers for maritime demolition and clearance projects) in the hole and fired it. The results, though spectacular, did not have the desired result of sinking the remains of the *Johanna Smith*. Topside, the explosion broke the keel and tore a 20 square-foot hole in the hull. Beneath the water, the blast blew out all the heavy equipment and machinery including the engines, boilers, and remaining gambling equipment, along with what was left of the decks and superstructure, allowing it to fall to the bottom 80 feet below. The Coast Guard continued blasting for several days until what remained of the *Johanna Smith* either sank to the bottom or was towed or drifted away. An article in the July 25 edition of the *News-Pilot* reported that beachcombers in Seal Beach had discovered "thousands" of nickels within the wreckage of the *Johanna Smith* that had come ashore. This precipitated an intense but short-lived treasure hunt along local beaches that left most participants with a nice tan but little else.

In the mid 70s I met an old gentleman who said he had been a diver for a San Pedro salvage company in the 1930s. When I asked about wrecks he had worked on or knew of, he said there was one job in his career that had been really special. He said his company had been hired to dive the remains of a gambling ship that had burned and sank just off Long Beach. The owners it seemed, were interested in recovering anything of value that could be found, but specifically the coins from the nearly 200 slot machines that went down with the ship.

Since he was senior diver for the company at that time, he did most of the diving himself. He mentioned that since the ship lay in about 80 feet of water he would only make two dives a day. He said that initially he had believed there might be some problem finding the slot machines and their silver cargo. Once on the wreck, this wasn't the case. He said that the decks, house, and hull structures were strewn across the bottom and sprinkled with the heavier equipment and machinery from the ship. Most of the ash and lighter debris either washed away in the sinking or were scoured out by the tides and currents. He found there was just a little overburden to contend with on the soggy old gambler.

As he dug through rubble and debris, he said he began to find numerous blackened chunks of melted metal. Closer examination showed them to be masses of silver coins melted together by the intense heat of the fire. Each dive, he said he managed to load several sacks with the silver lumps, some weighing 25

The steam schooner Johanna Smith *after her February 1919 conversion from a barge. Photo from the National Maritime Museum, San Francisco.*

or 30 pounds. On board his tender vessel, four men of substantial size who represented the owners of the sunken vessel immediately took charge of the bags as they were pulled aboard. The old man said that at the end of each day's diving he and his gear were courteously but thoroughly searched.

He went on to say that the job had lasted about two weeks and the customers had been quite pleased with the results. So pleased in fact, that on the final day of diving, one of the guardians of the salvaged silver gave him a fist-sized chunk of the melted coins as a souvenir.

He offered to show me the prized piece and I speedily accepted. Circumstances prevented me from meeting with the old gentleman the following weekend, but I was very anxious to learn more about the wreck and see his clump of coins. I made several later ef-

forts to contact him but never succeeded. I was never able to locate him again.

His story, of course, isn't proof of anything. My own feelings, admittedly unsupported, are that the old diver had worked on the remains of the *Johanna Smith*. Research indicates that four gambling ships burned in this area off Long Beach. One of them, the *Johanna Smith II* ex-*Yumuri*, has already been mentioned. The *Monfalcon* was another gambler that burned and sank but somewhat farther south, off Seal Beach; she has yet to be located. Another was the *Casino* ex-*James Tuft*, an ex-lumber barkentine that is discussed in the next section. And finally, the *Johanna Smith*. Though he never mentioned the name of the wreck he worked on, of the four ships. his description would seem to most closely fit that of the *Johanna Smith*.

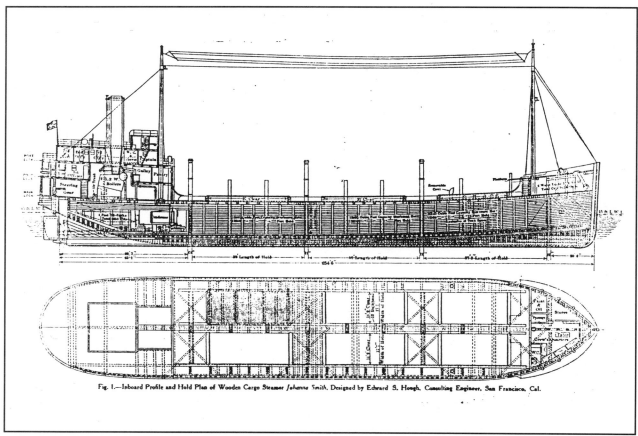

Fig. I.—Inboard Profile and Hold Plan of Wooden Cargo Steamer *Johanna Smith*. Designed by Edward S. Hough, Consulting Engineer, San Francisco, Cal.

Profile plan of the Johanna Smith. *From the Louis Hough collection.*

Telegraph repeater from the Johanna Smith *after the restoration. Photo from the P. Smith collection.*

I've been asked if perhaps this story might have been a tale created by the old gentlemen just to impress? Perhaps, but I doubt it. His familiarity with diving terms and jargon gave the impression of a man with intimate knowledge of the salvage profession and offshore diving conditions. The fact that there are the remains of a wooden steam-powered vessel, which had burned in just about that depth off Long Beach, might add a modicum of support to the old diver's story. Local divers call the site the 14-minute wreck since, at about 12 knots, it is just about 14 minutes off Long Beach Light.

Diving the Johanna Smith

Not one of the most beautiful spots on the coast, the wreck site does provide some interesting artifacts and lobster of bragging size. Because of the usually dark, murky water, visibility on the *Smith* averages around 10 feet with those rare mid-winter days where the visibility can range from 20 to 50 feet.

I had been diving the wreck for more than a year before I lucked into one of those 50 foot days. Prior to then I never really had a feeling for how the wreckage lay. On that day of exceptional visibility, I found that the wreck consisted of at least five major areas of debris, piping, and machinery approximately 20 feet apart, with smaller areas of debris scattered in between. Because the bottom consists of a silty mud, it is easy to stir up and care must be taken when moving around the wreck.

The wreckage lies generally in an east/west orientation in an area about 200 feet long and 50 feet wide. The western end is marked by a huge square structure, either a fuel tank or, perhaps, a fire box. The eastern end of the wreck is demarcated by a mass of large pipes, and is an area which produces many large lobster. In between are strewn large planks and timbers, masses of encrusted, rusting machinery, mounds of firebrick and all manner of unidentifiable objects sticking out of the mud; any identifiable structure has long disappeared.

Although unimpressive, the wreck has been slowly yet consistently producing interesting artifacts over the years. Portholes, equipment builder's plates, ornate hinges, glass and brass oilers, and a beautiful ship's telegraph are just some of the items salvaged from her. Since the consistency of the bottom and the usually poor conditions on the *Smith* tend to persuade most divers to go elsewhere, she has not been dived as much as some of the other local wrecks. As a consequence, her potential for interesting artifacts is higher than most. And, if one is inclined to accept the story related by the old salvage diver, then perhaps there is the potential for silver treasure, too. Certainly not enough to retire on, but definitely the material for salty tales for years to come.

P. S.

Casino

For crewman Walter Camlett of the gambling ship *Casino*, life was good. Along with fellow crew members Thomas Vermillyea and George Richardson he kept an eye on the ship, did light maintenance and made sure the gasoline generator that supplied power for the ship's lights was started every night.

Crewman Camlett surely had no idea what problems were awaiting him as he climbed down the companionway to the generator room on that early August evening in 1935.

Working by the ambient light coming through the companionway from the deck above, he casually reached down and threw the switch on the big gas engine that turned the ship's generator. Instead of the usual grind of the starter followed by the powerful roar of the engine starting, there was a tremendous explosion that turned the compartment into an inferno.

The force of the explosion had flung Camlett, unconscious with his clothing ablaze, to the foot of the companionway ladder. He was found there by Richardson and Vermillyea after they had fought their way through the flames. Working together, the two rescuers managed to move the severely burned Camlett up the ladder and to the momentary safety of the deck. By the time the three made the main deck, the rescuers' clothes, too, were ablaze; they were nearly as badly burned as the friend they had saved.

But time was running out; their respite from the flames was only temporary. Already great, oily black clouds of smoke were boiling from various openings in the *Casino*'s deck. Tongues of bright orange flame were licking out the open companionway just behind the charred crewmen. The flames, initially fed by the gasoline, found great favor with the dry wood and layers of paint on the 34 year old vessel; the conflagration grew.

By this time the unfortunate Camlett had regained consciousness, but even so, the task of launching a lifeboat was too much for the trio. As the fire spread with incredible speed, their options were reduced to but one: go over the side. The shock of the cold water on their burns must have been excruciating, yet the possibility of drowning held little threat compared to a sure death by the fire raging through the *Casino*.

Perhaps because they had been working on a gambling ship, a little luck rubbed off on those three ship-

The *Casino, fully ablaze off Long Beach, August 22, 1935. Note that the deckhouse has already been consumed by the flames. Photo from the P. Smith collection.*

mates. Just minutes after their plunge off the pyre-like gambler, they were plucked from the water by a boat from the *Monte Carlo*, another gambling ship anchored nearby. They were quickly transferred to a high speed water taxi, the *Bearcat III*, carried ashore and taken to Seaside Hospital in Long Beach.

Though seriously burned, all three eventually recovered. Their ship was not so fortunate.

Meanwhile, the pillar of smoke issuing from the *Casino* had brought the Coast Guard cutters *Hermes* and *Ewing* and the patrol boats No. 254 and No. 259 to the scene. In short order, it became obvious to the Coast Guard officers in charge that any attempt to save the blazing ship would be futile. With that decision made, one cutter remained with the blazing hulk while the remaining Coast Guard vessels continued their normal patrols.

In less than one hour, the *Casino* had burned to the waterline. The decision whether to tow the hulk to shore and beach it or sink it where it was with explosives resolved itself. The *Casino* slipped beneath the waves, and the problem of what to do with her was solved.

The *Casino* had begun her maritime career some 34 years prior to her sinking on August 22, 1935. She had been launched in 1901 from the Port Blakely, Washington yard of Hall Brothers as the *James Tuft*, a four-masted skysail barkentine of 1,274 tons. With a length of 215.5 feet and a beam of 42.5 feet, the *Tuft* had a cargo capacity of 1,400,000 board feet of lumber.

The Hall Brothers had built the *Tuft* for their own company, and she served them well both in the coastwise trade and trans-Pacific voyages. During the

The barkentine James Tuft, *prior to her conversion to the gambling ship* Casino. *Photo from the P. Smith collection.*

years 1920-21, the *Tuft* made two excellent passages from Fiji to San Francisco—one of 51 days, the other of 49 days. This is not to say that there weren't problems over the years.

In January 1923, while on a voyage from Kildonan, British Columbia to Callao, Peru with a lumber cargo, she suffered a severe stranding on that ominously named place off the Washington coast, Destruction Island. After enduring a heavy pounding from huge seas that basically reduced her to a waterlogged wreck, her crew was rescued by the Coast Guard cutter *Haida*. Though for a while it looked like the end of the line for the *Tuft*, the tug *Sea Monarch* managed to pull her free and tow her into Winslow, Washington, where she underwent extensive repairs. After reloading her cargo and reprovisioning, the *Tuft* continued her voyage to Callao with no further incidents. On her return trip to San Francisco, she blazed home in 37 days—a record that tied the third fastest time recorded for that route. It was a fitting end for her sailing career, for upon her arrival in San Francisco, the *Tuft* was taken from service and laid up.

In 1928, the old windjammer was sold to the G. E. Billings Company for use as a fishing barge in Santa Monica Bay. After her conversion at San Pedro, she was towed north and anchored off Venice, California. She had served well in this capacity for four years when her owners decided that their profits from the old barge could be enhanced with the addition of more exotic

diversions for their customers than halibut and mackerel. They were right. The installation of gambling tables, slot machines, booze, beer and scantily-clad women provided an instant, though short-lived boost to their profits. Though the "male only, ship smokers," as they were called by the *Los Angeles Examiner*, were only staged twice a month, they almost immediately caught the attention of local and federal law enforcement officials. In December 1932, Federal officers from the Deputy Federal Administrator and prohibition office along with local police, a vice squad unit, and the Coast Guard, staged a spectacular raid on the old four-master. Appearing suddenly out of the heavy fog aboard the cutter *Ewing*, officers reported that they struck just as four of the women on the *Tuft* were putting on their "unconventional art dances," which they immediately stopped; the officers were not fast enough to stop the dumping of "large quantities" of liquor overboard. In the final tally, out of the 300 who had been onboard the *Tuft* enjoying "high jinks on the high seas," four women and nineteen men were arrested and charged with violation of state liquor laws, the Volstead Act, vagrancy and participating in lewd and indecent exhibitions.

Early in 1933, the *James Tuft* was sold, converted into a gambling barge (apparently with very little work), and renamed *Casino*. The December 1932 raid was the first of many the old windship would endure, but despite almost constant harassment by local, state and federal law enforcement, she stayed in the "sin ship" business until the fire claimed her August 22, 1935 off Long Beach.

Diving the Casino

Just a short distance off the Long Beach breakwater, the *Casino* is within easy reach of divers, but is seldom visited. Her hull lies on a very silty bottom in about 80 feet of water. Because of her proximity to Long Beach Harbor, the conditions around the *Casino* are exceptionally poor. The water is usually dark, with visibility averaging around five feet. On some wrecks it's possible to look around and work in that amount of visibility, but the silt in which the *Casino* lies is so fine that the slightest disturbance, from fin or hands, stirs the bottom into inky blackness. The *Casino* is a relatively deep and arduous dive that is definitely not for novice divers.

The wooden hull of the *Casino* is surprisingly intact and rises about 18 feet off the bottom. Because of the fire, there is no deck or structures. The hull is open and few remains are visible beneath the many feet of silt and shell growth within. Some deck support timbers and numerous iron drift fastenings—festooned with clumps of shell growth and monofilament fishing line—are located along the inner edge of the hull.

Periodically during the winter offshore winds called Santa Anas, visibility on the *Casino* can increase to 50 feet or more. During these rare periods a diver can see and appreciate the size of the wreck and the amount of sea life she supports. Along with myriad smaller fish, sheephead, and bass—both calico and sand—are in residence in great numbers on the wreck. Although rarely seen in the normally poor visibility on the *Casino*, a good number of bragging size lobster also call the wreck home.

Though there are potentially a great number of interesting pieces on this ship—including, perhaps, gambling equipment—as far as could be determined, the only artifact ever recovered is a large bronze hawse pipe. Because of the lack of both material and aesthetic resources and the rarity of good visibility on the *Casino*, most divers choose other wrecks to visit.

P. S.

Seal Beach to Dana Point

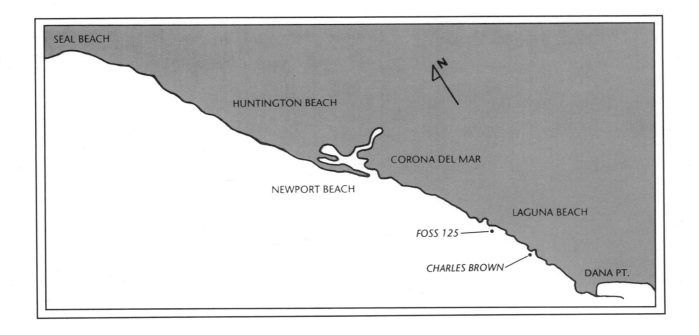

Foss 125

Research has yet to turn up many details on the sunken barge, *Foss 125*. Located just off Laguna Beach, the how and why of her loss have yet to be uncovered. Calls to the parent company, Foss Launch & Tug company, produced no information at all. They were congenial, but explained that over the years they had owned or managed thousands of barges, and that it was impossible to maintain records on all of them.

What is known about the *Foss 125* is that she was a steel barge of 432 gross tons. She was built in 1943 at Terminal Island, California, for the Foss Launch & Tug Company of Tacoma, Washington. She measured 130 feet in length by 38 in width and drew nearly 10 feet of water. Available records indicate she was lost in November, 1958, but offer no clue as to why she went down.

Diving the Foss 125

Because of her location just one-quarter mile offshore from Cleo Street in Laguna Beach, the *Foss* is a popular beach dive. To many divers who visit her, she is known only as the Cleo Street Wreck. She lies in 60 feet of water with the top of the wreck at about 40 feet. There are quite a few openings in the top and sides of the wreck that allow easy penetration. But, even though the *Foss* isn't large, no penetration should be made without the use of a guideline and a good light.

Despite the fact she was just a barge, a few very nice artifacts have been found on the wreck over the years. One of the nicest pieces to come up was a brass deck hatch with frame. Cast into the brass frame edge was the name *Foss 125*. As you might guess, this provided a fairly reliable clue as to the identity of the wreck. Also recovered was one beautiful, brass masthead light, along with various brass valves and handles.

Perhaps the most noticeable aspect of the *Foss* is the tremendous amount of sea life congregating on and about her. Numerous types of fish swarm through her hull, while lobster have found her to be an excellent shelter as well. The bottom around the wreck is sand, with rocky areas that provide scallops and, occasionally, abs. Visibility ranges from 10 to 60 feet with 20 being about average.

Though not a spectacular dive, a jump on the *Foss* is a good way for novice divers to get some wreck-diving experience without the extreme conditions encountered on some of the other local wrecks. Another benefit, of course, is that she is accessible as a beach dive—a convenience not available with many Southern California wrecks.

P. S.

Similar in size and style to the barge Foss 125 *sunk off Laguna Beach, is the* Foss 100, *here being escorted by the tug* Martha Foss. *Photo from the P. Smith collection.*

Charles Brown

The violent storm that swept the southern California coast in late April 1932 caused the destruction or stranding of numerous vessels. Some of those lost included the *Thomas P. Emigh* at Redondo Beach, as well as the *Gratia* and the *Melrose* along the Palos Verdes shores. Farther to the south, the storm took its toll as well, driving the little schooner *Charles Brown* to her destruction on the rocky coast near Laguna Beach.

Built in Japan in 1904 as the *Tokai Maru*, the little 72-ton vessel served as a fishing and trading vessel until sold to California owners in the early 20s.

The account of her years along the southern California coast is sketchy, but indications are that she served as a fishing barge in various areas. An article appearing in a February 1926 issue of the *Los Angeles Times* reported that four boys were "marooned in the storm-tossed sea on an old fishing schooner, the *Charles Brown*." The article said the vessel was some two miles off Santa Monica Canyon, and Venice police in power launches had been unsuccessful in attempting to reach the schooner or rescue the boys.

Though the *Charles Brown* obviously survived, searches through subsequent issues of the *Times* failed to reveal the fate of the four boys aboard.

Little else turns up concerning the *Charles Brown* until April 20, 1932, when she was listed as a victim of the massive storm that savaged the California coast. Few details were given, the most succinct information being her destruction by the huge seas on a rocky shore south of Laguna Beach.

The one watchman aboard her probably got the ride of his life when the *Brown* broke her mooring and was rapidly blown on to the rocks. Miraculously, he survived his ordeal with just bruises and abrasions; the *Charles Brown* was not so fortunate. The wild seas crushed and broke her apart, then dropped as much of her hull in the deeper water offshore as was cast up on the rocks ashore. The pieces of her hull that washed ashore were soon scavenged or burned during beach picnics the following summer. The remains of her hull offshore provided the local marine borers with a tasty oriental repast, while her fittings were driven into the bottom and covered with sand.

No photos are known of the little schooner *Charles Brown*, but this vessel, the *General Banning*, is very close to the descriptions of the *Brown*. Photo courtesy of the National Maritime Museum, San Francisco.

Diving the Charles Brown

What remains of the *Charles Brown* lies in 15 to 20 feet of water south of Laguna Beach. For the most part, very little remains above the seafloor and it takes a sharp eye to spot the protruding pieces of iron, steel, and brass that mark the wreck site. In spite of this, numerous artifacts have been recovered, including ornate hinges, large brass and copper fastenings, and portholes.

The best visibility in the area occurs during the summer and fall, but the bottom is most exposed after heavy winter storms. During the rest of the year, it usually requires extensive sand fanning and some work with a tool such as a rock hammer to uncover and remove artifacts from the site.

Visibility can range to 40 feet, but because of the shallowness of the *Brown*, sediment stirred up by the surge can be a problem.

The only other problem in diving the remains of the *Charles Brown* is finding a place to park on the crowded Laguna streets.

P. S.

La Jolla to Imperial Beach

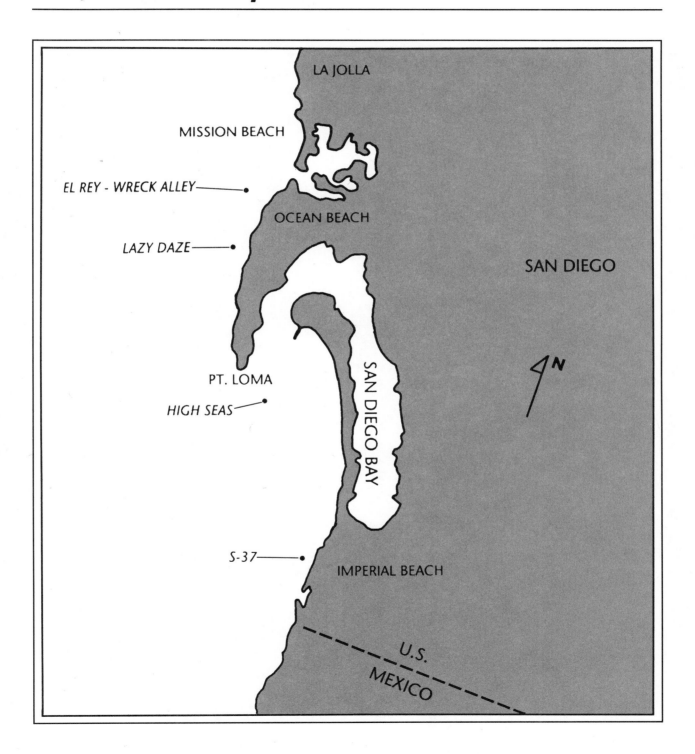

Wreck Alley

San Diego's hottest dive site is Wreck Alley. Three-quarters of a mile from the Mission Bay Channel entrance, it got its name because several vessels have been intentionally sunk there to function as artificial reefs. (Four were sunk the first year; more may have been added since this book went to press.)

Over the years it has been discovered that almost any sort of structure accidentally or purposely placed underwater in a sandy area will become a marine life haven; an artificial reef. Shipwrecks have proven excellent artificial reefs. Their exposed surfaces provide places on which sessile marine life can settle. Their many nooks and crannies provide homes and hiding places for crustaceans and fish. Smaller animals feed on the permanently attached residents and larger animals feed on the smaller animals.

Artificial reefs have replenished fishing grounds for years, now these reefs are being placed with divers in mind. Their primary purpose is not to provide hunting grounds but to promote sightseeing and photographic opportunities as well as interesting exploration.

Wreck Alley came into being as the result of the joint efforts of California's Department of Fish and Game and the San Diego Dive Instructors Association. Kelco, a kelp harvesting and processing company, donated the first vessel sunk, which was *El Rey*. The U.S. Navy provided advice on the sinking as well as the Underwater Demolition Team that actually sent the ship to the bottom on April 2, 1987.

El Rey was a kelp cutter built by Gunderson Brothers Shipyard in Portland, Oregon, in 1946. She was 100 feet long with a 32-foot beam. Her aft wheelhouse stood 36 feet high. *El Rey* was originally powered by two GMC 671s, which were eventually replaced by two 553 Caterpillars.

Only the canopy of *Macrocystis pyrifera*, giant kelp, is harvested. *El Rey*'s reciprocating blades would cut the kelp to a depth of less than three feet below the surface and conveyors would carry it to a bin in the middle section of the vessel that could hold about 300 tons of kelp.

For stability when traveling to a harvest site, *El Rey* would carry seawater in six special tanks. As kelp was deposited in the bin, the ballast water was dumped.

Since she spent so much time at sea, especially in remote, offshore areas, *El Rey* was called upon to rescue many people, including a movie star (who shall be nameless, to spare him embarassment) and a number of fishermen. She provided diesel fuel to boaters who misjudged their own supplies and allowed many of them to use her radio. She recovered several bodies as well. Also, according to Ron McPeak, senior marine biologist with Kelco, "Dr. Carl Hubbs, world renowned researcher from Scripps Institution of Oceanography, spent many days and nights aboard *El Rey* studying a variety of marine life including birds, migrating whales, fishes, and kelp forests."

Shooter's Fantasy was sent to the bottom to join *El Rey* on June 2, 1987. Originally named the *Betty Lou*, she was a steel-hulled charter sportsfisherman built in the early 1950s. Sixty-five feet in length, she was docked in Mission Bay. When she was converted for broadbill fishing, her new owners renamed her *Shooter's Fantasy*. Sold again and anchored off San Diego's Embarcadero, she became a home to an assortment of people. At least some of those living on her may have been thieves. No one bothered with her maintenance and she sank at anchor in 1985, her holds full of stereos, TVs, bicycles, and other goods thought to have been purloined from other vessels anchored around her.

Two years after she sank, *Shooter's Fantasy* was refloated so she could be towed to Wreck Alley, and resunk. Crews cleaning her holds and making her safe for divers after she was on the bottom threw a great number of items over the side. She is consequently surrounded by a number of diverse articles that had been stored in her holds over the years. Items recovered by divers working on her include a brass folding telescope and a German beer stein three feet tall.

Barge #1 became the third leg of the Wreck Valley triangle in June 1987. She was without a name during her lifetime on the seas, and is called *Barge #1* because she is the first of several barges expected to be sunk on the site. She is 65 feet long with a 22-foot beam. There are three open compartments below deck.

In July 1987, a 36-foot sailboat, *Strider*, was gutted by fire. It belonged to a friend of one of the divers who was instrumental in establishing Wreck Alley. After *Strider* was declared a total loss by its insurance company, it, too, was towed to Wreck Alley and sunk.

On January 17, 1988, a violent storm sent the 200-foot-tall Naval Ocean Systems Center Tower to the bottom, where it became the first unintentional addition to Wreck Alley. Now lying about 300 yards north of *El Rey*, the NOSC tower was erected in 1959, for oceanographic research and other navy studies. Late in 1987, jurisdiction of the tower was transferred to the Chief of Naval Research. Scripps Institution of Oceanography was chosen to operate it.

The wreckage lies in 60 feet of water with the highest part just 30 feet below the surface. There can be considerable surge and, on the surface, you should keep a sharp lookout for boat traffic. Recently, there was one buoy marking the site. The legs of the tower were covered with *Corynactis* anemones before it was knocked over, but at least one marine biologist who has visited the site believes the silt in the area will kill them.

In the forseeable future, the tower will probably be a safer dive. When it first went down, cables and twisted metal made visiting it hazardous but the cables, at least, can, and probably will, be removed.

Diving Wreck Alley

Wreck Alley is three-quarters of a mile from the Mission Bay Channel entrance. Three wrecks form a triangle on the bottom. *El Rey* sits upright, with her stern in 78 feet of water and her bow in 75. Before she was sunk, she was carefully prepared by Kelco to eliminate hazards to divers and the environment. Her engines were removed and she was steam-cleaned. Several holes were cut in her hull to facilitate her sinking and to allow divers easy entry and exit.

Barge #1 lies in 73 feet of water north of *El Rey*. *Shooter's Fantasy* lies in 68 feet of water 150 feet inshore of *El Rey* and north of *Shooter's Fantasy*.

The kelp harvester El Rey. *She was the first vessel to be purposely sunk for San Diego's Wreck Alley. Photo from Kelco, Inc.*

El Rey has a permanent buoy attached to the middle of her deck; *Shooter's Fantasy* has one attached to her bow. These are location buoys and are not to be used for mooring vessels.

Visibility in Wreck Alley can be as good as 20 feet, but is usually less. There can be currents, and boat traffic is always a hazard. For this reason, divers should descend and ascend along the buoys on the wrecks. Because of the depth and lack of visibility, this is not an area for novice divers.

Wreck Alley's success is proven by the number of charter boats, mostly six packs, that have gone into business since *El Rey* was sunk. You will find these listed in *Dive Boat Calendar and Travel Guide*. San Diego dive stores are also a good source of information about boat trips to Wreck Alley.

B. J. C.

Lazy Daze

The *Lazy Daze* really was the first vessel to sink in San Diego's Wreck Valley, although she is not usually recognized as such. The reasons she is not so credited are several: first, at the time of her loss, a wreck on the bottom was not considered a resource, and so she was generally ignored. Next, in the early 50s, when she went down, there were few recreational scuba divers—fewer still who were interested in diving the wreck of an old fishing barge. Finally, by the time the Wreck Valley project was implemented in early 1987—34 years after she sank—there was not a great amount of intact structure left on the *Lazy Daze*; in her condition, she didn't equal the glamor of the intact, newly-sunk vessels nearby.

Though the history of the 150 foot converted landing craft isn't known, it's probably a safe guess that she was a cast off veteran from the nearby naval facilities at San Diego. Like so many other vessels lost along the southern California coast, the old landing craft was given a new name—*Lazy Daze*—and converted to a fishing barge. After the addition of bait tanks and a galley, she was given a fresh coat of paint and moored on the edge of an offshore kelp bed some three quarters of a mile west of Sunset Cliffs, just south of Mission Bay.

During the night of May 11, 1953, the 93 ton *Lazy Daze* went down in about 75 feet of water with just a few pieces of floating wreckage to mark the site.

Diving the Lazy Daze

The years have been hard on the *Lazy Daze*. When I first visited the wreck in the mid 70s, a substantial amount of her remained. She was loaded with tons of brass and bronze plumbing, some of it obviously for the live bait tanks she had on board, but no purpose could be determined for the majority of the pipes. Hooked into the plumbing network at various places were large, heavy-duty, bronze marine pumps. Even after 20 years on the bottom, most of them were still in good shape. A San Diego commercial fisherman who received one as a gift, installed it in his boat and has been using it with no problems for over ten years.

Since the 70s, divers have slowly disconnected and carried away the various sections of pipe, so that no remnant of that vast network remains. Over the years, divers have recovered other items from the *Lazy Daze*, too. Several portholes, bronze valves of immense size, a bronze Very pistol, and several different types of lamps have been recovered from the old barge.

Today, most local divers dismiss the *Lazy Daze* as picked over and not worth a visit, but the wreck still has some surprises. A recent dive on the *Lazy Daze* for scallops and calico bass from adjacent reefs turned up a beautiful bronze deck light, with its dark green lens intact. Limits of scallops and several tasty calicos rounded out the catch.

The relief on the *Lazy Daze* is only about six or seven feet, making it difficult to locate her among the nearby reefs with fathometer alone. Loran numbers are the surest way to find her, though shore lineups are used by many locals, too.

Visibility on the wreck averages about 20 feet, though both greater and lesser extremes are common. Because she is located fairly close to Mission Bay, boat traffic is a concern. A divers down flag should always be used and descents and ascents should be made on the anchor line for safety.

P. S.

High Seas

It was just past sunset and already the friendly beacon of Point Loma Light was gleaming through the rapidly deepening early March dusk. On board the purse seiner *High Seas*, making her way outbound past the point, items that were not battened down began to skitter back and forth as she dipped her bow into the large Pacific swells. Skipper Joe Goulart was keeping extra alert as he guided the 392-ton vessel past the last of the channel marker buoys. He noted the position of a much larger vessel maneuvering nearby as he began to turn the *High Seas* north, toward San Pedro. He was well aware that a busy harbor entrance like San Diego's could be a place of danger for the seaman who wasn't alert.

The 13 crew members on board the seiner were in good spirits. They were on the final leg of an 80-day fishing trip. On their voyage they had ranged far up into the Gulf of California and as far south as Acapulco, in search of yellowfin and skipjack tuna. Luck had been with them, for when they arrived in San Diego at 4 that morning they carried some 250 tons of prime tuna on board; it looked as if 1970 was going to be a good year.

The stop in San Diego, the *High Seas'* home port, was a brief one to see family and loved ones and to take on fuel for the final leg of the cruise to the canneries in San Pedro. At the Star Kist or Van Camp cannery there, she would unload her cargo. Once

An early painting of the High Seas *before she was operated as a purse seiner. Note the large bait well on her aft deck. Photo from the P. Smith collection.*

empty, the *High Seas* would head south, back to San Diego, where her crew would begin preparing her for her next trip.

As Captain Goulart began his starboard turn around the flashing white light that marked San Diego channel buoy number 1, the full force of the choppy seas was felt. The large northwest swells struck heavily on the *High Seas'* port bow, causing the 128-foot vessel to lurch and roll like a drunk on New Year's Eve.

Suddenly, the movement of the boat changed from the lively roll and lurch motion to a sluggish stagger. A shout came from the stern, "We're taking on water!" The aft end of the seiner rapidly settled into the black choppy seas.

As the ocean inundated the stern of the *High Seas*, several crew members, including one of the owner's sons, 17-year-old Michael Reis, rushed aft to release the large, 20-foot skiff secured there. The skiff was used in the setting of the huge purse seine that was also stowed, looking like a large black hill, on the aft deck.

The next few minutes were mass confusion as crew members struggled to release the lashings holding the net tender, while the six-to-eight-foot seas swept across the decks of the rapidly settling *High Seas*. Matters grew substantially worse when the rising waters flooded the engine room and shorted out the electrical system. The beleaguered crew of the *High Seas* was plunged into blackness as all power was lost; the job of freeing the skiff continued under the intermittent beam of Point Loma Light and the gleam of flashlights.

Just a few minutes before the *High Seas* plunged beneath the cold, choppy seas, the net tender was freed and nine crew members managed to scramble aboard. John Reis, Jr. and his cousin Joe Reis, along with crewman Manuel Mamede were not as quick, and went into the chilly water. They made it to the skiff after the *High Seas* went down.

Nearby, Commander Ray Moses of the U.S. Coast and Geodetic Survey vessel *Davidson* had been keeping an eye on the bright lights of an outward-bound vessel. He, too, was an experienced seaman and was conning his vessel with caution as he made his approach to San Diego Harbor. When the lights on the other vessel went out, he figured they were in trouble. Not hesitating, Commander Moses ordered the *Davidson* to the area where the lights were last seen. Within a few minutes, the survey vessel was slowly moving through a large oil slick and an area of floating debris left by the recently departed purse seiner. Though the rough choppy water had been calmed considerably by the oil slick, it still took the crew of the *Davidson* several minutes to spot the *High Seas* survivors in the large swells and darkness.

Not wanting to risk a transfer of survivors in the large, rough seas, the *Davidson* moved in close to the net tender and passed over a tow line. Once the *Davidson* had made the calm and security of the harbor, the skiff was brought alongside and the *High Seas* crew was brought aboard the *Davidson*.

For the crew of the *High Seas* it had been an intense evening. In less than an hour they had gone from a happy crew on a well-found vessel with the prospect of profit looming bright, to a bunch of bedraggled castaways who had lost everything, yet were very thankful their lives had been spared.

The *High Seas* was built for the U.S. Navy at San Pedro Boatworks in 1945. She was a YP (Yard Patrol) that is, a small patrol craft, and during her stint in the navy she was only graced with a number, never a name: *YP 621*. Shortly after the end of the war, she was sold as surplus and purchased by Joao Reis, who converted her to a commercial tuna boat. Initially the *High Seas* was designed as a tuna clipper or bait boat. Such a vessel has several large tanks onboard to maintain the large quantities of live bait needed for this type of fishing. Clippers would cruise the Pacific waters off the west coast looking for signs of tuna: Birds feeding on the surface of the water; schools of dolphin; or tuna jumping on the surface. A chum line of live bait would be laid and the crew would grab stout cane poles with short, heavy lines and barbless lures, called squids, and scramble into the fishing racks mounted outside the hull. Live bait would be sprinkled liberally into the surrounding seas, bringing the tuna to a feeding frenzy. They would then strike at anything moving in the water, including the squid lures. When this happened, the greedy tuna were unceremoniously jerked from the water and flung over the fisherman's shoulder into the bins on deck. The fish's shaking and thrashing in the bin would free the barbless hook and the fisherman would whip the lure back into the water for the next unfortunate

Charlie. With really large tuna, the strength of two or three men working together was required to lift just one fish aboard.

Because this type of fishing was very labor intensive and therefore expensive, the owner eventually redesigned the boat as a purse seiner. In this type of fishing, a large circular net, with floats along the top edge and a weighted draw-string bottom, is maneuvered around an entire school of tuna, then slowly retrieved by the seiner. As the net is drawn aboard, the tuna are forced into a smaller and smaller space. Eventually the fish are crowded into a small area alongside the seiner, where they are scooped from the water in a smaller, sock-like net called a brail. Once aboard, the tuna are deposited directly into the refrigerated hold where they are stowed and frozen for the trip to the cannery. The *High Seas* had been doing this type of fishing on her last trip.

There was considerable speculation as to the cause of the *High Seas* sinking. Even though she was some 25-years-old, vessels don't just fall apart. When she was built for the Navy, only the best materials had been used and she had been assembled by some of the most knowledgeable and skilled shipwrights to be found anywhere. The vessels turned out by San Pedro Boatworks were staunch, well-made craft that were respected and sought after by private, commercial, and military seafarers alike. The loss of the *High Seas* raised eyebrows and questions up and down the coast.

Some of the oldtimers felt that for a vessel to sink like the *High Seas*, she would had to have been neglected to the point where dry rot had consumed a vast portion of her hull. But in fact, the *High Seas* had been very well maintained. She was the means by which many fishermen supported themselves. The *High Seas* was their survival; daily at sea and as a source of income for their families. She was a carefully looked-after vessel.

Though it was never conclusively proved, it appeared that an incident during the course of the final fishing trip may have caused the sinking. At one point, Captain Goulart had taken the *High Seas* into Acapulco to replenish fuel and supplies. While alongside the fuel dock, the *High Seas* was struck in the stern by a U.S. Navy tender. Although the blow was substantial, examination of the seiner's stern failed to turn up any visible damage. The incident was logged, then put aside. Both vessels had jobs to do. After the sinking, though, it was thought that perhaps some structural damage had gone undetected. It was speculated that in the rough seas, with nearly a full load of tuna and fuel aboard, the strain had been too much and the stern, weakened in the collision, had given way.

Diving the High Seas

I had my first opportunity to dive the *High Seas* in July 1974. A group of us had chartered the dive boat *Duchess*, out of San Diego, specifically because the skipper assured us he knew the position of the *High Seas*. He was as good as his word. After only 20 minutes of metering, he came across a reading that jumped from the bottom at 105 feet to nearly 50. He metered the spot twice more to pinpoint the wreck, then dropped the hook.

Though conditions were excellent, with flat seas and warm, sunny weather, there were other aspects to consider before diving. Most important was that we were anchored less than one-half mile from the San Diego Harbor channel buoy Number 1. The amount of traffic in the area—commercial, military and pleasure—made it imperative that descents to and ascents from the wreck be made on the anchor line. We made sure our divers down flag was prominently displayed, then suited up for the dive.

Because of the tremendous reading on the fathometer, all of us went down expecting to see a huge wreck. What we found was not what we expected. As we descended, we were able to make out the dim outline of something below us when we reached about 40 feet. I released the anchor line and swam toward the object, then stopped and quickly back pedaled. Our large fathometer reading was the *High Seas'* purse seine; part was tangled in the wreckage resting on the bottom, while the remainder, supported by its net floats, reached to within 50 feet of the surface. That black undulating mass of net, strewn with colorful yellow and orange floats, was a visage to frighten any diver with common sense. The thought of becoming enmeshed in that billowing web caused all of us to give it a wide berth. Even from a distance, I could see evidence of its effectiveness while bound to a dead ship. As we continued down the anchor line, I could easily make out bonito, bass,

Items recovered from the High Seas: *portholes, lamps, and a brass ice-cream scoop. Photo by Patrick Smith.*

sheepshead, and other types of fish caught within the net. Some were recent victims, still struggling. Others were rotted beyond identification, but still served the purpose of bait to lure still other fish into the deadly web. (By 1975, nearly all the net had disappeared from the wreck. On dives since then, only a few small areas of net can be found near the stern.)

Fortunately, when we reached the bottom, most of the wreck was free of net, with only the aftermost part of the stern entangled. In the 25-foot visibility, it was easy to identify large areas of the ship. As far back as the bridge, her bow section appeared quite intact and was lying on its port side. The white paint on the hull was still holding up well after four years underwater.

My buddy and I moved back toward the stern, noting the destruction of the bridge area and the remains of radio and radar gear on the sandy bottom next to the hull. When we reached the aft work-deck area, we turned and made a short penetration into what appeared to be a storage compartment. Strewn about were pieces of pipe, hose, fittings of all kinds, and several very nice brass deck lights, which we quickly bagged.

At this point, bottom time was growing short. We headed for the anchor line and the surface. While swimming across the sandy bottom for the anchor line, I spotted a ceramic plate with some type of logo on it, so I put it into the goodie bag. I saw that my buddy, too, had picked something up and stowed it safely in his bag. As we neared the anchor, more debris could be seen sticking out of the sand: bottles, plates and other types of ceramic objects, unidentifiable pieces of metal, and bones were scattered across the bottom.

Back on the surface, items recovered from the *High Seas* were proudly displayed and examined. Portholes, lights, brass oilers, a teakwood grating, and other fittings had been found. Also included were several embossed bottles (one had turned purple) and chinaware from the navy and several steamship companies. These items were obviously not from the *High Seas*, and for a while, a discussion of their origin raged hot and heavy. Eventually, we reached the conclusion that these items had been dropped over the years by ships entering San Diego Harbor. This area, just outside the channel entrance, was the last chance to dump shipboard trash before entering the harbor, and the first place it could be dumped on departure. For the sailors of yesteryear it was obviously much easier to shove trash over the side or out a scuttle, than to bundle it up, carry it ashore, and pay to have it hauled away. This practice must have been standard operating procedure for many vessels, both naval and commercial, judging by the diversity and amount of items seen and recovered. Because of this pre- and post-harbor disposal system, divers visiting the *High Seas* get the added bonus of perhaps finding embossed bottles, silverware, or logoed china from the early days of maritime transport along the west coast.

Diving conditions on the *High Seas* are usually quite acceptable, with visibilities ranging from 10 to 40 feet and the average about 20 feet. The major concern of anyone diving this wreck has to be the ship traffic in the area. It is absolutely mandatory to make all descents and ascents via your vessel's anchor line. It is equally important to fly the divers down or Alpha flag and to have a lookout at all times. By following these few rules, the *High Seas* can be a safe, exciting dive with the potential for a diversity of artifacts that can't be found elsewhere.

P. S.

S-37

Built at the end of World War I by Union Iron Works in San Francisco, the *S-37* would be 22 years old before she saw her first war patrol. The 219-foot long S Class submarine with a 20'8" beam, was launched on June 20, 1919, but wasn't commissioned until July 16, 1923. By August, she was in San Pedro, California and, as a member of Submarine Division 17, conducted exercises and tests off the southern California coast.

While recharging in San Pedro harbor in October of that year, however, there was an explosion in the *S-37*'s after-battery compartment. Three of the five crewmembers trapped by the dense smoke and flames died. Two of those who helped rescue two other crewmembers were seriously injured. Temporary repairs were made and the sub returned to her birthplace—Mare Island—for permanent repairs. She was back in San Pedro by December.

In 1924, SubDiv 17, including the *S-37*, participated in Fleet Problems II, III, and IV, moving through the Panama Canal, into the Caribbean, and then reversing direction. By the end of April, the division was back in San Francisco. Since it had been transferred to the Asiatic Fleet, the division prepared to travel to Manila Bay. Its vessels left San Francisco in September and arrived in the Philippines in November. For the next 16 years, the submarines' home port was Cavite. From there they cruised throughout the Philippines, the Netherlands East Indies (now Indonesia), and all the way to the coast of China.

When Pearl Harbor was bombed on December 8 (because they were west of the International Date Line), 1941, pulling the United States into World War II, the *S-37* was in Manila Bay. She was already old for a submarine as she prepared for her first war patrol. She saw her first enemy sub in January, but could not get close enough to fire her torpedoes. Her aging fittings and wiring caused other problems, also. On January 1, a fire broke out in her starboard main motor panel; four days later, she developed leaks in the air supply piping to the same panel.

By the beginning of February, she was in Java, where she was ordered to the coast of Borneo to patrol the Makassar Strait. On February 8, she finally saw the first real action of her nearly 23-year-old career. At 6 P.M. her crew sighted a destroyer. It was allowed

*The S-37 surfacing off Tsingtao, China, prior to
World War II. Photo by Bill Niedhamer, Steve Giles collection.*

safe passage, however, because it was thought to be
an advance guard unit for an enemy force en route
to Makassar City on the Island of Celebes.

At 6:13 P.M., three destroyers were sighted five
miles away. At 6:45, when no other vessels had appeared, the *S-37* went after the destroyers. She had
gotten to within 8,000 yards by 7:46 P.M. when she
saw four more destroyers just 4,000 yards away. Scanning the horizon carefully, the crew discovered the
dim outlines of three other large ships, three miles
away. At 7:51 the decision was made to go after these
last three ships, because they were thought to be
transports. Shortly after, however, the closest formation of destroyers increased speed, turned, and crossed
4,000 yards in front of the sub to provide cover for
the transports. Unable now to get a good shot at the
transports, the sub turned her attention to the
destroyers. By 8:40 P.M., she had fired all four of her
forward torpedoes, one at each of the destroyers. The
third one hit the third destroyer between the stacks,
buckling her in the middle so that her midship portion rose about 20 feet above the bow and stern. The
mortally wounded ship was the *Natsushio*, the first
enemy destroyer to be sunk by a U.S. sub in the
Pacific in World War II.

The fourth enemy destroyer sighted the *S-37* and
the sub was forced to submerge. She remained underwater, reaching a depth of 267 feet, for an hour and
a half while the three remaining destroyers dropped
depth charges at 10-to-15 minute intervals. Finally,
the enemy ships moved on and the *S-37* was able to
surface.

Although she remained in the area for another eight
days and saw several other Japanese ships, her lack of
speed and, on one occasion, faulty torpedo
mechanisms, eliminated the *S-37*'s chances of sinking
the enemy vessels. However, as she made her way
back to Java leaking oil, an enemy destroyer sighted
her. Although her captain, James Dempsey, had been
avoiding changes in depth because they made the oil
leak worse, he now was force to submerge, going as
deep as 150 feet. The *S-37* survived a five-hour attack
that included depth charges and aerial bombs. When
it was over, she headed for Surabaja Navy Yard on
Java, arriving February 21. Repairs on coolers, electrical steering, and starboard engine had barely been
completed when, six days later, she was forced to flee
as Japanese forces advanced on the island.

Early on the morning of February 28, the *S-37* was
off Java when she spotted two Japanese cruisers and
three destroyers leaving the vicinity after a victorious
battle with Allied forces. Once again, however, her
aging machinery slowed her down: Unable to control
her depth, she was forced to allow the enemy ships
to continue on their way unmolested. At mid-day she
came across an open, 50-foot boat from the Dutch
cruiser *DeRuyter* with Allied survivors aboard. Since
none of them was injured, she took the Americans
among them aboard, gave those in the boat some
provisions, and radioed their location to headquarters
before resuming her patrol. Later that day, she came
across more enemy ships, but was unable to attack
before they saw her, too. For the third time in her
career, she was forced to submerge and wait out the

*Bow torpedo room of the S-37. Photo by Bill Niedhamer, Steve
Giles collection.*

enemy's attempts to destroy her with depth charges and aerial bombs.

The *S-37* remained in the Java Sea during the first week of March. She was frequently attacked, and the depth charges and aerial bombings produced serious problems. When she was forced to submerge, there were leaks through disintegrating manhole and hatch gaskets. Although the crew had managed to slow the major oil leak through the engine room hatch to only one gallon every 20 minutes, the sub still left a telltale oil slick everywhere she went. On March 19 she arrived in Fremantle, Australia. In April, she sailed to Brisbane where she became part of Task Force 42. She was extensively overhauled and, in June, left for the Bismarck Archipelago for her fifth war patrol.

On July 8, the *S-37* was off the New Britain coast when she sighted a Japanese merchantman with a submarine chaser as an escort. For once, everything went right. The *S-37* fired three torpedoes, all of which hit their target, sending the 2,776-ton *Tenzan Maru* to the bottom. The *S-37* submerged to 110 feet, moving in a northerly direction, to escape the sub chaser's depth charges.

Ship's bell from the S-37. Photo from the P. Smith colleciton.

Diver recovering ship's helm from the submarine S-37. *Photo from the P. Smith collection.*

Six days later, a fire broke out in the starboard main motor. Then came a series of mechanical and electrical failures. By July 21, the sub was back in Brisbane harbor. After another overhaul, she departed on her sixth war patrol in the Savo Island area, supporting the Guadalcanal campaign. On September 2, she once again fired torpedoes, hitting the last destroyer in a column of four.

The latter part of October found the *S-37* on picket line station in defense of the Noumea, New Caledonia, base. This was not to be a long patrol, however. After a fire in her port main motor, mechanical failures, and tank trouble, the sub sailed for Pearl Harbor, and from there, to San Diego. She had returned to the West Coast after an absence of just more than 18 years.

That winter, the *S-37* underwent her second extensive overhaul. From then until the end of 1944, she served as an antisubmarine-warfare training ship. She was decommissioned February 6, 1945, at the ripe old age (for a sub) of 26. She was stripped and her hull prepared for towing. The navy had intended to use her as a target for aerial bombs, but this was not to be. The sub broke her tow and went aground near the city of Coronado. The navy sold her to a private salvage company. By placing large flotation tanks on either side, they managed to refloat her, but not for long. She broke her tow one final time and sank in 20-to-40 feet of water, off Imperial Beach, just north of the U.S.-Mexico border.

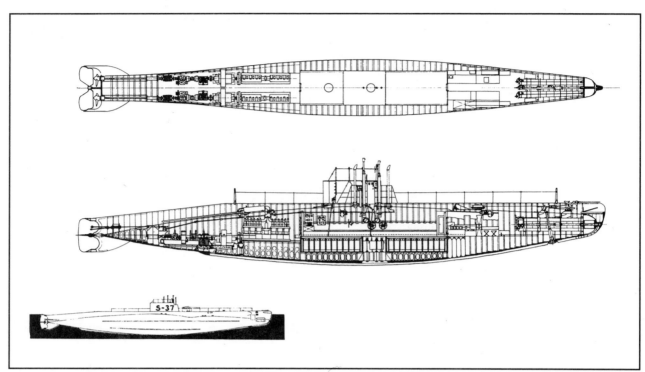

Outline plan of the S-37. Redrawn by R. Sperling from plans in the P. Smith collection.

Diving the S-37

Because the *S-37* is in shallow water only 200 yards from shore, diving her is always an adventure. On some days waves break right on shore; on others, 50 feet seaward. Diving should only be attempted when conditions are calm. Even then the area will be surgey. Visibility is predictably poor. Although the sub can be dived from the beach, she is very difficult to find from shore and is usually dived from private boats.

The *S-37* lies on her port side at about a 45-degree angle. The conning tower is about 10 feet below the surface on most days, but during a minus minus tide it will be out of the water. The rest of the wreck rises about 15 feet off the bottom. Many artifacts have been recovered from the sub over the years, including four telegraphs, portholes, assorted wheels and gauges, and the ship's wheel.

A six-by-three foot hole cut in the crew's quarters for the removal of the ship's wheel provides the only safe entrance. Although the hatches do not have doors, mussels have grown over them, making access impossible. Since the wreck is full of sand and very dark, only certified cave divers should explore the inside. Standard cave-diving equipment—redundant breathing systems, double tanks, extra lights, reel and line, etc.—must be used.

The *S-37* is in remarkably good shape and those who have dived her recently expect her to last at least another century. She was very solidly built. While a dive on her provides a rare opportunity to see an intact World War I submarine, visitors have discovered she also harbors a good population of lobsters.

B. J. C.

Channel Islands

San Miguel Island

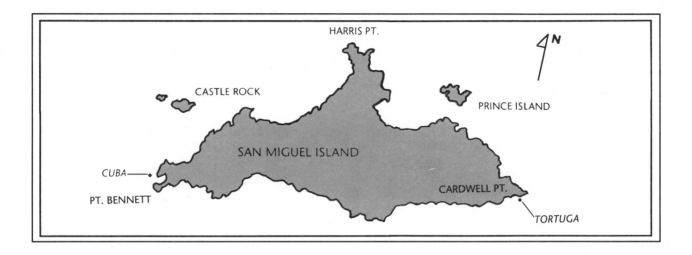

Cuba

On September 8, 1923, Ensign T. A. Kelly, quartermaster, U. S. Navy, had the afternoon wheelhouse watch. His ship, the U.S.S. *Reno*, a four-stack destroyer, was slicing through the huge, gray Pacific swells at 33 knots just west of Santa Rosa Island, one of the northern Channel Islands. For the past 15 hours, since she cleared the Golden Gate, the *Reno* and her crew had been involved in their annual smoke prevention and full-power trial. This yearly test run was required to evaluate maintenance levels and reliability over prolonged periods of time. So far, the run had been almost boringly routine. The only item of change had been the decision of the captain, Lieutenant Commander J. R. "Dick" Barry, to forego the scheduled Santa Barbara Channel passage and opt instead for the outside route seaward of the Channel Islands.

The patchy fog that is so common along the California coast had plagued the *Reno* since the Golden Gate, and had begun to thicken as she drew near the western entrance to the channel. To pass the speed trial, *Reno* had to maintain her top speed for the entire run from San Francisco to San Diego, or have the attempt disqualified. Captain Barry felt the safest course, where he could maintain speed, would be the longer but less traveled outside route. For the passengers and crew of the 3,000-ton Pacific Mail Steamship Company vessel *Cuba*, this decision proved to be most fortuitous.

At about 3 P.M., Ensign Kelly spotted a small boat off the *Reno*'s beam and brought it to the attention of Captain Barry, who later described the encounter in the October 10 issue of the *Los Angeles Examiner*:

> We thought it was a fishing boat at first. But
> as we dashed by I saw that it carried too
> many persons for such a craft . . . farther out
> we passed a second boat and knew then that
> they were in distress. Our speed was so ter-
> rific that we were forced to make a long
> circle of more than five miles to slow down
> before we reached the lifeboats. They
> proved to be two lifeboats from the S. S.
> *Cuba*—a Pacific Mail steamer out of Panama
> carrying passengers and cargo—that had
> grounded on the western end of San Miguel
> Island.

The Pacific Mail Steamship Company vessel Cuba *at her final port of call: the reefs off Point Bennett, San Miguel Island. Photo from the Santa Barbara Historical Society.*

One of the boats was under the command of the *Cuba*'s chief engineer, W. J. Owens, while the other was in charge of the second officer, John Rochou. All 68 survivors in the lifeboats were taken aboard the *Reno* and made as comfortable as possible in the little warship's limited space. Food, drink, and warm clothing were provided, and the officers and crew of the destroyer donated their bunks to the weary castaways.

Lacking only cutlasses in their belts and patches over one eye, Chief Engineer Owens and Second Officer Rochou nevertheless presented a suitably salty picture as they came aboard the *Reno*. Each had perched on his shoulder a large pet parrot that he had gathered up as he abandoned the *Cuba*. Though at first this appeared the thoughtful act of dedicated pet lovers, there was speculation later that Rochou and Owens had brought the birds along as an alternate food source should the lifeboat voyage run longer than the boat's supplies.

In speaking with Captain Barry, Chief Engineer Owens stated that although Captain Charles J. Holland of the *Cuba* hadn't been positive, he believed the ship had stranded on the south or west side of San Miguel Island. Following the captain's orders and steering by the boat's compass, the chief engineer reported that he had guided the lifeboats east, in the hopes of being picked up in the Santa Barbara Channel by some coastal vessel or perhaps making it to the mainland. Captain Barry gently pointed out there seemed to be a problem with the navigation, since when picked up, both boats were some 20 miles outside the Channel Islands and headed into the Pacific on a westerly heading, some 180 degrees from their desired destination.

Captain Barry then inquired as to the other passengers and crew of the *Cuba*. The chief engineer stated he believed most of the survivors had made it ashore near where the steamer had stranded. He said they were probably suffering from exposure and in need of assistance, since nearly every passenger, including a number of women, had abandoned the *Cuba* scantily clad in their nightclothes or bathrobes.

If there is anything that can stimulate the gallantry of a military officer, it's a situation with women in distress (scantily clad or otherwise). The *Reno* immediately began a search for the stranded *Cuba* as officers Rochou and Owens continued their story.

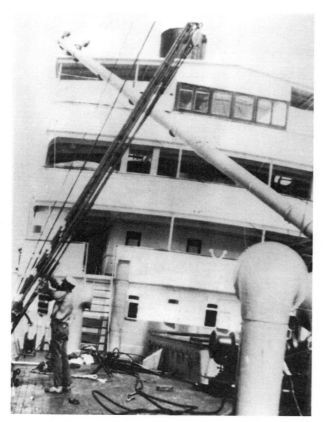

On the foredeck of the Cuba, *aground at San Miguel Island. Photo courtesy of M. and J. Bastian.*

When the *Cuba* struck, many of her lower decks flooded almost immediately. This prompted a short-lived panic by the passengers occupying these spaces, but fortunately no one was hurt. Calm was re-established when Stewardess Lottie Brown went below and guided the jittery passengers to safety on the main deck. Aside from that brief episode, the abandonment of the steamer was a tranquil and orderly exercise; there was no further panic and both passenger and crew morale was high.

On striking the reefs, the steamer was slewed around nearly 90 degrees by the large seas, which apparently contributed a major part of the hull damage sustained by the *Cuba*. As holds 1, 2, and 3, plus the engine room flooded, the mortally-wounded steamer began to list rather heavily to port; this played havoc with the launching of the starboard lifeboats. Because of the list, Chief Officer F. W. Wise, who was overseeing the starboard boats, found that the fully loaded boats couldn't be lowered. He ordered them emptied and all the passengers and crew in these boats reboarded the *Cuba*. The crew was then able to work the much-lightened boats into the water and around the port side of the ship, where the human cargo was reloaded. Despite the large seas and heavy fog, all passengers and crew were safely loaded aboard lifeboats, with Captain Holland, as tradition dictated, being the last to leave the *Cuba*. He then ordered the other boats to remain in the relative calm produced by the lee of the stranded Pacific Mail steamer, while his boat searched for a safe landing place for passengers and crew.

The *Cuba* was launched as the *Coblenz* in 1897 by Blohm & Voss at Hamburg, Germany. She was a medium-sized vessel of 3,168 tons, 307.7 feet long by 42.2 feet wide, with a crew of 52, and powered by a single, triple-expansion steam engine. Renamed *Sachem* while still under German ownership after the turn of the century, she came under the control of the Shipping Board at the close of World War I. Now called *Cuba*, in 1920, she was purchased by the Pacific Mail Steamship company and placed on the South American run.

The area near Point Bennett where the *Cuba* struck is designated as a "foul area" on coastal charts. This is an understatement of major proportions. Several acres large, it is a veritable labyrinth of reefs and shoals. That the *Cuba* was able to penetrate so far into this area before grounding is really amazing. Even with daylight, clear weather, and calm seas, navigating the area in even a small craft is a tricky and hazardous proposition. To attempt it with loaded lifeboats and succeed under the conditions encountered by Captain Holland and his crew, spoke reams of their skill as mariners, and noted them as a very fortunate crew as well.

After two attempts to work through the reefs, a safe channel of sorts was finally discovered. This path to safety was a narrow, foam-swept opening up to the rocky beach. Difficult enough in itself, the channel was nearly blocked with large, belligerent seals and sea lions. These animals were so aggressive that after only his boat and one other made the beach, Captain Holland ordered the other three not to risk landing. Instead, he commanded them to head out for the mainland via the Santa Barbara Channel, and seek rescue or assistance wherever they might find it.

Two of the boats, of course, were picked up by Captain Barry on the *Reno* after only 12 hours. The third boat carried 12 crew members and one passenger, and was under the command of the resourceful Chief Officer Wise of the *Cuba*. Though Wise's navigation was more accurate and his boat was at least headed east, toward the coast, these people did not have an easy time of it. They spent a nerve-wracking 28 hours struggling for survival against huge seas and curious whales before they were finally rescued by a passing tanker.

When interviewed by reporters, Luis Kemnitzer, the passenger on the third boat, and Chief Officer Wise described their encounter with the whales in the *Los Angeles Times* on October 11:

> We cast off at 4:30 o'clock Saturday morning and pulled for the lee of San Miguel Island, finally making San Miguel Passage with the aid of the current. Here, with Santa Rosa Island just visible through the fog, and San Miguel dimly outlined to the north, we were suddenly confronted by two spouting whales. At first neither was close enough to cause any grave fear. Then the one nearest us dived. When he came up, spouting and thrashing the water, he was much nearer. He dived again and came up within thirty feet of our frail craft, spouting and beating

> the waves as if angered by our presence. We were unable to even attempt rowing away, for all our energies were needed to keep the light craft afloat, to keep her headed right toward the enormous waves, each one of which threatened to engulf us. Then the current helped us, for we were borne into the main channel away from the whales.

Though forced to spend all night in an open boat, the "missing thirteen" as they were called by the newspapers, ate rather better than most shipwreck survivors. This was due to the foresight of one of the ship's waiters on board the lifeboat. Before he departed the *Cuba*, he gathered several pies and cakes to supplement the traditional lifeboat provisions of hardtack and water. This comparative gourmet fare was much enjoyed and appreciated by the 13 during their small-boat voyage on the briney.

Finally on Sunday morning, after being passed by several ships in the fog, Chief Officer Wise's boat was spotted by the San Francisco-bound, Standard Oil tanker *W. S. Miller*. the "missing thirteen" were quickly rescued and carried to San Francisco without further incident.

Meanwhile, back at the *Cuba*, the *Reno* had arrived at the scene and commenced ferrying the 25 stranded passengers and most of the remaining crew members from the island to the destroyer. Though the operation was made quite difficult by the large choppy seas, heavy surf, and numerous belligerent pinnipeds along the rocky beach, the rescue was completed in just two hours. Captain Holland and ten of his crew remained on San Miguel's barren shore to watch over the wreck and the $2.5 million cargo of silver bullion she carried.

One might imagine the depression felt by Captain Holland and his crewmen as the *Reno* pulled out of sight. They had just lost their ship. They were—for the moment—stranded on an inhospitable shore of rock and sand with the air filled with the unending cacophony of howling wind, crashing seas, and the barking, bellowing, and roaring of the thousands of seals, sea lions, and sea elephants that surrounded their little camp; their morale must have been pretty low. To add to the desolation, the shore was scattered with the remains of other ships that had come to grief on San Miguel's lethal coast as well as numerous human bones. Though the bones came from ancient Indian burial mounds nearby and were not those of the crews of those unfortunate ships, their presence nevertheless must have been more than a little disconcerting for the castaways.

When the *Cuba* struck the outer fangs of San Miguel Island, she was en route from Cristobal, Panama to San Francisco with passsengers and a general cargo of mail, mahogany, sugar, $300,000 worth of coffee and the silver bullion.

With all the passengers safely in the hands of Captain Barry and the U. S. Navy, Captain Holland turned toward the task of saving what he could from the *Cuba*. With diligence and back-breaking effort, the captain and his crew managed to recover most of the mail and all of the silver from the dying *Cuba*, and transfer them to their camp on the beach. The following day, the destroyer *Selfridge* hove to off Point Bennett and began operations to bring the mail and silver aboard. After many hours of hard work in cold, rough seas, the last of the bullion was safely loaded aboard the destroyer and locked away. Captain Holland asked and received permission for six of the remaining crew members to accompany the silver and mail to San Pedro. From there, all the passengers and crew rescued by both the *Selfridge* and the *Reno*, plus the silver and other salvaged materials, were picked up by the Pacific Mail Liner *Venezuela* and carried safely to San Francisco.

Meanwhile, word of the *Cuba*'s plight had spread, and salvage vessels from up and down the coast were converging on San Miguel Island. From San Francisco, two Red Stack tugs along with the salvage vessel *Homer* headed south for the site. From Los Angeles Harbor, the recently arrived sea-going salvage tug *Peacock* of Merritt, Chapman & Scott, was scheduled for the same destination, also with an escort of two Red Stack tugs. Initial attempts to locate the *Cuba* failed, due to darkness and fog around the island by the time the salvage ships arrived. After cursory and cautious circumnavigation of San Miguel failed to reveal the stricken liner, word was flashed by wireless that the Pacific Mail ship had sunk. Many newspapers up and down the coast carried the story that the *Cuba* had been torn to pieces by the heavy seas and wrenched from her reef-top perch into deep water. The *Homer*, more diligent than the other would-be salvors, stayed in the area and finally found the liner the following morning.

After making contact with Captain Holland on shore, the crew of the *Homer* moved its vessel alongside the *Cuba* and began salvaging those parts of the cargo and equipment they thought worth saving. The work continued almost without respite throughout the day and all the following night. Despite her flooded engine room, most of the *Cuba*'s wireless batteries still worked and were brought into operation to provide power for the deck and cargo lights, helping the task considerably.

About midnight, Captain Ira Eaton, Santa Barbara sea-dog and channel entrepreneur, arrived on the scene in his vessel, the *Sea Wolf*. Though the *Cuba* was plainly visible, all lights ablaze, Captain Eaton wisely deferred until daylight any attempt to navigate the "foul area" to the wreck. He pulled the *Sea Wolf* back into the protection of South Harbor and awaited morning.

With daylight, he could make out Captain Holland's tent encampment on shore, so a skiff was launched for the beach. Over a breakfast of "raw ham in scrambled eggs," the two captains exchanged information about the wreck and its circumstances.

Captain Holland explained that after fixing the *Cuba*'s position three days earlier with a sun sight, they had encountered heavy fog and had run on dead reckoning for the next 72 hours. He had left orders with Second Officer Rochou to be awakened at 3 A.M., so that he might try to establish a fix from Richardson Rock Light, but an hour later he still hadn't been called. Chief Officer Wise arrived on the bridge shortly after 4, and was amazed to find that the second officer had not called the captain. Wise immediately had the captain roused and within moments, Holland, still pajama-clad, was on the bridge. The captain said he immediately gave orders to change course to westward, but it was too late. They were already well within the "foul area"; they struck just a few moments later. After unsuccessfully trying to back the *Cuba* off, he gave the order to abandon ship. In concluding his narrative, Captain Holland said to Captain Eaton, "Young fellow, there is something unknown and sinister in the vicinity of San Miguel. Many times these rocks have taken their toll of ships and men who thought they were on the right course, but found to their sorrow that they were on the wrong one." After breakfast, Captain Eaton brought Captain Holland and his remaining crewmen aboard the *Sea Wolf* and took them out to the wreck.

While the two captains had been conversing, Horace Sexton, Captain Eaton's friend and partner on the *Cuba* caper, had struck a deal with the *Cuba*'s third officer for several cases of liquor. However, when the group arrived on board the grounded liner, they were disappointed to find that the crew of the *Homer* had already discovered the booze and liberated it during the night.

At about 9 A.M., when the *Homer* was loaded to capacity with coffee, mail, and apparently several cases of liquor, Captain Holland and the remainder of his crew boarded the salvage ship and departed for San Francisco. As the *Homer* pulled away, Captain Eaton was advised that a water taxi with guards for the wreck was on the way from San Pedro and would be arriving any minute.

To reassure the crew of the *Homer*, Captain Eaton pulled away from the wreck, but as soon as the salvage ship was out of sight, the *Sea Wolf* made fast back alongside the *Cuba*. Frantically, the *Sea Wolf*'s crew began loading anything that took their fancy: silverware, copper cooking kettles, linens, blankets, fixtures of all sorts, and tools.

Owing to the thoroughness of the *Homer*'s crew, no liquor was found, but several packages of marijuana were discovered in a paint locker and thrown overboard. Ironically, marijuana was legal at the time—though there was considerable stigma connected with its use—but because of Prohibition, alcohol was not.

In a short while, the water taxi carrying the guards came alongside. There were four guards, three of them armed, all of them big and mean-looking. They immediately ordered the *Sea Wolf*'s crew to return everything to the *Cuba*.

Captain Eaton looked at the guards, then at his crew, and told them to keep loading. The leader of the guards became abusive, but Captain Eaton's only response was, "Keep loading boys." In a frenzy, the guard threatened to shoot the next man who made a move. But with perfect calm, Captain Eaton asked the man, "What right have you to abuse us this way?"

The guard threw down a telegram saying, "Here is my authority." Cap Eaton read the telegram, handed it back, then turned around to his crew and said, "Keep loading."

Ira Eaton turned to the violently angry guard and said "Mister, that telegram says you were sent here to guard this ship and I figure you have not arrived here yet." When the guard figured out what this meant, he quickly jumped aboard the *Cuba*.

"Okay boys," said Cap Eaton. "Get aboard. The guard has arrived so we are through."

Though this was a legal technicality, Captain Eaton knew he was within his rights. Any vessel abandoned at sea (even though the *Cuba* was aground) with no anchor down, was fair game to whomever might find her. Though the salvor would have to turn everything recovered over to the Admirality Court, which would decide how the goods and equipment would be divided, the return on the effort was usually generous.

As the crew boarded the *Sea Wolf*, Captain Eaton pointed out to the guards that with the seas building and the *Cuba*'s bow and port rail already nearly under water, there was a good chance the wreck would go to pieces that night. Since the guards had no means to escape should the *Cuba* break up, Cap Eaton offered the use of the *Sea Wolf*'s skiff, if the guards would help load the rest of the items he wanted but hadn't had time to load.

With the water taxi rapidly disappearing over a dark and choppy horizon, and the sound of rivets being torn from the *Cuba*'s hull with every swell, the guards had little choice: they helped load.

Captain Eaton continued to salvage what he could from the wreck while glibly holding federal agents and representatives of Lloyd's of London at bay. In one case a rival freelance salvager who was denied, at gunpoint, access to the wreck, went back to San Pedro and spread the word that armed pirates were taking thousands of dollars of cargo and equipment from the doomed liner. Newspapers up and down the coast picked up the story and there ensued a brief but sensational run of mostly fabricated stories concerning Ira Eaton and the *Cuba*.

Shortly afterwards, Lloyd's advertised the wreck for sale, "as is, where is." Captain Eaton was high-bidder on the $500,000 vessel, at $800. He continued to salvage the wreck for the next several weeks with crews of young men from Santa Barbara.

One night after a violent wind-storm that produced large seas, the *Cuba* was gone. Washed from her position atop the reef, she sank into the deeper water nearby, beyond the reach of Cap Eaton and his salvage crews. Local sources said his profits from the liner were only slightly more than his costs on the venture.

Diving the Cuba

After numerous attempts to reach the *Cuba*, I was finally able to dive her in the mid-70s. On all previous attempts, either wind or large seas would turn us back even before we could manage to reach the "foul area" at San Miguel. On this trip, though the seas were flat and glassy with not even the merest whisper of wind, we had been beset by various mechanical problems on our 24-foot Thunderbird. Parts and pieces of the engine that had been carefully checked and maintained, for no apparent reason would suddenly melt, fly apart, or just die; the three-hour trip from Santa Barbara stretched to five.

Finally we reached Point Bennett. The final resting place of the Pacific Mail liner was just around the corner. I could hardly believe it. Despite the mechanical setbacks, we had made it to the site and the weather and seas were still calm and beautiful.

We turned the corner, and my heart sank deeper than the wreck we sought. Before us was line after line of churning, crashing white water: the "foul area." As I turned away deeply disappointed, Pat Gibson, a diver who had been on the *Cuba* before, chortled, "Far out, it's flat!" It was, he explained, some of the best conditions he had ever seen in the area.

I ran the boat carefully, as Pat stood on the bow and cautiously guided us through the maze of reefs until the *Cuba*'s huge engine appeared beneath our bow in the gin-clear water. Pat went in and placed the anchor. With the anchor securely set, we sat in an area of calm with the churning white maelstrom only yards away in nearly every direction.

Gearing up quickly, we were in the water in short order. And what water it was. Except across the tops of the reefs where there were foam and bubbles, the horizontal visibility was in excess of 100 feet. Apparently the eons of exposure to big seas and heavy currents has washed away all but the coarsest sand, so that even with rough seas, there is no sediment to be churned up to hamper visibility.

In the deeper areas between the reefs lay the *Cuba*. She appeared split in half like a spitted fish, with her immense engine the only part of her substantially

20-inch brass letters recovered and restored from the bow of the liner Cuba. *Photo by Patrick Smith.*

above the bottom. It rose nearly 20 feet from the rocky seafloor like a small reef itself. Spread out to either side of the engine were the sides of the liner. I found one area where the flattened hull plates with rows of portholes still in place undulate across the bottom in 50-to-70-foot sections. In other areas, large purple-and-white pebbled tiles lay scattered across the bottom along with all manner of shipboard fixtures. The *Cuba* is truly a wreck diver's paradise.

Though the fish in the area of the *Cuba* are large, plentiful, and nearly fearless of humans, most divers feel that spearfishing in the area is not a wise idea. Point Bennett is home to a large and diverse pinniped population: fur seals, sea lions, sea elephants, and others all make the Point their home. Many divers feel that arguing with a 600-pound bull sea lion over a fish dinner isn't the best use of their time. Similarly, there have been reports by commercial abalone and sea urchin divers of a great white shark that patrols the area around the Point Bennett rookeries. So unless one is really looking for the ultimate experience, ringing the underwater dinner bell by spearfishing in the area should be avoided.

Since the *Cuba* lies within Channel Islands National Park, no artifacts may be removed from the wreck. Regardless of the difficulties and dangers of the *Cuba*, it truly is a spectacular dive, one that I experience as often as I can.

P. S.

Tortuga

The new year of 1988 was greeted with high winds and stormy seas along the California coast. Beginning the previous December and continuing through mid-January of '88, a series of intense, powerful storms slammed southward from the Gulf of Alaska and pounded the ships and harbors of southern California. Newspapers, radio, and television carried stories of piers, homes, ships, and breakwaters damaged or destroyed by the violent seas and strong winds; damage estimates ranged into the multi-millions. Yet there was one victim of those storms that received little notice even though her story was one of the more interesting ones.

The victim was the U.S.S. *Tortuga* (LSD-26), and the only mention of her fate was made in the *Santa Bar-bara News-Press* under the headline, "Target Ship is Aground." The brief statement, a single column perhaps two inches long, stated that the "old hulk" had succumbed to the high seas and winds of the previous week's storms. It continued that the ship had gone aground on the southeast corner of San Miguel Island near Cardwell Point and had been "gutted," so it posed no environmental threat—poor eulogy indeed for a vessel that served the U. S. Navy for over 40 years.

The *Tortuga* was launched by the Boston Navy Yard on January 21, 1945, and was commissioned five months later. She was a Casa Grande Class Landing Ship Dock with a length of 457.9 feet, beam of 72.2 feet and a full-loaded displacement of 9,375 tons. The *Tortuga* cruised at 15 knots with a complement of 19 officers and 257 crew. For armament she car-

Landing ship dock 26. The U.S.S. Tortuga *was a veteran of Korea and Vietnam, and a victim at San Miguel Island. Photo from the U.S. Naval Institute.*

ried one 5-inch gun, two 40mm quad mounts, and twelve 20mm twin mounts.

She had completed her shakedown out of Norfolk, Virginia, and was en route to the Pacific combat area, when word reached her of Japan's surrender. Though she was too late to participate in World War II, she remained in the western Pacific. The *Tortuga* was attached to Amphibious Forces, Pacific Fleet, where she served as a mobile support and small-craft repair vessel. Though based out of Inchon, Korea, she conducted her support missions out of Tsingtao, Taku, and Shanghai, China; Hong Kong; and Yokosuka, Japan. In early 1947, the *Tortuga* returned to the United States by way of Guam and Pearl Harbor. She was decommissioned and placed in reserve at San Diego in August of that year.

In response to the communist invasion of South Korea in the summer of 1950, the *Tortuga* was recommissioned. After a brief refitting and shakedown, she sailed for Japan in December 1950. After stops at Pearl Harbor and Eniwetok, she arrived at Sasebo in February 1951. Almost immediately, she participated in a feint landing which was part of the operation to recapture the strategic port of Inchon.

During this time, intelligence reports suggested that with America preoccupied in Korea, the Chinese communists might take the offensive and mount an attack across the Taiwan Strait on the Nationalist-held island of Formosa. Intelligence experts believed the Chinese would utilize seagoing junks since they had proven to be nearly unsinkable during North Korean operations. In order to determine what ordnance would be most effective against such craft, the *Tortuga*'s mission was to raise eight 60-foot junks from the bottom of Inchon harbor and transport them to Yokosuka, Japan, for testing.

Throughout 1952, the *Tortuga* continued to supply support and amphibious services to United States and United Nations Forces in Korea. In 1953, she participated in the prisoner of war exchanges after the Panmunjom armistice. After conducting amphibious landing exercises and maneuvers in the Far East, the *Tortuga* returned to San Diego.

In 1954, the *Tortuga* was again assigned to the Western Pacific (WestPac) but en route, she was diverted to Haiphong, Vietnam, to take part in the massive evacuation of French nationals, in "Operation Passage to Freedom." The ship carried out four round

trips between Haiphong in the north and Da Nang, Saigon, and Nha Trang in the south before returning to Yokosuka, in October '54. For the remainder of the year, the *Tortuga* was involved in minesweeper support operations in Korean waters.

From 1955 through June 1966, the *Tortuga* was home-ported in San Diego and carried out regular, yearly cruises in support of WestPac. Between these deployments, she participated in exercises and equipment lifts out of west coast ports and underwent progressive upgrades and modifications. In July 1966, while the *Tortuga* was operating in Vietnamese waters, her home port was changed to Long Beach.

After the Gulf of Tonkin incident in August 1964, the *Tortuga* became part of the increasing American involvement in Vietnam. Though she had carried out several assignments in Vietnamese waters from late 1964 through 1965, in April 1966, the *Tortuga* was assigned to relieve the *Belle Grove* (LSD-2) as support ship for the Navy's operation "Game Warden." This operation was designed to interrupt and stop the flow of communist supplies along the coast of South Vietnam. She operated between Saigon and Vung Tau, helping to guard the shipping channels that ran through Viet Cong territory to the capital city.

In June, the *Tortuga* was shifted to the Mekong River Delta region to serve as a base for the Navy's fast river patrol boats (PBR's) of Task Force 116, and also to support a detachment of Army Huey (UH-1B) helicopter gunships. The heavily-armed gunships and patrol boats would work the rivers as teams with the PBRs stopping and checking river craft for contraband while the helicopters provided close support from above.

During the time the *Tortuga* was involved with the riverine assault groups, she received several visitors of note, including General William Westmoreland, Commander, Military Assistance Group; Rear Admiral N. G. Ward, Commander Naval Forces, Vietnam; and U. S. Ambassador to South Vietnam, Henry Cabot Lodge.

For the next three years, the *Tortuga* continued to support Allied amphibious, search and destroy, and cargo lift missions in the Vietnam Theater of Operations. Some of the operations she was involved in included "Fortress Sentry" and "Formation Leader" in the fall of 1967; "Daring Rebel" and "Gallant Leader" in May 1968; and "Keystone Eagle" in July of that

The U.S.S. Tortuga *aground at San Miguel Island, May 1988. Photo by M. and J. Bastian.*

year. Her final mission prior to heading stateside for the last time was "Operation Sea Float."

The *Tortuga* arrived at Seal Beach, California, in September 1968, where she unloaded her ordnance and then proceeded to Long Beach Naval Shipyard. On January 3, 1970, she departed Long Beach for the Inactivation Facility at Mare Island, where she was decommissioned three weeks later. She was then transferred into custody of the Maritime Administration (MARAD) and berthed at Suisun Bay. Her name was carried on the navy list until 1977, when it was removed.

Though it looked as if her then 32-year career was over, the Pacific Missile Test Center at Point Mugu needed a substantial-sized vessel to serve as a target for weapons tests. The *Tortuga* was chosen for the job. After being stripped and cleaned, the *Tortuga* was moored on the test range in deep water well off the Channel Islands. During the series of storms that swept the coast during the last two weeks of December, her ground tackle gave way and she drifted at the mercy of the wind and seas until she grounded high and dry on the southeast corner of San Miguel Island and broke in two.

On Board the Tortuga

Whatever spit-and-polish Navy neatness there once had been on the *Tortuga* was long gone. Though spokesmen for the Pacific Missile Test Range indicated that the old LSD was a target ship, the lack of damage to the vessel seemed to belie that description. She looked more like a sea-going junkyard with her mas-

sive aft deck piled high with sundry debris. Equipment and missile parts were scattered everywhere—piled over eight feet high in some places.

Inside the ship, the immenseness of the vessel was impressive. Long, gloomy corridors stretched out until they finally disappeared in the dim parallax. The *Tortuga*, though a dead ship, produced a cacophony of sounds producing unease in some visitors and curiosity in others. From somewhere below came a muffled sound reminiscent of a pump operating. Further on, a periodic wailing and whistling sound was tracked to a six-inch pipe running into the bowels of the ship. The rise and fall of the swells below forced air in and out of the pipe, producing the eerie sounds.

Though most of the areas were empty and stripped-out, there was an occasional compartment with a nice oak desk and chair, or file cabinets, or some other sign that the old ship hadn't been completely abandoned before her grounding on San Miguel.

One visitor to the ship described an incident he viewed from the starboard bridge. Down below in the calm, shallow lagoon that had formed in the lee of the wreck, two male sea elephants were fighting for the right to court one of the nearby females, who watched interestedly from the white sand beach. The battle raged for some time until a winner was determined and peace descended on the sea elephant herd again. The *Tortuga* was a dead ship, but her neighbors (who accepted her without reservation) were alive and well.

In her present location, the *Tortuga* should have lasted for years, providing those who were interested with a unique piece of military and maritime history to explore. Meanwhile the tradition will carry on: on June 11, 1988, a new *Tortuga* (LSD 46) was launched by Avondale Shipbuilding.

Epilogue

In the fall of 1988, the Navy, at the urging of the National Park Service, began operations to remove the *Tortuga* from her sandy berth adjacent to San Miguel Island. Under the blue-white flame of the cutter's torch, the old warrior quickly succumbed. Her superstructure was removed and placed aboard barges to be dumped in deep water. The forward two-thirds of her hull was patched, dragged from the beach and towed to deep water where it was sunk.

As of January 1989, only about 150 feet of the *Tortuga's* stern remains accessible. Because it was torn free during the grounding and settled more quickly into the sand, removal of this section was initially deemed too difficult. However, whether this section remains available is again under discussion. There is some talk that the Navy will try to remove the remaining stern section, but there has been no decision reached yet. Until they do decide to remove what is left, divers and others still have some remnant of the old warship to peruse.

P. S.

Santa Rosa Island

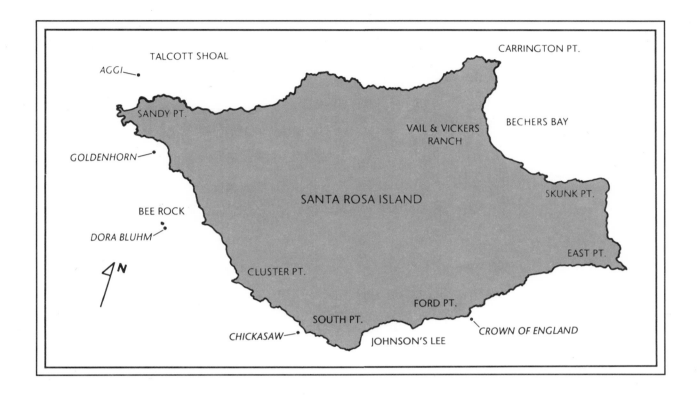

Aggi

It was a beautiful and prophetic sight, and because it was a vision of the future, it was sad as well.

The nondescript yet powerful steamer bulling her way through the morning chop of San Francisco Bay was a dramatic contrast to her tow, a sleek and graceful windship sitting well down on her marks. With her dependable engines, the steamer was the representative of a rapidly approaching future, while the sailing ship was a member of a dying breed, beautiful but uneconomical. The wind vessel was being called upon now because the war in Europe and that terrible new weapon, the U-boat, had destroyed so many vessels, that any ship that could carry a cargo could make a profit and hence was in demand.

The skipper of the full-rigged ship *Aggi*, Captain Anskar Olsen, was a conscientious and careful commander. Even as the towing steamer *Edgar H. Vance* moved steadily out of the security of San Francisco Bay and past the headlands known throughout the world as the Golden Gate, he was receiving reports from his ship's officers as they oversaw the final securing of the *Aggi*'s equipment and the chaffing gear on the towline forward (though it had all been checked several times already).

In her holds the *Aggi* was carrying 2,500 tons of barley and 600 tons of beans. On her hull, in white letters 12 feet high was the word "NORGE," which identified her as a neutral Norwegian ship. In spite of this precaution, this voyage was to be her last. She would not fall victim to a cruising U-boat, however, but to bad weather, bad luck, and the unforgiving shoals of the Santa Barbara Channel Islands.

The departure date for the *Aggi* and the steamer *Edgar H. Vance* was April 29, 1915. The plan was for the *Vance* to tow the heavily loaded *Aggi* as far as the Panama Canal, where the *Aggi* would hoist her sails and proceed to her destination in Sweden under canvas.

Unfortunately, shortly after clearing the Gate, the ships were struck by a storm of awesome intensity. The *Aggi* and *Vance* were caught in wind and seas of a velocity and size rarely if ever seen on this coast. There was also another rarity, snow; coastal mountains as far south as Santa Barbara were generously dusted and sailors up and down the coast agreed they had never experienced anything like this storm before.

The following morning, despite her powerful engines, the *Edgar H. Vance* was forced by the violence of the seas to release her tow, and only 75 miles out from San Francisco, unable to put about and make it back, the *Aggi* was on her own.

Several attempts to get some sail up to provide a little control were futile, so Captain Olsen and his crew of 20 plunged southward under "bare poles," doing their best to maintain themselves and their vessel. But, according to notes in the National Maritime Museum "the storm increased, the cargo began to shift, and before morning it was piled to leeward so that the guard rail was underwater and half the men's cabins were filled with the sea . . . the men had to double up in the dry berths on the windward side of the ship."

Four days later, on the afternoon of May 4, the *Aggi* was driven aground on Talcott Shoal at the west end of Santa Rosa Island. Despite, or perhaps because of the violence of the storm, the *Aggi* was hard and fast on the shoal with little movement, even though her decks were completely inundated with each huge wave. A boat was immediately launched and all the crew except for Captain Olsen and the first mate set out for the shelter of nearby Santa Rosa Island.

Shortly after the crew left the *Aggi*, Captain Ira Eaton of the vessel *Sea Wolf* noticed the ship's distress signal, and made for the wreck. After delivering the mate to Santa Barbara to arrange for salvage of the

The ship *Aggi lost by stranding at Santa Rosa Island, May 3, 1915. Photo from the P. Smith collection.*

Aggi, Captain Eaton returned to the island. He picked up the rest of the crew except for Captain Olsen, who remained with the *Aggi*, and brought them all to Santa Barbara.

As they were being interviewed by reporters in Santa Barbara, the *Aggi*'s crew said they weren't surprised at the outcome of their short-lived, ill-fated cruise, since there had been ominous signs foreshadowing such disaster from the beginning of the voyage.

They recounted that it began with the death of the ship's cabin boy at the start of the passage from Lyngor, Norway and continued with the desertion of the ship's cat on arrival in San Francisco. When they departed San Francisco under tow of the *Vance*, they were followed down the coast by strange sea birds uttering mournful cries, and finally a "strange-colored seagull had perched on the mast every minute down the coast until [they] were wrecked."

Aside from some personal belongings and the ship's pennants, which the crew took with them when they left, nothing had been removed from the *Aggi*. It was three days before crews could get out to begin salvage work on the ship. By that time, even though she appeared fairly intact from a distance, her hull had been pierced and broken in many places by the rocks on which she lay. Her cargo of grains was mostly ruined.

A salvage crew headed by Captain Eaton managed to save only about 300 tons out of the 3,100-ton cargo. The remaining grain served to hasten the *Aggi*'s destruction, for as it absorbed moisture, it expanded and literally tore the hull apart.

Even with the loss of the major portion of the *Aggi*'s cargo, there still remained substantial quantities of undamaged stores and equipment on board. Captain Eaton, with help from Captain Colis Vasquez of the 40 foot powerboat *Otter*, managed to secure numerous articles of considerable value and return them to Santa Barbara. Some of the items they documented included two small boats, two large anchors, five smaller anchors, chains, blocks and tackle, rope, a large amount of paints and oils, galvanized steel cable, and several tons of provisions. The *Santa Barbara Morning Press* also made mention of the ship's figurehead, which was described as "a beautifully carved full-sized figure of a woman, with streaming hair and long flowing robes," which would probably be saved as well.

The loss of a ship is always news and it was no different with the *Aggi*. Almost as soon as her whereabouts were known, representatives of Flying A Studios in Santa Barbara chartered a boat to take them across the still storm-tossed channel to visit the wreck site. They took motion picture footage both on and around the *Aggi*.

In the following weeks, footage of the wreck was shown in theaters around the world. Possibly as a result of this initial exposure, Universal Film Company purchased the remains of the *Aggi* for "photoplay" purposes. During the time she remained above the waves, several "swashbuckler" films, such as *The Sea Hawk* with Errol Flynn, were made on her decks. This worked out quite well for the studio, since with the *Aggi* so firmly aground, there was no need to worry about shooting schedules falling behind owing to *mal de mer*.

Her hull weakened by the expansion of her water-soaked cargo and the nearly constant pounding of the northwest swells, the *Aggi* eventually succumbed. She slipped from her rocky perch and disappeared beneath the kelp-bedecked waters of Talcott Shoal. There she remained, forgotten by all except for the few commercial ab divers who passed over her remains from time to time.

Then in 1966, the *Aggi* was rediscovered by charter-boat skipper Glenn Miller. Research in the local libraries provided all the information on the *Aggi*'s loss and some notes on her life, as well.

The *Aggi* began her career on February 21, 1894. She was built by Mackie & Thompson, hull number 77, and launched at Govan, Scotland, for R. J. Swyny of Liverpool under the name *Aspice*. Throughout her lifetime, she would be known by several names; after *Aspice* she became *Saint Erasmo*, then *Seerose* and finally, *Aggi*. She was a good-sized vessel of 1,921 gross tons, with a length of 265 feet, a breadth of 39.1 feet and a depth of 23.3 feet. Much care was taken with her construction and Lloyd's special survey gave her a 100A1 rating.

Since the area where the *Aggi* went down was excellent for fish, abs, and lobster and offered the added attraction of a shipwreck as well, it became another of Captain Glenn's exciting dive destinations.

In the late 60s, Captain Glenn freely offered his charter boat, the *Emerald*, and assembled a prestigious volunteer crew made up of, among others, such notables as Dr. Glen Egstrom, Dick Anderson, and Jim Joiner, to salvage one of the *Aggi*'s large stock and ball anchors. Despite the difficulty involved in salvaging an item weighing close to 5,000 pounds, the project was successful, and the end result was that the Santa Barbara Historical Society became the happy recipient of the historic old anchor.

Throughout the 60s and 70s, divers recovered all manner of artifacts from the *Aggi*'s broken hull. Such items as portholes, belaying pins, brass handrails and step-plates were recovered quite regularly. One of the nicest pieces to come up was the builder's plaque, a vessel's birth certificate in brass.

Other items (recovered from the *Aggi* at the time of her loss) are at Stoll House, a facility used by the Goleta Historical Society. On display there are the binnacle with compass and the ship's bell from the *Aggi*.

Diving the Aggi

Today the remains of the *Aggi* are strewn across a large area of sea bottom with portions of hull and masts scattered everywhere across the rocky reefs. Since she stranded on the shallowest area of the shoals, the maximum depth found in the vicinity is only about 50 feet. When seas are calm, visibility in excess of 50 feet is not uncommon. The reefs, kelp, and remains of the *Aggi* provide a spectacular underwater habitat with photo and game opportunities at every turn. During lobster season, Talcott Shoal is one of the premier spots on the coast for big bugs, rating with San Nicolas Island and Cortes Bank. However, since the *Aggi* lies within Channel Islands National Park, which is a marine sanctuary, there is except for game, a look but-don't-take provision in effect. Despite this prohibition on artifact removal, the *Aggi* is still one of the nicest wreck dives in the Channel Islands.

P. S.

Goldenhorn

A certain area on the west-central coast of Scotland has produced quality vessels of all types and sizes for over 100 years. Scattered for some 25 miles from Glasgow to Greenock along the banks of the River Clyde is the industrial community whose prolific production of ships helped make England the world power and mercantile leader she was in the 19th century. From the advent of iron ships to the present day, the label "Clyde-built" told a seafarin' man that the vessel—whether it was a warship or a cargo carrier, powered by turbine-electric, steam or wind—was the best obtainable.

In January 1883, the various shipbuilding yards along the Clyde launched six steamers and two sailing vessels. This represented a total launched tonnage for one month of 19,739 tons. The barque *Goldenhorn* counted for 1,840 tons of that total.

The *Goldenhorn* (268.8 by 40.2 feet) was an iron four-masted, barque-rigged, sailing vessel, launched on January 8 from the Russell & Company yard at Greenock. Though the company was young—not yet ten years old—and considered something of a newcomer by most Clyde shipbuilders, the contemporary trade paper, *Shipping World*, wrote in its November 1883 issue, ". . . they have already acquired an excellent reputation, more especially for the large and splendid sailing ships which they have turned out." It was this reputation for excellence that had brought the *Goldenhorn*'s proud owner, James R. de Wolf, to Russell & Company originally, and kept him returning as a satisfied customer.

The *Goldenhorn* was the second of three sister ships that Russell & Company would build for de Wolf's company for use in the Calcutta and San Francisco trades. The first vessel de Wolf commissioned was the *Matterhorn*, launched in 1882, and the third sister was the *Silberhorn*, launched in 1884. All three ships were iron, four-masted barque-rigged vessels of around 1,850 tons; all were good carriers with beautiful lines, but unfortunately were not particularly fast. All three vessels would become casualties of the sea.

The *Silberhorn* went missing on a voyage between Newcastle, New South Wales, and Iquique, Chile, in June 1907. Her cargo—coal—was a dangerous one. In the 19th and early 20th centuries, spontaneous combustion of such cargoes claimed the lives of a

The four-masted barque Goldenhorn. *She was the second of three ill-fated sister ships built for James de Wolf. Photo from the National Maritime Museum, San Francisco.*

good many sailors and ships. And from the scanty evidence that turned up, it was thought that was the fate of the *Silberhorn*.

In November 1909, a violent north Pacific storm caught the *Matterhorn* outbound from Portland, Oregon, to Ipswich with a full cargo of barley. Some 70 miles off the Washington coast, the huge seas swept the big square-rigger on her beam ends, causing the cargo of grain to shift. Efforts to get the ship upright were unsuccessful, and the violent seas soon tore the covers from her hatches, opening her hull to the chilly waters. When the *Matterhorn* foundered, she took the first mate, steward, and four seamen with her.

The crew of the *Goldenhorn* made out somewhat better when she came to the end of her career on the pinnacle rocks off Santa Rosa Island on the cold, foggy night of September 12, 1892.

The *Goldenhorn* was 72 days out of Newcastle, New South Wales, bound for San Pedro, California. Her cargo consisted of 2,808 tons of bituminous coal consigned to the Southern Pacific Railroad Company. Although the ship had been in fog and heavily overcast skies for the previous four days and the officers had been unable to take any kind of a navigational fix, Captain William Dunn wasn't too worried. The ship's dead-reckoning navigation had been carefully

watched with speed and course checks every hour. According to calculations, the *Goldenhorn* was at least 50 miles from the closest land. Captain Dunn's sense of well-being was brought to an abrupt end at 8:15 in the evening of September 12.

Under close-reefed sails, the *Horn* was ghosting along at about four knots through dark, heavy fog and choppy seas. Suddenly the cry of "Land ahead!" came from the fo'c'sle lookout. Captain Dunn ordered "about tack" in an attempt to beat off to windward from the rocky shore that threatened his ship. It was to no avail. What little wind there was died away, leaving the big windjammer no way to save herself. The heavy swell and her own forward momentum quickly drove the helpless ship hard on to the rocky pinnacles.

For the next hour, Captain Dunn and his crew maintained the most strenuous efforts to remove the mortally wounded ship from the rocks that held her, but their efforts were futile. A large rock had impaled the *Goldenhorn* nearly beneath her foremast like a bug on a board. The *Horn* had struck on the peak of the high tide, and as it began to ebb, each passing moment left the big vessel's bow more firmly impaled on the reef. As the afterpart of the ship began to fill and settle lower in the rough seas, the huge swells began to sweep completely over and through the *Horn*'s stern cabins.

Realizing the futility and danger of staying any longer, Captain Dunn ordered the crew into the lifeboats, and the *Goldenhorn* was abandoned to the sea. So quickly had the *Horn* been inundated, that neither food nor water was placed in the boats; the men cast off from the rapidly dying square-rigger with only what they had on their backs. The captain attempted to keep the boats together and close by the stranded *Horn*, with the hope they might reboard her the next morning, but with the heavy seas and the limited visibility in the fog and dark, the two boats were gradually swept down the coast of Santa Rosa Island.

Through the night, attempts were made to land on the island, but these were thwarted by the mostly rocky nature of the coast, the darkness, and the heavy seas. Some eight hours and 25 miles later, as dawn was breaking, Captain Dunn guided the two boats to shelter at Beacher's [sic] Cove. Exploration of the area revealed it to be barren of human habitation. When continued searching failed to turn up neither food nor water, the *Goldenhorn's* crew members took to their boats once again and began rowing for the mainland, some 28 miles away.

At 6 that evening, loungers on Stern's Wharf in Santa Barbara watched in amazement as the two boats with the 28 officers and crew of the *Goldenhorn* slowly made their way in. Most of the sailors, after a day and a night of exposure with no food or water, were in ragged shape.

A telegram was sent to the English Vice-Consul, C. W. Mortimer, in San Pedro, advising him of the situation even as the citizens of Santa Barbara transported the weary crew to the Arlington Hotel for rest and refreshments. Vice-Consul Mortimer wired back that he was departing immediately for Santa Barbara. Until he arrived he asked that all the needs and requirements of the castaways be seen to and said that the British government would be responsible for any costs.

By September 17, Vice-Consul Mortimer had surveyed the wreck of the *Goldenhorn*, convened a court of inquiry, and rendered the verdict that Captain Dunn was blameless in the loss of the big four-master. The wreck was attributed to heavy northeast currents setting toward the island and also the dense fog at the time she struck. The court noted that although these currents were known, they were not mentioned in the sailing directions or charts for that area of the coast. The court also stated that it appeared the ship would only last a few more days since the *Goldenhorn* was in very bad condition and breaking up fast.

Over the next week, before the wreck was sold to the Whitelaw Salvage Company of San Francisco, the local schooner *Ruby* made several trips to the wreck of the *Horn* and managed to salvage some stores, lines and cable, rigging and sails, and three anchors. The contemporary press noted that the items salvaged by the *Ruby* would be sold and the proceeds split between Captain Dunn and the owners of the little schooner.

By the end of September, the local press had milked everything of interest from the *Goldenhorn* incident, and mention of her had disappeared from the newspapers. From then on, except for a few salvors based in Santa Barbara and San Francisco, who would plunder the *Horn* (along with the *Gosford* and the *Winfield Scott*) each summer for whatever scrap they

The capstan cover and some of the brass letters that graced the bow of the Goldenhorn. *Photo by Patrick Smith.*

could find, she dropped from memory. By 1912, all mention of the ship ceased and she slipped into obscurity.

In January of 1970, Captain Glenn Miller, of the Santa Barbara dive boat *Emerald*, had a charter group on board that was looking for lobsters. The conditions on the backside of Santa Rosa Island were perfect: sunny and warm with the ocean dead-flat calm. Captain Glenn anchored where he had never visited before, in a reefy area on the southwest side of the island that was usually too rough to dive. He was hopeful that these reefs would be home to many naive lobsters for his eager divers. They were. The area was also the resting place of a large multi-masted, iron-hulled sailing ship.

Over the course of several dives that day, about 80 lobsters were captured; several brass portholes were also recovered. There was also a curiosity fired in Captain Glenn concerning the identiy of the old windship and the circumstances that had brought her to her briny grave, six fathoms down.

Captain Glenn was unable to return to his spot on the backside of Santa Rosa for nearly a month. During that time, he spent many hours asking old-timers around the harbor if they knew anything about a square-rigger lost off the west end of Santa Rosa. But no one knew anything of such a ship.

Early in February, he had a chance to get back to his mystery square-rigger with another charter group.

Again, conditions were excellent on the site. As divers splashed over the side, they could be seen clearly from the surface as they searched the reefs and wreckage 35 feet below. By the end of the first dive, the question of what ship was wrecked there was solved.

One diver had discovered the ship's brass capstan cover pinned beneath some wreckage on the bottom. Even through the heavy growth he could see there were letters engraved on it. When he got it to the surface and cleaned the growth off, the words, "Goldenhorn Liverpool," were revealed. A second dive produced the eight-inch brass letters H, O, R, and two Ns from the ship's bow.

The *Goldenhorn* had been found.

Diving the Goldenhorn

Today, the brine-soaked remains of the *Goldenhorn* are much the worse for their nearly 90 years underwater. Not only is the area where she grounded subject to moderate to heavy sea and weather conditions for a good part of each year, but the old coal-carrier was subjected to nearly two decades of salvage by crews who, as standard operating procedure, used dynamite and other explosives to remove what they wanted from the wreck. Despite the toll of time and salvage, however, there still remain substantial areas of the *Goldenhorn* to investigate.

A survey of the wreck by the National Park Service in the early '80s determined that the main sections lie in roughly a northeast to southwest orientation. The bottom is mostly sand with the rocky spines of reefs and pinnacle rocks scattered generously through the area. Depths over the wreck range from 18 to 36 feet and because of the shallowness of the area, surge can be a problem. Visibility on the *Goldenhorn* runs about 20 feet, but on occasion can range up to 50 feet or better.

In the early to mid-70s, divers on the *Horn* recovered such items as teak doors, brass hinges and portholes, ornate step plates, and even the ship's wheel. One fortunate beachcomber discovered the badly dry-rotted figurehead from the old square-rigger protruding from a sand dune just inshore from the wreck.

However, such activities are no longer condoned. The vessel is part of Channel Islands National Park and the policy (which is strictly enforced) is, "Look all you want, take nothing from the wreck." In spite of this, the *Goldenhorn* is still a fascinating dive. Immense sections of her hull and masts still remain, and for those who are interested, the reefs in the area are home to red, pink, and green abalone. Halibut in the 20-to-30-plus-pound range are often sighted and taken in the area, too. Fall and early winter seem to be the best seasons to dive the *Horn*, but those weather windows, calms between storms that occur in the early spring, can also provide excellent conditions.

P. S.

Dora Bluhm

It had been a good trip for Captain Oscar Johnson and the *Dora Bluhm*. The stout little schooner had departed Coos Bay, Oregon, May 19, 1910, with a capacity cargo of 350,000 board-feet of lumber consigned to the Golden State Lumber Company of San Pedro, California. The run south had been made in good time under the blustery push of the springtime northwesterlies. Six days out, in the vicinity of the Santa Barbara Channel Islands, the *Dora Bluhm*, still moving well through choppy seas built up by a heavy westerly wind, sailed into heavy mist. Captain Johnson, a careful seaman with many years of coastal sailing experience, took the necessary precautions of shortening sail to reduce the *Bluhm*'s speed and placing an extra lookout forward.

Unfortunately, these efforts were not enough to save the *Bluhm*. At about 9 that evening, with no warning whatever, the vessel crashed hard onto Bee Rock, an outlying pinnacle on the south side of Santa Rosa Island. The strong wind, choppy seas, and large swell forced the *Bluhm*'s entire length across the top of the rocks, then deposited the heavily damaged ship on the other side. The *Bluhm* immediately began listing as the sea rushed into her shattered hull. Captain Johnson ordered the crew to cut away the masts and rigging to reduce topside weight in an attempt to bring the vessel back to an even keel. Even though each of the heavy wooden masts was nearly the circumference of a 50-gallon barrel, the crew had them cut away in less than 20 minutes. The incentive of staying out of the cold, choppy waters produced all the adrenalin necessary for the crew to perform this feat. But, even before the task was completed, Captain Johnson realized it was to no avail. With the last few axe strokes, the *Bluhm*'s heavy masts and rigging went overboard and quickly sank. She righted herself only slightly for a moment and then continued settling rapidly into the choppy black seas.

In most cases her cargo of lumber would have been more than adequate to keep her afloat despite her ravaged hull. On this trip, however, her cargo was fresh cut, unseasoned wood with little or no buoyancy. Instead of helping to keep her afloat, the *Bluhm*'s cargo was rapidly dragging her to destruction.

Captain Johnson had no options. He gave the order all sailors hope they'll never hear: "Abandon ship!" The crew responded quickly, and just 30 minutes after the *Dora Bluhm* had struck, Captain Johnson and all seven crewmen cast off from the mortally wounded ship. They paused after they had rowed a short distance away and looked back. The *Bluhm*, her shape barely visible through the mist and dark, slipped lower, then disappeared beneath the choppy seas as they watched. The *Bluhm*'s journey was over, but her crew had a way yet to go.

Not being sure of his location because of fog and darkness, Captain Johnson guided the lifeboat north. Soon the men could hear the sound of heavy surf pounding a beach they couldn't see. Deciding against trying to negotiate the heavy surf in pitch darkness in an overloaded lifeboat, Captain Johnson reversed course away from the dangerous shore. He realized his best chance of surviving was to get into the Santa Barbara Channel (which he knew should be nearby) where he and his crew might be picked up by a coastal vessel or perhaps make it all the way to the mainland.

Twenty-four hours later, the crew of the *Dora Bluhm* was picked up, still in heavy fog, by a power launch operated by the Santa Rosa Island Company. After the group had been given food and water—which they hadn't had since the *Bluhm* sank—the same launch carried the captain and crew to San Pedro, where the loss was reported. Since no lives were lost and no valuable cargo was involved, there was very little stir caused by the loss of the *Dora Bluhm*; barely 20 lines in the local paper. She was just another hard-working coastal vessel that went the way of so many of her sisters.

Launched in 1883 by the Hall Brothers of Port Blakely, Washington, the *Dora Bluhm* was a typical Pacific Coast three-masted schooner of 330 tons. Since she was only 133.7 feet by 33.3 feet, and drew only 10.5 feet of water, she was small enough to get into the dangerous but profitable "doghole" lumber ports along the northwest coast. These ports were in nearly any small declivity along the coast that was adjacent to virgin timber. After the logging operations began to cut and mill lumber, the only way to get their product to the lucrative markets south was by sea. One schooner skipper, on seeing where he had to take this

Photographs of the Dora Bluhm *are unobtainable; this three-masted schooner, the* Fred E. Sanders, *was also built by Hall Brothers, and, except for being slightly larger, is very similar to the* Bluhm. *Photo from the National Maritime Museum, San Francisco.*

vessel to receive his load of lumber, commented that there was hardly enough room for a large dog to crawl in and turn around, let along for his ship. "Why it's only as big as a doghole," he said. and the name stuck.

The *Bluhm*, built for William G. Bluhm, engaged in this dangerous but profitable trade until 1892. Up until that time, she had never had a problem. Strangely, when she did get into trouble it wasn't on the dangerous northwest coast, but in the usually milder waters of the south.

In November of 1892, the *Bluhm* was cast ashore and wrecked at Topolobampo, Mexico. She was dragged off the beach and afterward towed to San Francisco, where she was deposited on Rotten Row in Oakland Creek. There she languished until July 1894, when she was purchased by the well-known shipbuilder, Hans Bendixsen. He had the *Bluhm* towed to his facility on Humboldt Bay where she arrived on August 2. Just 11 weeks later, completely refurbished, she was sold to W. H. Smith and continued with her lumber-carrying career.

In 1906, the *Dora Bluhm* was sold to the Pacific States Trading Company and for the following two years operated as a codfisher in Alaska waters during the summer months. Later, she once again went back into the lumber trade until her loss, May 25, 1910, at Santa Rosa Island.

Diving the Dora Bluhm

In late 1972, a group of wreck divers heard about a newly-discovered wreck at Santa Rosa Island from a Santa Barbara dive boat captain. He thought it was probably a steam-powered vessel of some sort, owing to the large amount of what looked like pipes and plumbing lying all over the bottom. Since the wreck was in the vicinity of Bee Rock, an area that is very exposed and can be quite rough, we scheduled a trip for the first open weekend and prayed for good weather. Luck was with us, for on the day of our charter the wind was calm and the seas had only a moderate swell.

On the five-hour trip to Santa Rosa, all of us pumped the skipper for more detailed information on what he had found. However, since his only interest in wrecks was limited to knowing their locations for his customers, we learned very little more.

Once at the site, the anchor was quickly set. We listened to the skipper's last-minute briefing as we geared up. He said that although he thought he had anchored very close to the wreck, if we didn't see the pipes immediately, we should move inshore. My buddy and I soon followed the anchor over the side. Conditions were excellent. Depth was about 50 feet, with 40-foot visibility and a slight surge that tugged us back and forth on the sandy bottom. Not spotting anything immediately, my buddy and I headed off in the direction the skipper had indicated. A few minutes later we found it. Spread across the bottom was a spaghetti-like mass of twisted pipe. Various lengths and diameters were knotted together and strewn everywhere. I didn't understand what I was looking at. It didn't appear to be the condenser pipes from a steam engine and there was no machinery or equipment lying around. It looked more like a plumbing truck had dumped its load here. As we swam closer, it dawned on me what I was seeing. It wasn't pipe on the bottom but rope, a sailing vessel's rigging strewn about in piles and covered with sea growth. I swam closer, grabbed a two-inch line and gave it a pull; the whole tangle moved and sediment clouded the water. As the slight surge carried the cloud away, I noticed I had pulled something from the bottom. It was round and black and for a moment I thought it was an old kelp holdfast that had grown on the line. As the last of the silt was carried off, I could see that what I held was a rigging deadeye.

It was traditional in design with its three holes giving it a skull-like appearance. It was about nine inches across and quite heavy. It appeared to be in excellent shape with no worm damage and only a little light growth covering its surface. Looking more closely at the mass of lines, I began to make out many other deadeyes of different sizes, plus pulley blocks of various types and sizes, and the wooden grommets used on sailing vessels called bullseyes. I knew the history of the *Dora Bluhm* and it was obvious we were sitting on what remained of her rigging. It had been cut away in that desperate attempt to save her on that dark foggy night more than 60 years earlier. As we swam through the area, the thought crossed my mind: Where was the rest of the *Dora Bluhm*?

We followed the rigging debris down swell until it disappeared. Although we continued on for some distance beyond, we never found another clue. Since that time I have searched downswell and down the prevailing wind path in the hopes of discovering the *Dora Bluhm*'s final resting place, but to no avail. It's possible she was carried across the bottom by the surge and broke up in shallow water. If this happened, then there would be no indication of her destruction except, perhaps, for some of her timbers or cargo cast ashore. It is also possible that with her heavy load of lumber, she was driven into the bottom and covered with sand. In that case, perhaps one day after a heavy storm season, a diver will swim through the area and come across the nearly intact remains of that maritime workhorse, the *Dora Bluhm*.

P. S.

Chickasaw

At first glance, the grounding and subsequent loss of the *Chickasaw* seems to be a story that would provide little interest. A 20-year-old freighter with a cargo of cheap toys and imitation flowers, bound for Wilmington, California, from Yokohama, Japan, loses her way and crashes ashore on the west side of Santa Rosa Island.

To be sure, there were tense and exciting moments during the rescue of the 46 crewmen and four elderly tourist passengers, but she was no new expensive liner crashing to her doom with hundreds on board. There were no lives lost, nor even really threatened. And no valuable cargo nor treasure.

But first glances can be misleading, which is the case with the *Chickasaw*. A little probing and research reveals that the old freighter really is a treasure ship—a cache of maritime history.

The *Chickasaw*'s life began, like nearly all modern ships, with a piece of paper. In her case, it was a Maritime Commission contract calling for the construction of MC hull number 134 for the Mississippi Shipping Company. The name of the vessel was to be the *Del Santos*. Construction began just two days after Pearl Harbor, December 9, 1941, at the Kearney, New Jersey, yard of the Federal Shipbuilding & Drydock Company, and was completed just under four months later on April 4, 1942. The *Del Santos* was 459 feet in length, 63 feet in breadth, drew 27 feet of water and displaced 6,131 gross tons.

On July 11, after fitting-out and shakedown runs, the *Del Santos* was turned over to her owners, the Mississippi Shipping Company. It is doubtful, however, that she completed even one voyage for her new owners before she was passed to the Navy under the auspices of the War Shipping Administration. On September 16, 1942, the *Del Santos* was renamed *Dauphin* and designated AP-77 (auxiliary transport). However, it was discovered there was a Canadian ship with the same name, and to prevent confusion, two days later her name was changed from *Dauphin* to *Thurston*. The *Thurston* (ex-*Del Santos*, ex-*Dauphin*), was commissioned into the U. S. Navy on September 19, 1942.

The *Thurston* was moved to the Atlantic Basin Ironworks in Brooklyn, New York, where she was modified to fit her documented description. The work was

The Chickasaw *is shown in this photo with her war paint and her war name, U.S.S.* Thurston, *awaiting her next load in New York Harbor. Photo from the National Archives.*

minimal and took just five days. It consisted of the installation of metal pipe bunks and other facilities to accommodate 1,306 troops and the mounting of her rather modest armament. Total weaponry for the *Thurston* was made up of four 3" deck guns and four 40mm antiaircraft guns—not much protection to run the iron gauntlet that Hitler's Atlantic U-boat wolfpacks maintained in the early days of the war.

On October 24, after completing several shakedown cruises out of Little Creek, Virginia, and participating in amphibious landing exercises with Army units at Solomons Island, Maryland, the *Thurston* joined an east-bound convoy designated Task Group 34.9. This group was to be known as the Center Attack Force in the invasion of North Africa. On November 8, TG 34.9 arrived off Fedhala, French Morocco. Five days later, the *Thurston* entered Casablanca Harbor and quickly completed unloading her cargo of troops, equipment, and supplies. Two days later she departed for the States, arriving at Hampton Roads, Virginia, on November 26, 1942. Over the next three months,

she completed two more trans-Atlantic trips carrying reinforcements to the North African campaign. In March and April of '43, the *Thurston* was hauled out for drydocking and repairs.

The *Thurston*'s next task was carrying troops to Oran, Algeria, in preparation for the invasion of Sicily. After landing rehearsals with the 16th Infantry Regiment off Algiers, she joined Task Force 81 and on July 10 began unloading troops and supplies off Gela, on the southern coast of Sicily. Another trip back to New York for troops and equipment, and the *Thurston* was back in Oran on September 2. After she was unloaded, she embarked 600 German prisoners of war—destination: New York. Once again the *Thurston* survived the Atlantic run, safely depositing her prisoners in New York on September 22.

On October 8, the *Thurston*, loaded with American troops, departed New York for Gourock, Scotland, where she arrived nine days later. After disembarking the American GIs, she immediately sailed for Glasgow where she took on board a number of Canadian troops. Then the *Thurston* returned to Gourock where she joined a convoy for North Africa. Almost as soon as the convoy arrived at Algiers, it came under heavy German air attack. During the course of the raid, three ships were torpedoed and sunk—the destroyer *Beatty* and two transports, the *Santa Elena* and the Dutch ship *Mornix Van St. Aldegonde*—and six German aircraft were downed. The convoy, somewhat depleted, departed Algiers and arrived in Naples on November 8, where the *Thurston* offloaded her Canadian troops. With barely time to refuel, she was ordered south to Palermo, Sicily, where she picked up elements of the American 1st Armored Division and transported them to Scotland. Following a week's layover in Gourock, she departed for the States, arriving in New York on December 9, 1943.

Beginning in January 1944, the *Thurston* began a frenzied four-month period of dashing back and forth across the North Atlantic carrying cargoes of troops and supplies. She began with a New York–Liverpool run; in February, she ran round trip New York to Gourock; and April found her again in Great Britain, this time gracing the harbor at Cardiff, Wales. After unloading, AP-77 headed to Loch Long, Scotland, for three weeks of landing exercises in preparation for the Allied invasion of Hitler's "Fortress Europe."

Late in May while the *Thurston* was loading in the harbor at Portland, England, she suffered some minor damage when a German bomb exploded close to her port side. After a brief interruption for repairs, loading was completed and on June 5, the veteran transport joined Assault Group O-3, part of the vast D-day armada making the channel crossing to Normandy. By 3:30 the following morning, the *Thurston* was anchored some ten miles off Omaha Beach. There her troops disembarked onto LCIs, and hit the heavily defended beaches at H-hour as scheduled. During the initial assault, three of the *Thurston*'s boats were lost; two more were lost in the second wave. That evening the transport was ordered back to Portland where she remained "on-call" until late June.

On July 4, she departed Portland for Naples, via Oran. Her cargo on this trip consisted of heavy trucks and M-4 tanks that she successfully delivered in Naples on July 17. She remained there until August 13 when she loaded assault troops and joined Task Force 84 for the invasion of southern France. She continued operating in the Mediterranean between

North Africa, Italy, and southern France until late October, when she joined a convoy headed to the United States.

Arriving in New York on November 6, the *Thurston* was placed in drydock for overhaul. Five weeks later she was headed back to duty, this time in the Pacific.

After making a quick stop at Norfolk, Virginia, the *Thurston* passed through the Panama Canal and arrived in San Francisco on January 5, 1945. Seventeen days later she anchored in Pearl Harbor and began offloading passengers and cargo. With the war in the Pacific rushing to a climax, the *Thurston* and her crew had no time for rest. Once she was empty, she took on fuel, supplies, and troops, and headed west to the Marianas via Eniwetok.

On February 16, after five days at Saipan, AP-77 joined with Transport Group Able of the Attack Force for the assault on Iwo Jima. For five days the *Thurston* remained offshore from the Iwo beaches before she was ordered to land her troops and offload her supplies. Finally on February 27, she completed her unloading and was ordered to the Solomons by way of Saipan and Guam, where she delivered many battle casualties. She continued on her way, making stops at Tulagi and Espiritu Santo to load elements of the Army's 27th Infantry Division, and then transported them via Ulithi to Okinawa.

The *Thurston* then retraced her previous route, making stops at Ulithi, Manus, and New Caledonia, collecting some 917 homeward-bound service personnel and battle casualties. From there, it was back across the Pacific where she arrived on May 26. After unloading, she immediately embarked troops for the Philippines and headed back to the Pacific war zone.

After disembarking her Army troops in Manila on July 8, transport AP-77 was routed to Tacloban where she loaded homeward-bound naval personnel. She arrived in San Francisco on August 14, as the war ended. Ten days later, the *Thurston* began another troop-transport trip to the Philippines with Army personnel. After she arrived in Manila on September 15, she was assigned to "Magic Carpet" duty, returning servicemen home from overseas as quickly as possible.

Her routing home included a stop in the Solomon Islands at Guadalcanal. While en route there, her watch spotted a drifting, 28-foot dory, apparently without anyone alive on board. The suspicions of the *Thurston*'s deck officer were aroused, however, because of a blanket covering something in the forward area of the drifting boat. He sent a landing craft to check the apparent derelict. The LCVP circled the dory several times at very close range before moving alongside. As the boarding officer stepped aboard the dory, three Japanese emerged from beneath the cover and began throwing hand grenades at the officer and the LCVP. As the officer dove overboard, the LCVP crew hastily abandoned their boat before the grenades exploded. A second LCVP was quickly launched to rescue the crew of the first boat. This boat carried a heavily armed crew and suceeded in recovering all members of the first craft. As soon as the second boat completed her rescue and cleared the area, the *Thurston* opened fire on the dory and sank it with a three-inch shell. Despite the proximity and violence of the grenade attack, the boat crews suffered no casualties and the *Thurston* was able to recover her LCVP, too. After this violent interlude, the transport made stops at Guadalcanal and Espiritu Santo, New Caledonia, before arriving at Seattle on October 30.

The *Thurston* made three more "Magic Carpet" voyages; two to the Philippines and one to Japan. She completed her final trip in San Francisco on June 20, 1946, and immediately thereafter was prepared for decommissioning. She was returned to the War Shipping Administration on August 1 and took back her old name, *Del Santos*. For her service in the war, she received seven battle stars.

The End of the Chickasaw

In 1948, *Del Santos* was purchased by the Waterman Steamship Company, and the following year renamed *Chickasaw*. Under that name, she carried out general merchant trading until her loss in 1962.

The evening of February 7, 1962 was the beginning of the end for the venerable freighter. At 9:18 P.M., she was groping her way down the California coast through eight-to-ten-foot seas and the rain and fog of a rather severe series of winter storms, when her career came crashing to an end. Despite the fact that she carried radar, a radio direction finder, a fathometer, and an experienced captain, in the dark and violence of the storm she lost her way and drove onto the exposed western reefs of Santa Rosa Island.

Calls for assistance from the doomed ship found response from the Coast Guard, which dispatched two

S.S. Chickasaw, *gutted on the reefs at Santa Rosa Island, circa 1970. Photo by M. and J. Bastian.*

cutters, the 125-foot *Morris* from Long Beach and a 95 footer from Santa Barbara. The U.S. Navy directed the salvage ship *Gear* to proceed to the scene from her San Diego base, while commercial firms in Los Angeles dispatched the tugs *Sea Ranger* and *Judd* to help free the freighter, if conditions allowed. But they didn't. The *Chickasaw* had stranded in an extremely dangerous and difficult area. Her hull had dragged over several razor-sharp reefs before coming to rest against the base of the nearly vertical sea cliffs that marked the rugged edge of the island. Almost all the freighter's holds and lower compartments had been damaged and were taking on water. Fortunately, almost three-quarters of the *Chickasaw*'s hull was supported by the very reefs that had torn the bottom from her. If there was little likelihood of her sinking, there was also little chance of her ever coming free of her rocky perch.

Attempts at rescue from seaward were hampered by limited visibility, large storm-generated seas, and the fangs of outlying reefs, which prevented vessels from coming close enough to the stranded freighter to do any good. Even though there was an Air Force station less than four miles from the *Chickasaw*, rescue from the island was hampered by the ruggedness of the terrain and the continuing storms that had turned the island's soil into a quagmire.

With quiet efficiency, the *Chickasaw*'s crew prepared the ship's lifeboats for launching and then waited for the arrival of the various rescue vessels. It turned out to be a long wait. For the next 90 hours, the passengers and crew of the *Chickasaw* remained marooned aboard the storm-tossed freighter. Storm-generated waves of a reported 18 feet swept the area and pounded the old war-horse heavily on Santa Rosa's reefs. It wasn't until three days later that a breeches buoy was rigged from the nearby island cliffs to the battered ship, and it was another 24 hours after that before Captain Emmanuel Patronas allowed his four passengers and 32 of his 46 crewmen to evacuate the ship over this 200-foot-long aerial link to the island. Despite high winds and stormy conditions, the rescue effort was completed in just four hours. On shore, the passengers and crew were assisted by 20 members of the 669th Air Control and Warning Squadron who escorted the weary castaways through the rain on an arduous, muddy, three and a half mile hike back to the island Air Force station. After some hot food and dry clothing, the passengers and crew of the *Chickasaw* were transferred to a Coast Guard cutter and arrived in Santa Barbara that evening.

By February 18, marine surveyors hired by Waterman Steamship Company believed there was only a small chance that the vessel might be saved, but more likely she would remain where she was.

To take advantage of whatever chance there was, one of the most experienced and successful salvage companies on the Pacific Coast was brought in—salvage master Fred Devine and his powerful vessel, the *Salvage*

The sea claims more of the S.S. Chickasaw, *circa 1984. Photo by M. and J. Bastian.*

Chief. Devine and his ship came to the *Chickasaw* with dozens of successful operations behind them in some of the most difficult and dangerous places on the coast. Some of their better-known recoveries over a 20-year span included the vessels *Semar, C-Trader, Lipari, Nozima Maru, Yorkmar,* and *Venerator.*

Because of the outlying reefs, Devine used the services of Columbia Helicopters, and the experience of pilot Wes Lamatta—who had worked with him on several other salvage projects—to carry cables and lines between the *Chickasaw* and the salvage ship offshore. Despite huge anchors placed offshore and the tremendous power of her twin 1,800-horsepower, 10-cylinder Fairbanks-Morse diesels, the *Salvage Chief* was unable to remove the *Chickasaw* from the rocky ledge. Attempts at removing the freighter's cargo were considerably more successful, with the *Salvage Chief* recovering nearly all of it.

With her cargo removed, the underwriters sold the salvage rights to the *Chickasaw* to self-styled salvage master Al Kidman for the bargain basement price of $2,500. Unfortunately for Kidman, his salvage attempts on the *Chickasaw,* like so many of his other salvage endeavors, came to naught. After losing his barge to heavy seas in the area, he wrote the project off. The *Chickasaw* was then abandoned to the elements. Occasionally, a few dedicated scroungers would visit the ship whenever conditions would allow. With flashlights and curiosity, they would prowl and poke through the old ship, usually unaware of the history of the ex-navy vessel. When the curious departed, the local gulls and pelicans would go back to their long-term project of covering every exposed square inch of the wreck with their odoriferous whitewash, while the sea slowly pounded the ship into submission. The gallant ship that had survived some of the most hazardous duty during World War II, had finally succumbed—a victim of fog and storm and the tenacious reefs of southern California's Channel Islands.

Visiting the Chickasaw

You'll note that I say "visiting" rather than "diving" the *Chickasaw.* Until recently, the majority of the wreck remained above the surface. For years, during calm weather, adventurous souls would paddle their way in and make their way on board the old freighter in search of brass souvenirs. Lights, valves, coat

The Chickasaw *in January 1988. Photo by M. and J. Bastian.*

hooks, locksets, plaques, and even a sextant were recovered from her. Even in the mid-'70s, the rusted remains of some of her cargo of toys could be found in the corners of her holds. In the mid-80s, her bow and stern sections finally fell away, leaving only the *Chickasaw*'s midships section—including her bridge—upright. The storms of the winter of '87–'88 caused even this stalwart section to begin to fall. With the exposure to the prevailing winds and sea it's likely that soon the sea will claim all of the old transport and nothing will show above the surface.

As for diving the remains of the *Chickasaw*, it's not a wise idea for several reasons. First, the area is dangerous because of violent seas around numerous reefs and pinnacles. Second, because of almost constant wave action on the clay-like rocks that can be found in the area, the visibility is usually pretty poor—with ten feet about maximum. Third, the tons of steel that made up the *Chickasaw* now lie scattered across the bottom, each edge rusted to knife-like sharpness. Any diver with the least bit of common sense should begin to get an idea of how dangerous a dive on this site would be. Finally, the *Chickasaw* lies within Channel Islands National Park, which means that removal of artifacts or even disturbing the site is strictly forbidden.

Until the last section of the old ship makes its final plunge, she will remain one of the most photogenic subjects in the Channel Islands, but one that should be seen strictly from above water, not below.

P. S.

Crown of England

Even before seaman Emil Smith, forward lookout on the steamer *Crown of England*, could shout the warning, "Breakers ahead!" the foggy night air in November, 1894 was rent by the grinding and tearing sounds of the ship running across the reef. As the vessel ground to a halt, the engines stopped and there was a brief moment of silence before orders were shouted and the sea began to pound its victim. It passed in a flash, the noise returned, and engulfed the stranded *Crown of England* like the waves slamming into her. Captain James Hamilton was too late shouting orders trying to back her off. The night air was filled with violent sounds: the hollow drumming boom of the swells slamming into the empty hull, the tortuous grinding as the waves slid the ship broadside across the jagged reef against gravity and the pull of her engines. In a short time it became obvious to Captain Hamilton that the situation was hopeless; not only was he unable to extract his ship from the reef where she was so precariously perched, but the huge and violent surf pounding the *Crown* made him fear for the lives of his crew. Surrounded by the gray-black mistiness of heavy fog and crashing waves, and with his ship starting to go to pieces around him, Captain Hamilton gave the order to abandon ship. But how? To try to launch a lifeboat in the surrounding maelstrom would be suicidal. Just when it appeared that the options had been narrowed by the fates to just one—staying with the *Crown of England* until daylight, and hoping the vessel held together under the terrific pounding—another hope was offered. Seaman Fred Frandberg, a common sailor with uncommon courage, volunteered to try to swim a line to the beach, which could be seen dimly through the fog. After several attempts, seaman Frandberg was successful. Soon after he rigged the line, all the *Crown*'s company were safely landed on what seemed an inhospitable shore.

Almost immediately, the captain organized the crew into small groups and sent them to search out the area for inhabitants who might be able to render assistance. Not only were the search parties unsuccessful, but somehow during the quest, Captain Hamilton became separated from the others and had great difficulty finding his way back to the camp. Apparently, it wasn't his night for navigation. The cold, miserable crew spent the remainder of the night huddled together on the lonely beach.

By daybreak, Captain Hamilton and First Mate Poole had concluded that they had stranded on the south side of Santa Rosa Island. Since there seemed to be no possibility of local assistance, it was decided that the next day, Poole and five crewmen should take one of the lifeboats and attempt to reach Santa Monica.

The doughty Poole and his crew of five manned the oars and spent the next two days and nights moving south under the "ash breeze." On Monday morning, November 11, 1894, the few early risers and fishermen scattered along the end of Santa Monica's Long Wharf were surprised at the unexpected appearance of a small boat containing six bedraggled sailors. Their surprise was heightened by the fact there were no vessels anchored in the roadstead from where the little boat might have come. Word spread quickly, and by the time the boat was alongside the wharf, quite a crowd had gathered to learn the story behind its arrival and its strange-looking crew. First Mate Poole related the story of the stranding of the *Crown of England* and the situation facing Captain Hamilton and the 14 crew members who remained on Santa Rosa Island. After telling how he and his crew had, in fact, only located the Long Wharf by following the sounds of the locomotive whistles operating there, the men were hustled away for some rest and a well-deserved meal. The story of the *Crown*'s voyage to disaster was related to curious reporters who soon arrived on the scene.

The *Crown of England* was a relatively new vessel, having been built by Richardson, Duck & Company, at Stockton-on-Tees, in May 1891, for the Crown Steamship Company of Belfast, Limited. She was strong and modern, constructed of tough iron plates over steel ribs, and she was powered by a triple-expansion steam engine of 200 horsepower. After her survey by Lloyd's she was rated 100A1, the best possible. Though not of great size—297 feet in length, 40 feet in breadth, 19 feet in depth and 1,658 net tons—she was built for cargo carrying.

Immediately after her launching and shakedown, she was chartered by Samuel Samuels & Company for the north Pacific route between the Orient and Seattle. Failing to make a success of this route, she was chartered by John Rosenfeld & Company of San Fran-

cisco and from late '93 until her loss in November '94, she engaged in coal transport along the Pacific Coast. At the time of her stranding she had been en route to Nanaimo, British Columbia, in ballast from San Diego.

Word went out to Rosenfeld & Co, in San Francisco and the tug *Fearless* under command of Captain Dan Haskell was dispatched to the scene of the wreck. Despite Mate Poole's speculation that the *Crown* would be a total loss, there was considerable hope the vessel might be saved. However, by the time the *Fearless* arrived at the location, the *Crown of England* was already too far gone.

The *Crown* had perched herself atop the jagged reef just east of Ford Point on Santa Rosa's south shore. On his arrival, Captain Haskell noted that nearly the entire length of the *Crown*'s keel could be seen at low tide, and he was able to board the wreck without getting wet, by ladder from the beach. On board remained only the second mate, the third assistant engineer, and five seamen, the rest of the crew having been transported to Santa Monica by the tug *Warrior*.

After making a thorough examination of the *Crown of England*, Captain Haskell reported to the underwriters that the ship was a total constructive loss. He found both the rudder and stem posts broken and the engine had shifted off her mounts. Examining the cargo areas, he found the watertight bulkheads broken in, numerous large holes pounded through her tough iron hull, and the heavy four-inch between-decks steel stanchions twisted and bent.

It was amazing that such a well-built ship should break up so rapidly, but there were several unfortunate circumstances that combined to seal the *Crown*'s fate. First, she was travelling in ballast, which meant she drew very little water. Added to an extreme winter high tide, this placed her very high on the reef, in an exposed location. Next, the heavy seas that were running when she was stranded pounded the vessel heavily, and even the toughest hull has its limits. Finally, the amount of time the *Crown* lay on the reef guaranteed her destruction; she worked across the rocks for nearly a week until a salvage tug arrived. When Captain Haskell was interviewed after returning from the wreck, he noted, "Had the vessel's course been 50 feet further seaward, she would have cleared the rocks, and had she struck 50 feet closer to shore, her position would have been much more favorable to saving the wrecked vessel." It seemed that all the fates had been against Captain Hamilton and his ship on the night of November 7, 1894.

Since the *Crown of England* was a British ship, the Court of Inquiry was headed by the Honorable C. White Mortimer, British vice-consul, and held in the city where the *Crown*'s crew came ashore, Santa Monica. The testimony contained no information of a spectacular nature, but did serve to emphasize the extent and degree of the fog that obscured the coast on the *Crown*'s last run.

Captain Hamilton was the first witness. He stated his vessel was in heavy fog from the moment she left the wharf in San Diego until she struck that fatal reef near Santa Rosa Island. He pointed out that the fog was so thick the harbor pilot who guided the *Crown of England* out of San Diego Harbor became lost twice, before guiding the ship safely beyond Point Loma.

Other witnesses included First Mate Poole, First Engineer McHaffy and several other officers and crew members of the *Crown*. They all corroborated the captain's statements as to the poor visibility and the care that was taken in navigating the ship. Captain A. Smith, a mariner from San Pedro and local maritime expert with 27 years of experience in local waters, stated that the *Crown of England* had probably encountered an unknown current and been forced off her course. He finished his testimony by saying, "... any of the best of captains might have come to the same disaster through the same cause." The following day, a statement was received from the second officer of the steamship *Corona*, which had sailed from San Diego to San Francisco a few days prior to the *Crown*. He said that a current they encountered in the area of the Channel Islands persisted all the way up the coast, and by the time they reached San Francisco, it had thrown off their navigation by more than 12 miles.

After that statement was read to the court, testimony was closed and a finding exonerating Captain Hamilton and his crew from all blame in the loss of the *Crown of England* was promptly presented.

While the court was carrying out its inquiry into the loss of the *Crown*, Captain Metcalf, the local Lloyd's agent, arrived at the wreck site to determine if anything could be done to free the ship. Almost as soon as he saw the vessel, he realized that Captain Haskell had been correct in his assessment; there was nothing to be done but salvage whatever machinery, equipment, and fittings could be rescued, and write off the rest. Quickly concluding his survey of the *Crown*, he soon reboarded the tug *Valiant* and returned to Santa Monica with his recommendations.

Once the underwriters assumed the loss, they wasted little time in auctioning off the remains of the poor old *Crown* to the highest bidder. The California Iron and Wrecking Company made a determined attempt to win the contest and were successful in their efforts. They, too, wasted little time, and by December 7th, the one month anniversary of the stranding, they had five vessels on site, including the San Francisco tug *Katie O'Neil*, the schooner *Anna*, three lighters, and 40 men engaged in the dismantling of the *Crown*. The company representative, Henry J. Rogers, stated to the Los Angeles papers that they were making excellent progress in their endeavor, having already recovered the main engines, steam hoists, steering gear, anchors, chains, and much other valuable equipment.

Because of her proximity to the bluff-edged shore, much of the salvage work was carried out from the island. Like Uroboros, the mythic Greek dragon that consumed itself, the *Crown*'s own equipment became the major instruments of her dismantling. One of her steam donkey engines was somehow maneuvered from the *Crown* to the nearby bluffs, where the powerful machine, in conjunction with a mast from the wreck, was used to remove even the heaviest equipment from the *Crown*. One of the first things to be brought from the wreck was her huge cast-iron stove. The salvage crew appropriated it for their own use, in short order installing it in the salvage camp on the bluffs where it provided hot meals for the 40-man crew.

California Iron and Wrecking Company's plan was to break apart the hull of the *Crown* after all the machinery had been removed, but this did not come to pass. Although the salvage crew managed to get most of the *Crown of England*'s machinery and equipment, the sea snatched the battered and gutted hull away from them before they managed to claim it.

Diving the Crown of England

Unfortunately, the *Crown of England* doesn't offer a great deal for divers. Not an exciting or pretty wreck, she isn't visited often. Since she lies within Channel Islands National Park, where it is unlawful to remove anything from any wreck site, it's probably fortunate that the temptation of removing artifacts doesn't exist on the *Crown*. What remains of the ship, mostly the tough iron plates that made up her hull, lies in 12 to 18 feet of water within the shadow of Ford Point. These plates are scattered across the bottom and provide little for photographer, hunter, or wreck diver.

When the weather is calm, visibility can range up to 20 feet, but the average is usually somewhat less. During these calm periods some of the other reefs in the area can provide abs and kelp bass that are so scarce around the *Crown*.

Unlike most shipwrecks whose final resting places are unmarked once the ship disappears beneath the waves, the *Crown of England* has a marker—several in fact. The steam donkey engine, mast, and cook stove remain on the bluff where they were left. They seem quite appropriate as a good example of man's pragmatism when he loses a battle to the sea.

P. S.

Santa Cruz Island

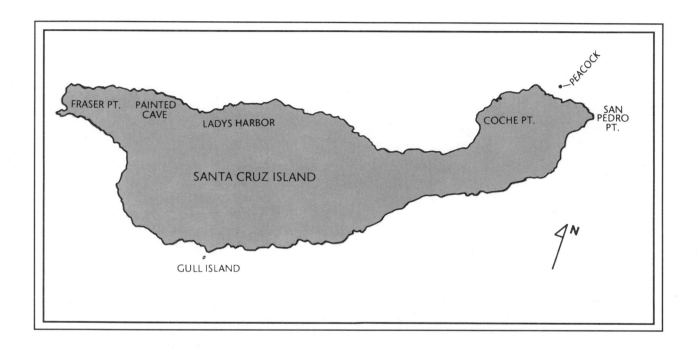

FRASER PT. PAINTED
CAVE

LADYS HARBOR

PEACOCK

COCHE PT.

SAN
PEDRO
PT.

SANTA CRUZ ISLAND

GULL ISLAND

N

The *Peacock*

Mystery surrounds this vessel. Knowledgeable wreck divers agree on one point: She is a World War II minesweeper. One man, who researched her identity when she first went down, is sure she is the *Peacock*. No one else has presented information that disputes this. Thus, until it is proven otherwise, the Scorpion Anchorage wreck will be known by that name.

If the ship is the *Peacock*, her early years are well documented. The 136 foot long motor minesweeper was originally known as the YMS-371. She had a beam of 24.4 feet and a wood/composite hull. Built by Weaver Shipyards in Orange, Texas, she was launched November 27, 1943, and commissioned the following February. Lt. J. L. Grace was her captain, conning her through operations in the Gulf of Mexico until the summer of 1945, when her orders sent her to Okinawa.

The YMS-371 traveled to Okinawa via the Panama Canal. From July until August she was involved in minesweeping operations in that area. Then she was

The Peacock *(also known as* Los Buscaderos; *the* Hornbill [Ams-19]; *and, its original name,* YMS-371) *on August 21, 1944. Photo from the National Archives.*

A closer look at the Peacock's *deteriorating wooden hull.*
Photo by Bonnie J. Cardone.

sent to Japan's Honoshu Island to sweep mines around the island, in Tokyo Bay, and at the naval base of Sasebo. On February 16, 1946 her duties were finished. She sailed for San Pedro, California and arrived in April. For her service in World War II she earned two battle stars.

On February 7, 1947, the YMS-371 became the *Hornbill* and was reclassified AMS-19. She was actually the second *Hornbill*. The first one sank in San Francisco Bay after colliding with a lumber schooner in June 1942.

The *Hornbill* served as a training ship on the West Coast and at Pearl Harbor until 1953, when she began duty with the U. S. Naval Schools of Mine Warfare in Yorktown, Virginia. When her duties there were finished in February 1955, she was reclassified MSC(0)-19. She was decommissioned in September 1955.

On June 30, 1960, C.D. Anderson of Corpus Christi, Texas bought the *Hornbill*. He renamed her *Los Buscaderos* and used her for towing. In 1968, the San Juan Towing and Salvage Corporation bought *Los Buscaderos*, and renamed her *Peacock*. She became a freighter with a home port of Miami, Florida. She had a $20,000 mortgage on her when she was seized by the government of the Dominican Republic a year later. Why she was seized and what happened next remain mysteries. Ten years later, however, in December 1979, a World War II minesweeper fitting the description of the *Peacock* sank in Scorpion Anchorage off Santa Cruz Island. Is this wreck the *Peacock-Los Buscaderos-Hornbill*-AMS-371? We may never know!

Diving the Peacock

Today the vessel we call the *Peacock* sits upright in 60-70 feet of water. The top of her deck is just 40 feet below the surface. Because a sandy bottom surrounds her, she has become an artificial reef, a haven for marine life. Schools of blacksmith swim around her, anemones decorate her deteriorating wooden hull, while other fish and invertebrates seek shelter inside.

Her bow points out to sea. The current usually runs from bow to stern. Because of her depth, surge is rarely a problem. Because she is in Scorpion Anchorage, the waters around her are usually calm. From the sand in front of her, even on a not-so-clear day, she is impressive. Seen from that angle she is reminiscent of Catalina's *Valiant*, although the *Valiant* has a slight list to starboard and the *Peacock* lists to port.

The wreck is fully penetrable but it is recommended divers do not go into areas requiring a light. Also, bring a sharp knife because there is monofilament fishing line snagged on the vessel in various places. Pieces of the ship's fittings are found inside and scattered outside on the sand. But beware: this wreck is in the Channel Islands National Park and Marine Sanctuary. Taking anything but game described in the California Sportfishing Regulations is strictly forbidden. Bringing up so much as a plastic handle from a drawer could net you a fine and a jail sentence!

B. J. C.

Anacapa Island

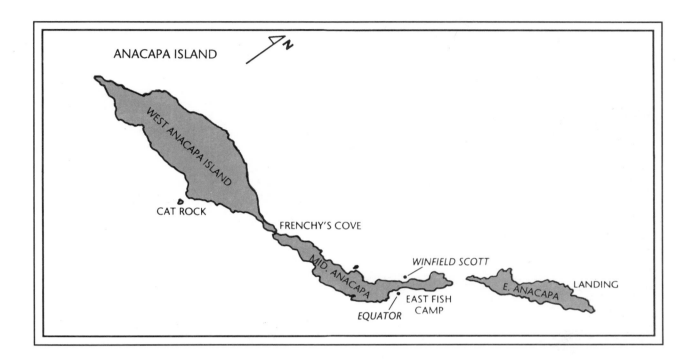

ANACAPA ISLAND

N

WEST ANACAPA ISLAND

CAT ROCK

FRENCHY'S COVE

MID. ANACAPA

WINFIELD SCOTT

EAST FISH CAMP

EQUATOR

E. ANACAPA

LANDING

Winfield Scott

A shipwreck that strands its passengers on a deserted island has formed the plot of several wonderful novels, including *The Swiss Family Robinson* and *Blue Lagoon*. The hardships incurred by such an event in real life, however, are far less romantic. That was the case for the 450 gold rush-era passengers and crew who boarded the side-wheeler *Winfield Scott* in San Francisco on December 1, 1853, bound for Panama and, eventually, the East Coast.

According to *Memoirs of Edward Bosqui*, there were 300 passengers on board, including a number of army officers ordered east from Oregon and other parts of the northwest. There were also "distinguished

veterans of the Mexican War" and several of Colonel Fremont's guides and mountaineers.

Recalling the trip some 42 years later, passenger F. S. Crane told the *Ventura Free Press*: "The cabins was full and I took a berth in the steerage with 350 to 400 others, principally miners returning East, nearly all of whom had specie belts well filled. There were a good many hard characters among them and life for the first 24 hours was anything but pleasant."

Although the number of passengers the *Winnie* carried on her fatal voyage varies from account to account, the stories of the disaster that wrecked her are remarkably consistent. Passenger Richard Keen, in his *Account of a Journey Overland to California: From Logan Indiana, in 1852 and return Voyage via Panama*

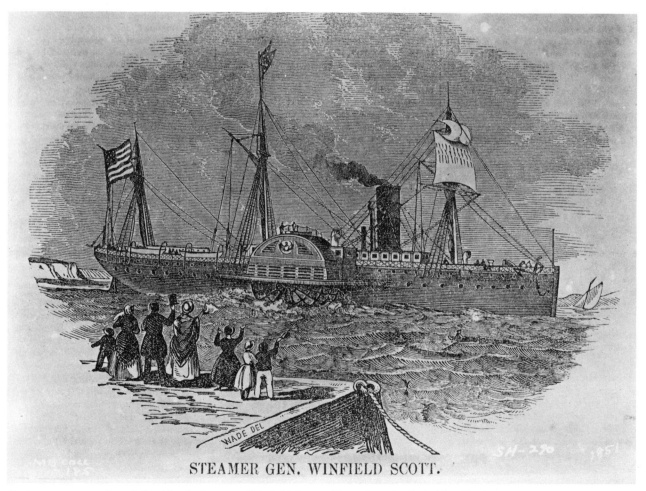

STEAMER GEN. WINFIELD SCOTT.

Contemporary engraving of the side-wheel steamer Winfield Scott. *Photo from the P. Smith collection.*

to New York, wrote that on the evening of December 2, the fog was so dense he could not see from one end of the ship to the other. It was so heavy, "it could wet a person in a few minutes." Although a lookout was posted in the crow's nest and an officer stood watch on the deck as well, the *Scott* struck a rock just off Middle Island, Anacapa. None of the accounts of the tragedy agree on the exact time this happened; it is said to have occurred anywhere from 9 P.M. to 2 A.M.

The captain ordered the ship's engines to back her off the rock, which was done. Passenger Asa Cyrus Call noted in his diary "There was a great breach in the steamer and the water was pouring in like a river." The water flooded the engine room, killing the engine fires. The vessel drifted helplessly, until her stern went aground. Although there was great confusion on deck, where all the passengers and crew had rushed, Captain Simon Frazer Blunt ordered the *Scott*'s longboat lowered. When men rushed wildly for it, the captain took out his pistol and demanded that women and children be allowed to board first.

The longboat set out in the night, looking for a safe place to unload its passengers, but the pounding surf and the steep cliffs made this difficult. A landing was finally found about a mile west of the wreck. After debarking its passengers, the longboat returned to the *Winnie*, where it and the side-wheeler's five other boats were lowered and loaded. Most accounts tell of disorder and panic accompanying this. Because there were so many people and so little space in the boats, no one was allowed to bring much except the clothes on his or her back. Most of the passengers had gotten ready in haste, and many were incompletely dressed. Richard Keen commented: "We were a miserable looking set of mortals."

The five boats held about 150 people, according to the diary of Asa Cyrus Call. While the boats were involved in ferrying the second shift of passengers to land, life preservers were handed out to those still on board. Eventually, everyone was safely ashore on a rock that Call estimated was 50 yards long and 25 yards wide. It was about 200 yards off Anacapa.

When daylight came, the seas calmed and the survivors were ferried to a larger rock, about one-half mile long and 100 yards wide. At the same time, a boat with at least two men, according to one account, or an officer and some sailors, according to another,

set off for Santa Barbara, on the mainland. Since they would have had to row some 22 miles, it is probable there were more than two men. The plan was for a horseman to be dispatched from Santa Barbara to San Francisco to seek help.

Meanwhile on the deserted island, a shortage of food and water soon became a problem. According to Richard Keen, potatoes, pork, and water were salvaged from the *Winnie* which according to Edward Bosqui, ". . . rested on a shelf of rock and . . . her stern overhung a precipice." There were 3 to 4 fathoms of water under the bow; 22 under the stern. Keen and Asa Call both recall that a seal was shot, skinned, and cooked. Keen added, "We also saw a lot of black fish. They have white spots around the eye. They looked as large as an ox and they move through the water very sluggishly. There was a general fusilade [sic] at them and they went down." This would seem to indicate the presence of many black sea bass, which are rarely seen today, and never in great numbers.

According to passenger Bosqui, a small sailboat showed up the morning after the wreck with "an old otter hunter" named George Nidever aboard. Nidever gave Bosqui "all the lines and fish hooks he had; and later Captain Blunt readily complied with my request to let me have one of the ship's boats to go fishing off the island. I got three or four to accompany me and in a very short time we caught a fine mess of fish. After this, relays of crews were engaged in fishing from morning till night while we remained on the island." It seems unlikely the men could catch enough fish to feed approximately 450 people every day. Bosqui does not say who ate the fish, but it was most certainly not Asa Cyrus Call nor Richard Keen, both of whom complained that their food consisted of small portions of pork and a potato or two.

Call also wrote: "Robbery and plunder has been the order of the day since the wreck. But today we appointed a committee of investigation and had everything searched. A good deal of property has come to light and two thieves have been flogged."

Other passengers reported that only officers, firemen, and sailors were allowed to board the *Winnie* and remove luggage. Beacause very few of their effects had come ashore by the morning of the second day, the passengers took matters into their own hands, appointing a committee to visit the ship and bring back what it could. First, however, the group had to seize one of the lifeboats and eject the crew members in it. Then the committee members rowed out to the *Winnie*. This is Richard Keen's account of what happened when the committee returned: ". . . they . . . reported that we were all robbed, the deck was literally strewed with papers, letters and etc. Carpet sacks were ripped open, trunks and chests were knocked to pieces, and everything of value taken." The irate passengers demanded the captain speak to them, which he did, explaining that the firemen and sailors were responsible for the ship's plunder. Luckily for the thieves, the steamer *California* was spotted in the distance and the impromptu trial was abandoned, as everyone scrambled to the top of the island in hopes of hailing her.

The *California*, sailing from Panama to San Francisco, was signaled and came within one-half mile of Anacapa. She already had many passengers aboard, but managed to also take the women and children from the *Winnie*, along with the gold dust, according to one account. While on the island, Richard Keen had accidentally come across the gold dust in "a pile of iron-bound boxes with a man standing guard over them. . . ."

The *California* returned to the wreck on December 9. The rest of the passengers, some mail, baggage, and express matter was ferried from the island shore to the *California*. The effort took about seven hours, according to newspaper accounts of the period. Richard Keen reports that when Captain Leroy of the *California* requested the passengers give Captain Blunt three cheers "... some of them did so but a majority I think remained silent." Although Captain Blunt had many friends in high places, he was not given the command of another vessel, and is said to have died of a broken heart six months later. If the passengers' accounts are to be believed, Captain Blunt, an 1849 graduate of Annapolis, had little control over his crew.

One account of the period said that $746,000.54 of the *Winnie*'s treasure, presumably the gold dust in the iron-bound boxes, was forwarded to New York; $138,860.96 went to England.

The *Scott*'s crew remained on the island, awaiting the arrival of the steamer *Republic*, sent from San Francisco to help salvage the ship. By the time the *Republic* arrived (December 10 or 11), however, the

rocks had taken their toll; the *Winnie* was beyond saving. Blunt directed the stripping of what was left. By December 12 this work was completed. Blunt and his crew departed Anacapa aboard the *Republic*.

When the salvage work began, some 25 mail bags, which contained about 10,000 letters, were 14 feet underwater. Captain Blunt thought that since two weeks had elapsed, the mail was beyond saving. However, a postal clerk dispatched from San Francisco by Postmaster Colonel Henley, thought it was possible, and offered the crew of the *Republic* $10 per salvaged bag. Blunt agreed to pay this out of his own money, until the Pacific Mail Steamship (PMS) Company could reimburse him. The salvage crew members eventually earned $220 for the bags they recovered.

The PMS Co. soon had 10,000 soggy letters. According to the *Daily California Chronicle* of December 24, 1853: "These letters were brought to this city, a room taken, a hot fire built, frames with network(s) of strings formed, upon which the letters are laid, one by one, to dry. . ." When this had been done, the letters were resealed, restamped, and sent on their way. Only one could not be forwarded. This was said to be because ". . . the superscription (was) so destroyed . . . this was done by the wax used in sealing a letter which was packed with it."

It should be noted that the wreck survivors were visited several times while they were camped on Anacapa. Besides George Nidever in his small sailboat, the *California*, the *Republic*, the *Southerner* and the *Goliah* stopped by the island.

Gold coins and mother lode nuggets recovered from the wreck of the Winfield Scott. *Photo from the P. Smith collection.*

Launched October 27, 1850, the *Winfield Scott* was built by Westervelt and Mackay in New York. She was a wooden side-wheel steamer 225 feet long, with a beam of more than 34 feet. She had three decks, three masts, and a rounded stern, on which there was an American eagle coat of arms. She had no bowsprit, but her straight stem was decorated with a bust of the man for whom she was named, Major General Winfield Scott, who had distinguished himself in the Mexican American War.

The *Scott* could accommodate 165 cabin passengers and 150 steerage passengers. The dining saloon could seat more than 100 and was 96 feet long. The drawing room was 80 feet long and 14 feet wide.

The *Scott* was specifically built to carry passengers between New York and New Orleans, and this is how she spent her first year at sea. Then she was sent to San Francisco, where she operated as the West Coast connection for the New York and San Francisco Steamship Company. The California gold rush was just two years old: The fastest, safest, and easiest way to get from one coast to the other was to sail from New York to Chagres, Panama, travel overland to Panama City, and sail north to San Francisco. The latter part of the journey took about two weeks. First cabin passengers were charged $350 for the trip, while the cheapest bunks went for just $75.

The *Scott* arrived in San Francisco, via Cape Horn, for the first time on April 28, 1852. She carried passengers and cargo up and down the coast for the New York and San Francisco Steamship Company for just more than a year. Then, in July 1853, the Pacific Mail Steamship Company bought the steamers of its rival company, including the *Winfield Scott*. She would not be of service to them for long.

With Captain Simon Frazer Blunt in charge, the *Scott* left San Francisco on December 1, 1853. By the evening of December 2, her brief life was ebbing.

Diving the Winnie

After the *Republic* had salvaged what she could of the *Scott*, the ship was abandoned, and others moved in. A resident of Santa Cruz Island took food, wine, and other goods. A Santa Barbara resident removed wood from the wreck and used it to build his home.

The first hardhat divers to visit the *Winnie* were probably those from the wrecking scow *San Pedro*. Ac-

This immense shaft recovered from the Winfield Scott *was only part of the booty brought back to San Francisco by these 1894 salvors. Photo from the National Maritime Museum, San Francisco.*

cording to James P. Delgado, writing in the *Pacific Historian*, a quarterly magazine, they recovered five-foot copper bolts, tons of iron wreckage, and the ship's figurehead. They had to dynamite the ship in order to salvage her, however.

From time to time, other items were salvaged from the *Winnie*. The remaining brass, copper, and heavy machinery were supposedly taken from her during World War II by a Santa Barbara diver. He sold the metal as scrap.

The first scuba divers on the *Winnie* may have been E. R. Cross and Dick Anderson. Although Cross remembers a 1957 dive on her, Anderson does not. Cross believes they were the first because the wreck looked virgin.

The wreck was rediscovered in the middle '60s by lobster hunters aboard Glenn Miller's charter dive boat, the *Emerald*. In the March 1967 issue of *Skin Diver Magazine*, he wrote: "A few of them talked of

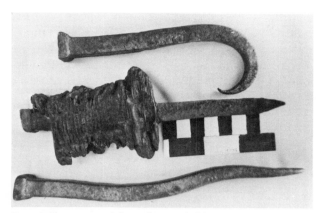

Brass spikes recovered from the Winfield Scott. *Photo by Patrick Smith.*

swimming through a strewn mass of wreckage but my friend Ed Larralde was more explicit. On the way back to port he dropped a big copper spike into my hand and told of seeing an enormous wheel with giant spokes standing upright in the rubble. That could mean only one thing; the ship had been a sidewheeler." Miller did some research at the Santa Barbara Historical Society, and decided the vessel the spike came from had to be the *Winfield Scott.*

According to the *Skin Diver* article, Miller and a friend, Jim Gurdy, brought a dredge to the spot and did some serious work. They found portholes, gold coins and nuggets, a ceramic spitoon, and a variety of other artifacts.

Dick Anderson also dived the wreck and, in an article that ran in the September 1969 issue of *Skin Diver*, claimed to have found gold coins. Divers on the trip with him were said to have found a number of copper nails, used to secure copper plating to the *Scott's* wooden hull. Anderson even made a movie, starring Glenn Miller. Entitled *Gold from the Winfield Scott*, it was a hilarious account of diving on the vessel. It is still shown occasionally at film festivals.

In 1938, Anacapa and Santa Barbara Islands formed the Channel Islands National Monument. In 1980, Anacapa and Santa Barbara, along with the waters surrounding San Miguel, Santa Cruz, and Santa Rosa, became the Channel Islands National Park. Since 1938 it has been a federal offense to remove artifacts from the *Scott*, but little or nothing was done to those who did. Divers today, however, must be satisfied with sightseeing and/or photography only. The area is patrolled by Park Service rangers and those who remove artifacts are prosecuted.

In recent years, because of the heavy kelp in the area, it was believed not much of the *Winnie* remained. This idea was proved false during the winter of '85–'86, when large swells and unusual currents devastated the kelp as well as removing sand and overburden from the wreck site. Large sections of the hull and machinery were exposed. Artifacts such as bottles, plates, fastenings, and hardware were found. Department of Interior marine historians and archaeologists examined and mapped the site for future reference, as well as collecting all loose, exposed artifacts. Since that time, the sand has returned and the kelp has re-established itself, obscuring the site once more. Today it consists mostly of indistinct mounds that hide whatever decomposing machinery or hardware lies beneath.

The rest of the wreck is scattered across about an acre of sea bottom, ranging in depth from 25 feet to the surfline. The bottom is rocky, with an even coating of coarse dark sand. Because of the wave action over the years, most of the wreckage has settled into rocky depressions and been covered over by the sand.

Kelp is usually heavy in the area, so the marine life it supports is abundant. Visibility runs from 10 to 40 feet, with 15 to 20 feet the average.

B. J. C.

Equator

As if cursed from the beginning, the *Equator* was definitely a hard-luck ship. In her short career that spanned less than a year, she provided her owners with little other than problems and disappointment.

Launched in early 1949 at Tacoma, Washington, for the Columbia River Packers Association, the *Equator* foreshadowed her blighted career by crushing the ways that supported her during her launch. Just moments after the traditional bottle of champagne crashed across her bow, she surprised everyone by collapsing her launch cradle and rolling over on her side, instead of proceeding down the ramp into the water. Eventually the 92.7-by-26.5-foot, 238-ton *Equator* was righted and finally deposited into Tacoma Harbor.

For the next few months she apparently carried out her fishing assignments in an acceptable manner. The end of June 1949 saw the *Equator* southbound from Astoria, Oregon, with a full load of fish for the San Pedro canneries.

On July 2, she crashed ashore near East Fish Camp, Anacapa Island. Distress calls to the Coast Guard brought prompt rescue for the *Equator*'s crew, but the ship's position precluded any attempt at pulling her free. The owners were paid off and the *Equator* became the insurance underwriters' headache. Her valuable cargo of fish was a total loss. Because of her position and the damage she received when she went ashore, there was no possibility of refloating her. The only option left was selling the rights to a salvage company willing to gamble on a profitable recovery of equipment.

The records indicate some disagreement as to why the *Equator* went aground. One source suggests that reduced visibility because of fog caused the unintentional stranding and subsequent loss. Another account states that an uncontrollable leak developed, and the grounding was intentional to prevent the loss of the vessel in deep water. Whatever the reason, the reefs in the area guaranteed that the *Equator* would never sail again. She was less than six-months-old, and her life as a commercial fisher was over. Her life as a dive spot was about to begin.

The underwriters sold the wreck to a salvage firm that moved onto the site to recover what it could from the unlucky vessel. Using explosives to open her hull, the salvage divers were successful in recovering the *Equator*'s huge Enterprise diesel. It was practically new, and despite its saltwater soaking, almost showroom-fresh. Additional equipment recovered included numerous pumps, winches, and deck equipment. Before a total equipment salvage could be completed, however, the weather deteriorated. The risk of remaining on the site wasn't worth the possible return. The salvage company called the job complete and abandoned to the sea what remained of the short-lived *Equator*.

Diving the Equator

Today the remains of the *Equator* lie scattered across a rocky reef and sand bottom just 150 feet offshore Anacapa's middle island. Visibility in the area averages 30 feet, but often is 60 feet or better. The site, which usually has a moderate growth of kelp, covers an area perhaps 75 yards square. The remains consist of steel plates, some wood beams, steel and copper pipe, chain, welding tanks, electric cables, a toilet (that constantly flushes), and the remains of some type of radio equipment.

Storms and heavy swells can and do change the amount of sand in the area of the wreck site. As a consequence, the amount of wreckage to be seen varies from season to season and storm to storm. Sometimes the area appears for the most part to be an expanse of sand with just a few kelp holdfast-covered rocks and a few pieces of pipe and plating poking out of the sand.

On other occasions, the area appears to be totally made up of rocky bottom and reef, with only scattered pockets of sand. During these periods, nearly all the mortal remains of the *Equator* are on display for any skin or scuba diver to view. The key word here is view, for the *Equator* is within the confines of the Channel Islands National Park and removing or even touching the wreckage is strictly forbidden.

Because the island provides a lee against the prevailing northwesterly winds, the site is usually well protected. Depending on the state of the tide and the amount of sand on the site, the depth over the wreck ranges from about 20 to 28 feet. With its calm, clear water, the wreck of the *Equator* is an excellent spot for a beginning diver, either skin or scuba, to experience a wreck site.

P. S.

Santa Catalina Island

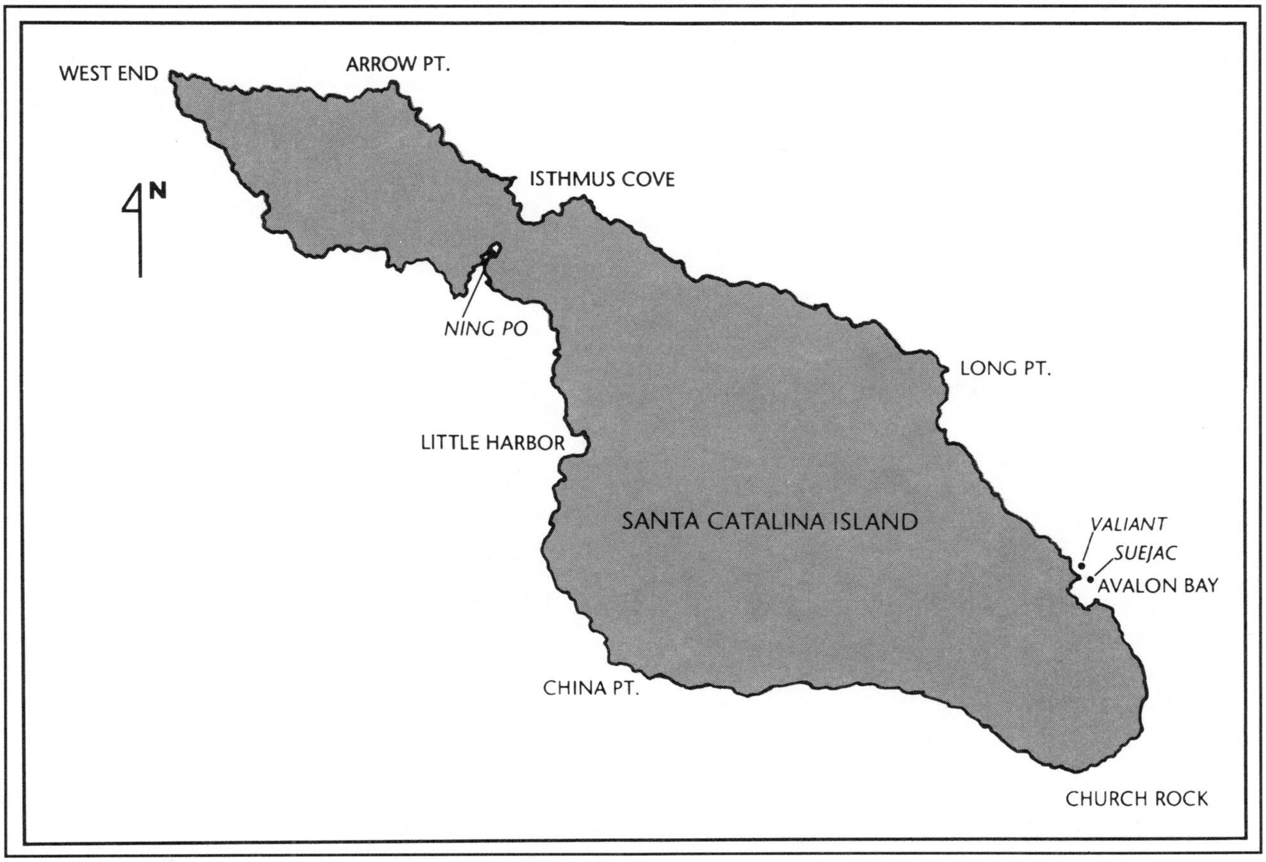

WEST END
ARROW PT.
ISTHMUS COVE
N
NING PO
LONG PT.
LITTLE HARBOR
SANTA CATALINA ISLAND
VALIANT
SUEJAC
AVALON BAY
CHINA PT.
CHURCH ROCK

Ning Po

None of the other wrecks discussed in this book had as long or as colorful a career as the *Ning Po*. It is the only Chinese junk—at least the only one we know of—wrecked off the southern California coast.

Built in 1753 in China, the *Ning Po* was 158 feet long. She had a beam of 37 feet. Her mainmast, 90 feet high and 9 feet in circumference, was made of ironwood and estimated to weigh 20 tons. Those who saw her afloat said she was a masterpiece of construction. Her ribs were camphor wood and a strip of mahogany braced her amidships. According to Della Phillips, writing in the *Overland Monthly* in April 1917, "No bolts were used in the ship's construction. Instead, sharp-pointed iron spikes, about one foot in length, were driven slantingly into the wood." The ship had nine watertight compartments, an innovation that wouldn't be used on Western vessels until more than 100 years had passed.

The *Ning Po* was designed to resemble a sea monster and her captain steered the vessel from the remarkably high stern, which was the monster's tail.

Launched as the *Kin Tai Fong*, the *Ning Po* began her career as a merchant ship. But because she was so well equipped and fast, she was soon being used as a smuggler and a slaver. Pirates, too, commanded her. According to one source, between 1796 and 1861, she not only took part in a rebellion against the emperor but was seized for illegal activities six times. At one point the British held her, but she was recaptured by the Chinese who then used her as a prison ship for smugglers and pirates. In 1861, she was commandeered by Taipei rebels. Colonel Charles "Chinese" Gordon, commander of the British Imperial forces, recaptured her. He also renamed her *Ning Po*, which means calm or peaceful wave, and was also the name of a Chinese city.

Later in 1861 the vessel was damaged by a typhoon. In 1911 the *Ning Po* was once again seized by rebels. Later that same year, a group of tourists decided to buy her, intending to sail her to the U.S. and put her on exhibition. Before the journey her matting sails were replaced with schooner type, gaff-headed sails. A mutiny and two typhoons delayed her departure, but finally, under the command of Danish Captain Ues Toft, and with a crew of 14 Scandinavians and Orientals, she left Yokohama, Japan. After sailing

The ornate stern of the Ning Po *in drydock at the Craig Shipyards, Long Beach, 1913. Photo from the S. Lawson collection.*

7,000 miles in 59 days, she arrived in San Pedro on February 19, 1913.

Ning Po was first exhibited in Venice, then towed to San Diego. By October, she was once again in San Pedro, moored off the breakwater. Although her owner, W. M. Milne, had hoped to take her first to San Francisco and then to the East Coast, she was still in San Pedro on November 18, this time anchored off Dead Man's Island (removed from the harbor in 1928.) It was the day a southeaster moved in. During the storm the *Ning Po* went aground in about 12 feet of water about one-quarter mile east of Dead Man's.

It took considerable effort to get the boat off the rocks at Dead Man's and keep her afloat. She was eventually towed to Long Beach and, two months later, had been made seaworthy once more. Shortly thereafter, Milne sold the *Ning Po* to the Meteor Boat Company which secured permission for the junk to be tied alongside the municipal pier. She received visitors there for about a year, then was towed to San Diego, where she was also exhibited.

The *Ning Po*'s history for the next 20 years is fuzzy. She was apparently towed to Catalina Island where she was a cafe and museum for awhile. Then she was towed to Catalina Harbor, at the isthmus on the backside of the island, where it is said she was an "extra" in various movies. In 1935, she was ravaged by fire. Then, according to the exhibit devoted to her in the Catalina Island Museum, she was "dismantled." Some of her camphor wood beams were carved into such souvenirs as boxes and napkin rings. Some of these are displayed at the museum along with nails, photographs, and a beheading spear from the vessel.

All that's left of the *Ning Po* today lies under mud and five to ten feet of water just inside Ballast Point, Catalina Harbor. Visibility is always poor because the muddy bottom is easily stirred up.

    B. J. C.

M/Y *Valiant*

The *Valiant*'s life on the sea was brief: She was less than five years old when an explosion started the fire that ended it. They were magnificent years, however.

Built in 1926 by Newport News Shipbuilding in Newport News, Virginia, the *Valiant* was designed by Cox & Stevens. The 444-gross-ton, twin-screwed vessel was powered by a Winton 950-h.p. diesel engines. She was 162 feet, 3 inches long and had a 26-foot beam. Her cruising speed was estimated at 16 miles per hour and her cruising radius was 5,500 miles. She is said to have been the first American yacht built with a double bottom for storage of water and fuel, safety, and stability.

The *Valiant* was originally christened the *Aras*, which is Sara spelled backward. Sara Chrisholm was the wife of the first owner, millionaire Hugh Chrisholm, of Portland, Maine. The yacht, with its 13 tiled bathrooms and a playroom designed especially for the Chrisholm children, cost more than $750,000.

For unknown reasons, the Chrisholms sold the *Aras* to Charles S. Howard the same year she was built. Owner of Howard Motor Company, Buick distributors for the West Coast. Howard renamed his new yacht the *Valiant*. She was sailed through the Panama Canal to San Francisco. Although her home port was San Francisco, California, she was a frequent visitor to Santa Barbara, Los Angeles, and Catalina, according to newspaper clippings from the time.

In 1930, the Howards spent several months cruising Mexico, Central America, and the South Pacific. Afterward, they stopped in Los Angeles to prepare for the final leg of their journey. Before starting home, the Howards sailed to Catalina for a weekend pleasure cruise with several prominent Angelenos as their guests.

On Saturday, December 13, 1930, the *Valiant* was anchored in Descanso Bay, just in front of St. Catherine's Hotel. In addition to the Howards and a crew of 22, Mr. and Mrs. Ellis Wilkes and Mr. and Mrs. Paul Franklin were aboard.

The Howards and their guests had spent the day fishing and had returned to Descanso, near the town of Avalon, to spend the night. Dinner was being prepared and the passengers were enjoying cocktails and dancing. Some of the crew members were ap-

The yacht Valiant. *Photo from the P. Smith collection.*

parently playing cards when the lights on the vessel dimmed and went out: The gas generator's fuel tank was empty.

One of the crew interrupted the card game to run to the engine room. He opened a valve that started gasoline flowing by gravity into the generator's fuel tank, then restarted the engine and left. He either forgot to turn off the fuel valve or, anxious to return to the game, planned to return later to do so.

Very shortly, the fuel tank overflowed and gasoline flooded the floor of the engine room. A spark ignited it and around 7:50 P.M. there was an enormous explosion. The entire midships of the *Valiant* was ablaze in minutes. Charles Howard quickly ushered his guests to the bow, where they hurriedly boarded one of the vessel's four launches.

Howard could hear screams coming from the galley and once his guests were safe, he ran there to help. The Filipino baker, Hugo Pebulay, his clothes on fire, was trapped in an 18-inch split in the deck. Howard smothered the flames, then pulled Pebulay to safety.

A second explosion occurred. Speeding toward the burning vessel, harbormaster Francis McGrath pulled several crew members into his boat. Other vessels rescued the rest. McGrath decided it was too risky to leave the burning *Valiant* in Descanso Bay, where it posed a threat to other boats. Quickly he attached a tow line and proceeded to tow the ship toward the open sea. He had not gotten very far, however, when the port anchor came unsecured and plunged into

the ocean. A third explosion occurred aboard the *Valiant*, causing McGrath to abandon his plan and flee for the safety of Avalon.

Five crew members were taken to Avalon hospital, treated and released. Pebulay's stay there was longer.

The *Valiant* burned for three days, the fire fueled by the 8,000 gallons of diesel she carried, before the flames finally died out on December 17. According to the *Long Beach Telegram*: "Amid clouds of steam and sparks, the palatial yacht, *Valiant*, sunk at 8:10 A.M. today. The yacht had been burning fiercely after exploding and bursting into flames Saturday evening. No loss of life or serious injuries were suffered by any of the persons on board. However, it is reported that an undetermined amount estimated in excess of $75,000 in cash and gems has gone to the bottom in this, one of the most costly shipwrecks in recent years."

In 1955, a group of divers led by Bob Bell applied for salvage rights on the *Valiant*. They had learned that Mrs. Howard's pewter jewelry box, containing $67,000 in diamonds, had gone to the bottom with the vessel. Bell's first group brought up one of the bronze propellers. (Mel Fisher, owner of Mel's Aqua Shop in Redondo Beach, had already removed the other. Fisher would find the incredible treasure of *Nuestra Senora de Atocha* off the Marquesas Keys 30 years later.) Each of the props weighed about 1,000 pounds. The salvors also spent more than four

Coins recovered from the yacht Valiant. *In the upper right is one of the "free drink" tokens. The five coins, lower center, were melted together by the fire. Photo by Patrick Smith.*

A display built from the recovered remains of the Valiant's *telegraph. Photo by Bonnie J. Cardone.*

months in 1957 trying to find the diamonds. They removed the wreck's superstructure and most of the main deck. Seven and a half tons of brass and bronze were brought up. Although the divers found a number of Howard's Good-for-One-Drink tokens, the diamonds eluded them. If the jewels have been found since, their recovery is a well-kept secret.

According to an article by Bob Bell in the now defunct *Dive Magazine*: "In 1967 a well-known sport diver, Bill Stach, made one short dive to the wreck and found a strip of solid gold about 28 inches in length, three and one-half inches wide and an eighth-inch thick. [It was] the *Valiant*'s Commission Plate.

This, ten years after we made hundreds of dives without finding anything of value."

This was not the last of the treasured artifacts to be found, however. In 1973, Dan Chambers was making yet another dive on the *Valiant*. He'd been on it about 30 times in six years. The charter boat *Scuba Queen* had carried him and other wreck divers to the site and dropped its anchor right in the wreck. The chain was draped over the gunwale on the starboard side about three-quarters of the way from the bow. Dan swam over to the chain, and grabbing a hold of it, rested there a minute. As his eyes wandered over the wreck, he noticed a plate on the gunwale. He scraped it with his knife and part of a letter—a W, he thought—appeared. He knew immediately that he had found a boarding plate, presumably with the word "Welcome" on it. He had only a small crowbar with him, so he surfaced and came back with one that was four feet long. With it, he popped the plate off easily. Dan attached a lift bag to his find and sent it topside. Underneath it was the metal part of one of the ship's boat hooks.

Once the object was on the deck of the *Queen*, Dan was in for a surprise. Made of brass, it weighed 30 pounds, was three feet long, ten inches wide, and one-half inch thick. Engraved on it was the name *Valiant*. On subsequent dives, Dan looked for a similar plate on the port side of the wreck, but never found another.

Diving the Valiant

The *Valiant* lies in 90 feet of water, parallel to the shore. She is upright, with her bow pointing northwest. Sand surrounds her. She is in the lee of the island and is generally an easy dive. Unless there's a northeaster, the waters are almost always calm, and divable when many other areas are not. There is a current on occasion. Visibility is nearly always good—about 30 feet—and sometimes even better. Since the current tends to run from the bow to the stern, the visibility is usually better at the bow.

The top of the stern—what remains of it—is in about 60 feet of water, as is the top of the bow. Spectacular pictures of the bow can be taken from the sand on good days. The brass bow chocks are missing, having been salvaged by a California Wreck Diver. The hull is covered with growth: gorgonians,

Some of the objects recovered from the Valiant. *Photo by Bonnie J. Cardone.*

scallops, strawberry anemones, tube worms, yellow encrusting anemones, and two species of hard corals. A school of blacksmith usually swims above her. Inside the wreck there are orange garibaldi, small sheepshead, and calico bass. Small lobster can be found in certain areas. At the bow, a ladder leads from inside the wreck to an open hatch, which is too small for a diver with a tank to pass through.

The best time to dive the *Valiant* is from after Labor Day in September up to Memorial Day in May. In the summer, Avalon Harbor is extremely busy. Every size boat can be expected there. Although licensed skippers know the meaning of the divers down flag, many of those running smaller boats do not. They may even motor over to see what divers are doing! For this reason, a lookout should always be left on the deck to watch and warn off approaching vessels. Whether you plan to dive the *Valiant* from the shore or by boats permission must be granted by the Avalon Harbor Master whose offices are on the pleasure pier. Contact him by radio as you approach the harbor by boat or, if on shore, walk out to end of the pier and ask permission in person.

B. J. C.

SueJac

On Sunday, November 14, 1980, the 54-foot-long gaff-rigged schooner *SueJac* was anchored just off Catalina's Casino Point. A northeast windstorm was buffeting normally calm Avalon Harbor and six-foot seas were running. The lifeguard boat *Baywatch Avalon* was busy. By 9:30 A.M. lifeguards Steve Wagner, Steve Lockwood, and Dennis Zimmerman had assisted in the rescue of 30 people from vessels inside the harbor. Then, alerted by calls from tourists watching the storm's rampage, they turned their attention to the *SueJac*, the only ship anchored outside the harbor.

Three crew members were aboard the ferrocement-hulled schooner: Captain Richard Gill, First Mate Jeffrey Left, and Daniel Gill. The ship had been provisioned for a six-month Pacific cruise and had sailed to Catalina from Puget Sound, Washington. She was a beauty. Built in 1968 and owned by George Boalanger of Mar Vista, California, her hand-tooled wood fittings and tile recalled a more elegant era.

As the *Baywatch* boat approached the *SueJac*, the lifeguards could see the reports of her trouble were not exaggerated. The vessel had dragged anchor and was now dangerously close to the rocky shoreline. The crew and its dog were trying to get away from the doomed vessel in a dinghy. As the *Baywatch* crew watched, a wave crashed into the little boat and it sank. Dennis Zimmerman jumped into the water and rescued all three men and their mascot. By the time the *SueJac*'s crew was aboard the *Baywatch* boat, their ship was 60 feet beneath the sea.

The end came quickly. Three times the *SueJac* hit the boulders that protect Casino Point from heavy seas. The third hit opened a hole on her port side that quickly filled with water. She spun around and sank in less than three minutes.

Salvage of the *SueJac* started as soon as the storm cleared and diving was feasible. Two different companies worked on her for a share of the salvaged goods. Those items brought up by the divers were taken to Avalon's Pleasure Pier and sold. The whole operation took less than two weeks.

Of course, the salvage companies took only those items that might bring a profit. Not long after her sinking, the *SueJac* was visited by the California Wreck Divers, who arrived at her site via the charter dive boat *Scuba Queen*. One member of the club, Steve

The schooner SueJac. *Photo from the Steve Giles collection.*

Giles, found Polaroid pictures floating on the ceiling inside the ship. When dried, these photos of the vessel were still in almost perfect condition.

Not long afterward, the city of Avalon hired Jon Hardy and his son Alec to remove all the *SueJac*'s doors and hatches so divers visiting her would never get trapped inside. The Hardys brought up a lot of kitchen utensils, including many plastic dishes. The name of the Melmac pattern? Catalina!

Diving the SueJac

In the winter of '85–'86, Jon Hardy was again hired by the city of Avalon, this time to move the floats enclosing the Catalina Underwater Park to include the *SueJac*. The buoy marking the southern end leads divers right down to the ship. She lies on her starboard side with her stern in 60 feet of water and her bow in 90. Her small cabin can be safely entered. Visibility ranges from spectacular—75 feet—to poor— 10 to 15. The kelp forest is dense around her and the canopy overhead greatly reduces the light level. It is usually quite dark.

Since her sinking, the *SueJac* has been visited by hundreds of divers. Dennis Zimmerman, the lifeguard who rescued her crew and mascot, made his scuba certification check-out dive on her just months after her sinking. Almost every weekend, the underwater park is the scene of similar check-out dives made by

An unknown diver pauses in the hatch of the SueJac's *cabin.
Photo by Bonnie J. Cardone.*

students and their instructors who come over to the island on either Catalina Express or Catalina Cruise Lines ships. These classes enter the water from rocky Casino Point. Catalina Diver's Supply stations a truck on the point that provides air fills and rental gear. Its main store is on the Pleasure Pier.

The *SueJac* is also visited by private and charter dive boats. Those aboard such vessels should be aware that the best time to dive her is during the off-season. From May through September, Avalon Harbor is extremely busy and anchoring near the underwater park is hazardous because of the boat traffic. Many of those running small skiffs, dinghies, and fast cigarette-type vessels seem not to understand the meaning of the divers down flag. Also when nearing Avalon, the captains of all visiting vessels must request, by radio, permission to anchor near and dive the *SueJac*.

Several movies have been filmed using the *SueJac* as an underwater set. She's also appeared on such TV shows as "Rip Tide."

SueJac *Mysteries*

Although nothing was ever proven, rumors flew regarding the *SueJac* immediately after her sinking. There was a great deal of speculation regarding her anchorage off Casino Point. Why was she there instead of inside the much safer harbor? Why were two salvage teams hired instead of only one? The ship was visited by a SWAT team shortly after she went down. Was this just a training mission or were the team members looking for something special? The vessel was valued at $250,000, but according to reports, she was uninsured why? Her owner, George Boalanger, never had time to discuss these matters with me, though I spoke with him (briefly) by phone three times and left several messages. Thus, these and other questions regarding the *SueJac* are unlikely to ever be answered.

B. J. C.

San Clemente Island

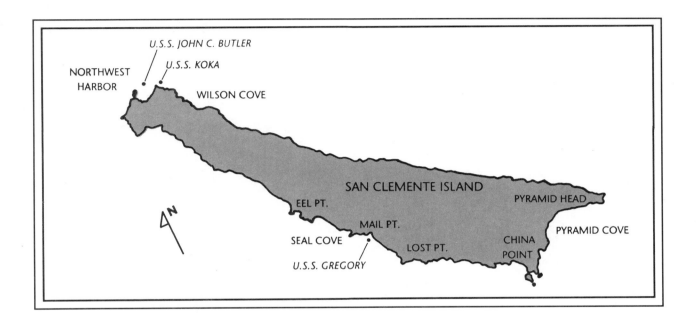

U.S.S. *John C. Butler*

Not all the wrecks found in California waters are the results of "acts of God" or accidents. This is especially true of those found off San Clemente Island, some 60 miles from the mainland. Clemente is owned by the Federal Government and administered by the Department of the Navy. War games are periodically held here. Recruits practice necessary war skills—including target practice—here, too. One of their victims was the U.S.S. *John C. Butler*, a destroyer escort with an impressive history.

Built by Consolidated Steel Corp, Ltd., in Orange, Texas, the *John C. Butler* (DE-339) was launched November 12, 1943. Commissioned March 31, 1944, she was named in honor of a Navy pilot posthumously awarded the Navy Cross for extraordinary heroism in the battle of Midway. A destroyer escort, she was 306 feet long, with a beam of 36'8" and displaced 1,350 tons. Her shakedown cruise was conducted off Bermuda.

By the end of June, the *Butler* had sailed through the Panama Canal and reached Pearl Harbor, where more training operations were conducted. In August, she escorted transports to Tulagi in the Solomon Islands. She then joined escort carriers out of Manus Island, Papua New Guinea, on preinvasion strikes. She also provided antisubmarine and antiaircraft protection for carriers involved in the invasion of Morotai and Peleliu.

In October 1944, the *Butler* was one of a fleet of 13 ships, known as Taffy III, stationed in Leyte Harbor off the island of Samar in the Philippines. On the 25th, Taffy III became the heroes of the Battle of Leyte Gulf, classified by many as the "Greatest Battle in American Naval History."

In addition to the *Butler*, under Lt. Commander J. E. Pace, Taffy III consisted of the carriers *Gambier Bay*, *St. Lo*, *Fanshaw Bay*, *White Plains*, *Kalinin Bay*, and *Kitkun Bay*; destroyers *Johnston*, *Hoel*, and *Heerman*; destroyer escorts *Samuel B. Roberts*, *Raymond*, and *Dennis*. Rear Admiral C. A. F. "Ziggy" Sprague was Taffy III's leader.

On October 25th, Taffy III was surprised by a much superior Japanese fleet that had managed to elude other units protecting the Leyte landing area. The enemy armada numbered 22 ships: 7 cruisers, 11

The U.S.S. John C. Butler, *circa the 1950s. Photo from the Steve Giles collection.*

Depth charge racks on the U.S.S. John C. Butler. *Photo by Bonnie Cardone.*

destroyers, and 4 battleships including the feared *Yamato*, the largest battleship ever built. Her 70-foot-long barrels could fire 3,220-pound shells. The *Butler* and her three sister destroyer escorts had only five-inch diameter guns.

Nonetheless, the four destroyer escorts charged the Japanese, laying heavy smoke to protect the six carriers. Every available gun was pressed into service; torpedoes were launched at every possible target. The attack surprised and confused the enemy fleet, which retreated to the North. Lost in the attack were the *Gambier Bay*, *Johnston*, *Hoel*, and the *Samuel B. Roberts*. An hour later, the *St. Lo* was sunk by kamikaze pilots.

For her part in the battle, the *Butler* received the Presidential Unit Citation.

In addition to the Battle of Leyte Gulf, the *Butler* saw action in Morotai and Luzon. She was in Iwo Jima when the flag was raised in victory. Later, assigned to A54A Picket Duty north of Okinawa, she was attacked by 13 kamikaze planes. Although damaged in the process, she managed to shoot down six of them and was awarded the Navy Commendation. She also earned five battle stars for her World War II service.

The *Butler* returned to San Pedro, California in November 1945, and, decommissioned in June of 1946, became a member of the Pacific Reserve Fleet in San Diego.

In December 1950, six months after the Korean conflict broke out, the *Butler* was recommissioned. Assigned to the 11th Naval District, she took naval reservists on short training cruises. Later, she was part of the Fleet Sonar School training program in San Diego. She was decommissioned for the last time in December 1957.

It seems ironic that such a distinguished vessel would end up being used for target and demolition exercises, but that's exactly what happened to the *Butler*. No longer a state-of-the-art warship in 1970, she was anchored off San Clemente, where Navy personnel practiced aerial and surface gunnery on her. As the result of the damage received during these exercises, she broke in half and sank in 80 feet of water inside Northwest Harbor. Even underwater she was not allowed to rest in peace. UDT and SEAL teams visited her there, learning war-time skills by using explosives on her. Her bow section was later towed to deeper water and sunk.

Diving the Butler

What remains of the stern of the *Butler* is easy to find because it is buoyed. This section is less than 70 feet long and sits upright on a sandy bottom. The depth charge racks are still recognizable. Off to one side, a 5-inch deck gun sits all alone. Visibility here is usually poor. When there are long, rolling swells, the site is not only surgey but, because of the sandy bottom, reminiscent of an underwater snow storm. The outside of the wreck is covered with growth, including bull kelp, gorgonian fans, and several species of algae. Since this is the only high profile structure in the area, fish are common, especially sheephead and blacksmith.

Although I have never been inside the *Butler*, I have been told there are lots of electrical cables that make diving hazardous. There is also lots of silt. Penetration of the wreckage is not recommended without special training. Some dive shops use the *Butler* in their wreck diving classes. To avoid stirring up the silt inside, they make students leave their fins outside. Experienced wreck divers who attempt this should make sure their fins are secure, so they don't float off while the wreck is being explored. (This has happened!)

B. J. C.

U.S.S. *Koka*

Seven eager divers with loaded tanks left aboard the Doja, *skippered by Theron Huish, from the boat dock at Long Beach, November 9, hoping for two day's good diving for bugs in the waters of San Clemente Island.*

Saturday morning, after a hearty breakfast, the divers, who were Pete Greenwood, John Chancellor (Little John), Bill Goodwin, Don Fish, Mike Darling, Jack McLeod and John Rhoades, took the plunge, literally, in calm water to a rocky reef. Underwater visibility was 60-70 feet. They were disappointed as they could find no bugs of legal size, although diving conditions were excellent and they enjoyed exploring several caves and numerous crevices.

They were almost ready to call it quits but decided instead to 'up anchor' and move to another location farther down the island. Again they anchored on a kelp bed above another rocky area and could find no legal size bugs, then it happened: They found a wreck. Who found it first is difficult to determine, but all the divers spent the remainder of the day until sunset bringing up brass and bronze souvenirs.

Sunday morning they continued diving and found the anchor and screw still to be salvaged. John Chancellor recovered a porthole intact with glass. It was so heavy he could not manage to bring it up alone, yet would not relinquish it, if necessary was all set to stay down for days, but Pete Greenwood arrived on the scene and gave him a helping hand. Tubes and bug bags were used to bring up the souvenirs, which completely ruined said tubes and bug bags.

Footnote: All efforts to trace the wreck so far have been unsuccessful, but investigation is still going on. Future plans include a return trip to gather more souvenirs (purely in the interest of research), information, and anything else that can be salvaged . . .

Pete Greenwood eventually recovered the propeller of the wreck, blade by blade, then set about trying to identify the ship. The prop had its weight—1,915 pounds—serial numbers, and the name of the American Ship Building Company engraved on it. Greenwood wrote to the company and in January 1965, received a letter telling him the prop had been

* From the *Sea Dog Digest*, published by the Amberjacks Diving Club, 1962.

The reverse side of a medal found on the Koka, *showing the owner's name, Paul Louis Morin. His name is also on the station watch bill that was recovered from the wreck. Photo by Bonnie J. Cardone.*

"originally on the vessel *Tioga*, our Hull No. 39, built in Buffalo, New York, around the year 1885. The vessel was a steel tug 285 feet long with a 39 foot beam and had a 14 foot depth. It is believed that this vessel was lost in that area of the Pacific in the year 1919. It was owned by the Union Shipbuilding Company."

Thus, the San Clemente wreck was known as the *Tioga* for several years. Additional information, however, was accumulating. The American Ship Building Company had suggested Greenwood write Captain H. C. Inches at the Museum of the Great Lakes Historical Society in Vermilion, Ohio, for further information. Greenwood learned from the society that the *Tioga* carried miscellaneous railroad freight between Buffalo, New York, and Chicago, Illinois. She had been owned by the Erie Railroad.

Meanwhile, another wreck diver, co-author Pat Smith, was conducting his own research. And he wondered: how had a Great Lakes vessel ended up wrecked on California's San Clemente Island? He, too, wrote Captain Inches, who dug deeper into the files and told Smith the *Tioga* had been wrecked on Sawtooth Reef in Lake Superior in 1919. She had been cut up for scrap, which was sold. Obviously, Smith decided, she couldn't have been reassembled,

The U.S. Navy tug Koka *in San Diego Bay, circa 1930. Photo from the National Archives.*

so the Clemente wreck must only have some of the *Tioga*'s parts.

Some time in the early 1970s, Smith learned the *Tioga*'s props had been sold at auction, apparently to the Puget Sound Navy Yard where the Navy tugboat U.S.S. *Koka*, had been built in 1919. Because of Smith's discovery, the wreck once known as the *Tioga* was identified as the *Koka*.

California wreck diver Steve Giles' discovery of a brass bearing block with the tugboat's name on it cinched the ship's indentification. Later, Pat Smith recovered the brass Station Watch Bill, which had U.S.S. *Koka* engraved on it, along with the names of various crew members and their stations.

After her launching in 1919, the *Koka* (AT-31) was assigned to the 11th Naval District in San Diego. She sailed throughout California waters, towing targets and performing other duties required of her by the Navy. At least one of them was unusual. In his book, *I Cover The Waterfront*, Max Miller writes: "Each year we go after elephant seals for the Zoo. Sometimes we go in the navy's tugboat, *Koka*, sometimes in the navy's Eagle boat 34. We cruise to the Mexican island of Guadalupe." Miller's book, originally published in 1932, chronicles his adventures as a waterfront reporter for a San Diego newspaper.

On December 7, 1937, the *Koka*'s duties were more mundane. Her destination was Wilson Cove, San

Clemente Island, a trip she had already made 55 times. Her cargo included mail, passengers, fresh water, and provisions.

The trip was uneventful until the very end. Although the day started out clear, heavy fog reduced visibility for the last two hours. According to Court of Inquiry Records the tug was traveling slightly faster than her CO thought she was: He estimated her speed at 10.9 knots, but it was actually 11.1. The *Koka* had been underway for seven hours when, also according to Court of Inquiry records, the Commanding Officer (who was also the Officer of the Deck and the Navigator) sighted rocks off the port bow. Thinking he knew where he was and that there was clear water to starboard, the CO gave the order, "Full right rudder, ahead standard speed." One minute later, his ship was aground on the northeast point of Clemente. She was declared a total loss and decommissioned that same day, although some equipment was salvaged from her in the next few weeks.

The grounding of the *Koka* on Clemente was not a first for this 156-foot-8-inch-long, 30-foot-wide, 1,000-ton vessel. She had previously grounded near San Diego on April 9, 1921. Fog was also a factor in that incident, but the only damage sustained by the boat was a lost propeller blade.

Diving the Koka

After more than 50 years at the mercy of surge and waves, not much remains of the *Koka*. Also, navy UDT

Wreck divers check to see whether an object is brass or iron and steel by hitting it with a hammer. If rust floats up, the object is ferrous metal. If no rust appears, the object may be brass. Photo by Bonnie J. Cardone.

and SEAL teams used her wreckage to practice their skills. Today, part of her lies on the shore of protected Northwest Harbor; the rest of the *Koka* is in shallow water no more than 15 feet deep. Because the area has a rocky bottom, visibility is consistently good—20 to 60 feet.

Although she is often divable, there is almost always surge. Eel grass covers some of the remains. After all these years beneath the ocean, the *Koka* blends in with the seascape. It takes a practiced eye to distinguish manmade debris from nature. The largest recognizable part of the ship is her engine. There are still artifacts to be found, however. In 1983, another of the ship's 21-inch portholes was recovered. Keys and other small items are occasionally brought to light by those with the patience to overturn rocks and larger pieces of wreckage. Thirty-caliber ammunition is found here now and then, but leave it on the bottom: It can still be detonated. Although it seems unlikely the state will declare the remains of the *Koka* "historic"

The Navy tug Koka *trapped and dying near Northwest Harbor, San Clemente Island. Photo from the National Archives.*

30-caliber ammunition and ceramic tiles recovered from the U.S.S. Koka. Photo by Patrick Smith.

or "archaeologically significant," should you consider taking artifacts found on her, remember, she is more than 50 years old.

B. J. C.

U.S.S. *Gregory*

San Clemente Island is the final resting place of two Navy ships, both of which served with distinction in World War II and the Korean War. While the *John C. Butler* lies inside Northwest Harbor, the *Gregory* is on the backside of the island, between Mail Point and Lost Point. She is easy to find as some of her wreckage is on the shore.

A Fletcher-class destroyer, the *Gregory* (DD-802) was 376 feet long, with a beam of almost 30 feet and displaced 2,050 tons. She was built by Todd-Pacific in Tacoma, Washington, and launched in May 1944. Commander Bruce McCandless was her captain. Her shakedown cruise took place off the West Coast, and by October of that year she was in Pearl Harbor. After two months in Hawaii, she sailed to Iwo Jima to take part in one of the last great campaigns of the Pacific war. Arriving there on D-Day, February 19, she survived a month of almost constant fire as she protected transports and provided support for the forces invading the tiny Japanese island.

The *Gregory* also took part in the war's largest amphibious effort, the Okinawa campaign. She was one of more than 1,000 ships commanded by Admiral R. A. Spruance. The *Gregory* left Saipan on March 27 and arrived off Okinawa April 1. As Marines waded ashore on the island's western coast, she was part of a task force conducting a diversion landing off the southeast coast, hoping to distract some Japanese attention from the actual invasion. Once this operation was completed, the *Gregory* patrolled Okinawa on radar picket station.

As the sun was setting April 8, the ship's lookouts sighted three kamikaze planes heading toward her. Although hit several times by the *Gregory*'s guns, one plane crashed into her amidships just above the waterline. Although she had no power in her forward engine and her fire rooms were flooded, the ship continued her battle, managing to shoot down the other two Japanese planes.

Temporary repairs were made in Kerema, Papua New Guinea, but the *Gregory* was asked to escort the carrier *Intrepid* to Pearl Harbor before heading for San Diego and permanent repairs. The war ended before she was ready to return to service. For her efforts, she was awarded two battle stars.

The U.S.S. Gregory *in Puget Sound, Washington, 1944. Photo from the National Archives.*

The *Gregory* was placed in inactive status and decommissioned in January 1947. In June 1950, the Korean war officially began and the U.S. Navy once again needed the *Gregory.* She was recommissioned in April 1951, and commanded by H. C. Lank.

By August of 1951, the *Gregory* was on patrol duty off the Korean coast. She protected aircraft carriers from attack and was among the ships that bombarded the coast. She also patrolled the Chinese Nationalist island of Formosa.

In August 1953, the armistice was signed and the *Gregory* returned to San Diego, having earned four battle stars for her part in the Korean conflict. Until 1964, she made yearly trips, usually six months long, to the Far East, taking part in training maneuvers with both American and foreign ships. In February 1964, the *Gregory* was decommissioned and entered the reserve. In May of 1966, she was renamed the *Indoctrinator* and, safely and securely tied to a dock in San Diego, served as a training facility for Navy personnel.

In 1972, the Navy found a new use for her old sailor. Now nearly 30 years old, the *Gregory* was

towed to San Clemente. On the last leg of her journey, she broke her tow and washed ashore the island near Mail Point. Navy SEAL and UDT teams practiced demolition on her, literally blowing her to pieces.

Diving the Gregory

The very first time I saw the *Gregory* in 1983, the water was calm and the day, sunny. We made three jumps under ideal conditions. There was surge, especially in the stern area, which is less than ten feet deep, but it was manageable as long as you were careful. The water around the other pieces of wreckage averages 20 feet deep.

The kelp covering the wreck was gone, the result of an especially rough winter. Visibility was about 75 feet. Brass, polished by the winter storms, was all over the bottom, shining like gold. Divers could actually choose among the artifacts that lay about. I shot three rolls of film and picked up a shackle and a small pulley.

The *Gregory* was extremely photogenic then, resembling a wreck at Truk Lagoon without all the encrus-

Hull plates, the U.S.S. Gregory. *Photo by Bonnie J. Cardone.*

tations. But it was the last time I was able to dive her. Since she is so close to shore and on the weather side of the island, wind and waves often create water conditions that make diving dangerous.

Because she isn't dived all that much, the *Gregory* still yields nice artifacts. And if you do get the chance to make a jump on her, treasure it—it's likely to be some time before you have an opportunity to do it again.

B. J. C.

Appendix: Charter Dive Boats

Southern California has good diving all year-round. This is the major reason there are so many excellent charter dive boats. These range from "six packs," so called because they carry up to six passengers, to modern vessels 90 feet long, designed and built specifically for diving.

Large Boats

The larger boats can carry up to 50 passengers, but usually limit multi-day trips to between 30 and 40. Docked primarily in the San Diego area, San Pedro–Long Beach, Port Hueneme–Ventura, and Santa Barbara, most, but not all, have galleys, bunks, and compressors. On multi-day trips, the cost includes food and air fills; on most single-day trips, these are separate and you pay for them on the trip home. The San Diego boats usually supply weights, weightbelts, and tanks, but you bring your own on most of the other boats. Truth Aquatics' three boats, docked in Santa Barbara, do not sell alcoholic beverages, but you may bring your own. Most of the other boats sell beer when the diving day is over.

Bunks are almost always furnished with pillows, pillowcases, and blankets, but on multi-day trips your own sleeping bag may be more comfortable: for practicality, most of the bunks have vinyl-coated pads that are cold and stick to bare skin.

Almost all the boats have freshwater showers. On the older boats these are out on the deck. Truth Aquatics' *Vision* and *Conception*, however, have showers below decks. Some of the other boats—the *Atlantis*, *Charisma*, *Encore*, *Cee-Ray*, and *Spectre* for example—have showers in the heads. The freshwater capacity of all of the boats is limited, and long, lingering showers are not encouraged.

Few of the boats allow ice chests aboard because their modern galleys have versatile menus and the cooks are usually willing to prepare food to accommodate almost all tastes and diets. If you have special requests, talk to the skipper ahead of time.

Each of the boats has a unique personality and a cadre of loyal followers. One, the *Peace*, even has a saltwater hot tub!

Boat Calendars

All of the larger boats publish monthly calendars that list the dates they have trips, the planned destinations, and the group or groups that have chartered the particular dates. If a trip is listed as "open," it means there is no chartering group and you call the boat directly to reserve space. Otherwise you are expected to call the chartering group to sign on a trip. You can receive a calendar by calling and requesting one.

Six Pack Boats

The smaller boats offer personalized dive trips for an instructor with students or other small groups. Services vary. When you book a trip, ask if there is a compressor on board or if you will need to bring a tank for each dive. Ask about the galley, if any. Discuss destinations. Six packs are ideal for those who do not like diving with a lot of other people, who want to dive only with people they know, or who have specific destinations in mind that are off the beaten path of the bigger boats.

Destinations

It should be noted that all destinations are tentative, and are never guaranteed! The weather is unpredictable and last minute destination changes, made for the comfort and safety of the passengers, are not unusual.

Almost all of the larger boats can be chartered to visit any Channel Island, off-island, or coastal dive site. It is two hours to the nearest islands (Santa Catalina and Anacapa), and six-to-nine hours to the outermost (San Clemente and San Nicolas). For this reason, the boats usually board passengers the evening before the dive—either at 8 or 10 P.M.—and travel to the destination while they sleep. When you book a trip, always ask when you can board and when the boat will depart. Catalina and Anacapa trips usually board early in the morning—6 to 7 A.M.—and leave then. Not all the boats allow guests to board the night before on these trips.

Miscellaneous

Extra Equipment

As modern and well equipped as the boats are, most of them do not carry spare gear, nor do they sell or rent it. Thus, guests should bring everything they think they will need. This includes such things as extra straps, etc. If something breaks or fails to function properly, your only option is fixing it yourself or borrowing gear from someone else.

Fish and Game Licenses

If you think you might be spearing fish or collecting any other game, buy a California Sportfishing License. These are available at sporting goods stores, some drug stores, and from most of the landings at which the dive boats are docked. You can get a yearly license or a one-, five-, or ten-day license. Fishing licenses cannot be bought on board the boats.

Diving Conditions

Wreck diving takes place in southern California waters year-round. Since water temperatures range from 42 to 64 degrees F, thermal protection is a must. Most divers wear either one-quarter inch neoprene wetsuits or drysuits. Hoods, booties, and a good pair of gloves are also necessary. The water tends to be the warmest and visibility the best in September and October. Warm Santa Ana winds, however, can flatten the Pacific any time of year. And when they occur, diving conditions are usually optimal.

The waters around the four southern Channel Islands are usually about 10 degrees warmer than those of the northern Channel Islands. The southern islands also tend to offer better visibility than their northern counterparts.

Dive Boat List

Listed below are the boats that were available for charter at this writing. New boats are constantly being added to the fleet and some boats go out of business every year, so this list will be incomplete. We have included only the larger charter boats; all of them and most of the six packs advertise in either the *Dive Boat Calendar and Travel Guide, California Diving News,* or *Discover California Diving.*

Santa Barbara—Sea Landing Breakwater

> *Conception*
> *Truth*
> *Vision*
> Truth Aquatics
> Sea Landing Breakwater
> Santa Barbara, CA 93109
> (805) 962-1127

Ventura—Cisco's Landing

> *Captain Midnight*
> Cisco's Landing
> (805) 644-7763

> *Vaya con Dios*
> Aqua Ventures
> 2172 Pickwick Drive
> Camarillo, CA 93010
> (805) 484-1594

Ventura—Ventura Harbor

> *Liberty*
> P.O. Box H
> South Gate, CA 90280
> (805) 642-1233

> *Peace*
> Ventura Harbor
> 1559 Spinnaker Dr. #108
> Ventura, CA 93001
> (805) 658-8286

Scuba Luv'er
704 Thousand Oaks Blvd.
Thousand Oaks, CA 91360
(805) 496-1014

Spectre
935 Maplewood Way
Port Hueneme, CA 93041
(805) 642-1233

Port Hueneme—Sport Fishing Landing

Sea Ventures
P.O. Box 8
Port Hueneme, CA 93041
(805) 985-1100

Los Angeles—22nd Street Landing

Atlantis
1740 Palacios Drive
San Pedro, CA 90732
(213) 831-6666

Cee Ray
22nd Street Landing
141 W. 22nd Street
San Pedro, CA 90731
(213) 519-0880

Charisma
Encore
26302 Senator Avenue
Harbor City, CA 90710
(213) 326-7460

Golden Dubloon
112 Ninth Street, #4
Huntington Beach, CA 92648
(714) 969-1289
(714) 963-4378

Magician
741 W. 37th Street
San Pedro, CA 90731
(213) 548-6129

Maverick
663 W. 35th, #1
San Pedro, CA 90731
(213) 547-3824

Westerly
22nd Street Landing
141 W. 22nd Street
San Pedro, CA 90731
(213) 833-6048

Wild Wave
P.O. Box 667
San Pedro, CA 90733
(213) 534-0034

Los Angeles—Cabrillo Marina

Scuba Queen
600 Laura Street
La Habra, CA 90631
(213) 691-0423

Los Angeles—Queen's Wharf

Mr. C
P.O. Box H
South Gate, CA 90280
(213) 831-9449

Los Angeles—Ports O'Call

Bold Contender
Ports O'Call
Berth 76
San Pedro, CA 90731
(818) 366-2611

San Diego—Point Loma Sportfishing

Bottom Scratcher
Sand Dollar
P.O. Box 6374
San Diego, CA 92106
(619) 224-4997

San Diego—H & M Landing

> *Horizon*
> 2803 Emerson Street
> San Diego, CA 92106
> (619) 277-7823

San Diego—Commercial Basin

> *Betsy M*
> 7920 Windsor Drive
> La Mesa, CA 92041
> (619) 632-0407
> (619) 753-6928

Catalina—Avalon

> *King Neptune*
> P.O. Box 1017
> Avalon, CA 90704
> (213) 510-2616
> (800) 262-DIVE

Bibliography

Books

Adamson, Hans Christian. *Keepers of the Lights*. New York: Greenberg Publisher, 1955.

Allen, Oliver E. *The Windjammers*. Alexandria, Va.: Time-Life Books, 1978.

Benson, Richard M. *Steamships and Motorships of the West Coast*. Seattle: Superior Publishing Company, 1968.

Berman, Bruce. *Encyclopedia of American Shipwrecks*. Boston: Mariners Press Inc., 1972.

Best, Gerald M. *Ships and Narrow Gauge Rails*. Berkeley: Howell-North, 1964.

Bosqui, Edward. *Memoirs of Edward Bosqui*. Oakland, Calif.: The Holmes Book Company, 1952.

Botting, Douglas. *The U-Boats*. Alexandria, Va.: Time-Life Books, 1979.

Bronson, William. *Still Flying and Nailed to the Mast*. Garden City, N.Y.: Doubleday & Company, 1963.

Brown, Giles T. *Ships That Sail No More*. Lexington: University of Kentucky Press, 1966.

Chatterton, Keble E. *Q-Ships and Their Story*. Annapolis: Naval Institute Press, 1972.

Eaton, Margaret Holden. *Diary of a Sea Captain's Wife*. Santa Barbara: McNally & Loftin, 1980.

Gibbs, James. *Disaster Log of Ships*. New York: Bonanza Books, 1971.

————. *Pacific Square-Riggers*. Seattle: Superior Publishing, 1969.

————. *Shipwrecks of the Pacific Coast*. Portland: Binfords & Mort, 1971.

————. *West Coast Lighthouses*. Seattle: Superior Publishing, 1974.

————. *West Coast Windjammers*. Seattle: Superior Publishing, 1968.

Gleason, Duncan. *The Islands and Ports of California*. New York: Devin-Adair Company, 1958.

Harlan, George H. *San Francisco Bay Ferryboats*. Berkeley: Howell-North, 1967.

Harlan, George, and Fisher, Clement. *Of Walking Beams and Paddlewheels*. San Francisco: Bay Books, Ltd., 1951.

Heyl, Erik. *Early American Steamers*. Buffalo, N.Y.: N.p., 1953.

Hice, Charles. *The Last Hours of Seven Four-Stackers*. Distributed by The Ohioan Company, 1967.

Houston, John M. *Early Excursion Ships to Santa Catalina*. San Pedro, Calif.: Advertising Ink, 1980.

Jackson, Walter A. *The Dog Hole Schooners*. Mendocino, Calif.: Bear & Stebbins, 1977.

Keatts, Henry. *Field Reference to Sunken U-Boats*. Kings Point, N.Y.: American Merchant Marine Press, 1987.

Keatts, Henry, and Farr, George. *Dive into History— U-Boats*. Kings Point, N.Y.: American Merchant Marine Press, 1986.

Keen, Richard. Personal Diary—*Account of a Journey Overland to California from Logan, Indiana, in 1852 and Return Voyage Via Panama to N.Y.*[sic] Copied for the California State Library, 1942.

Kemble, John H. *The Panama Route, 1848–1869*. New York: Da Capo Press, 1972.

Kortum, Karl, and Olmsted, Roger. *Sailing Days on the Redwood Coast*. San Francisco: California Historical Society, 1971.

LeFleming, H. M. *Warships of World War I*. London: Ian Allan Ltd. Revised, 1961.

Lenton, H. T. *American Fleet and Escort Destroyers, vol. 1 & 2*. Garden City, N.Y.: Doubleday & Company, 1971.

Lloyd's of London. *Lloyd's Register of Shipping*, 1850–1975. London.

Lockwood, Charles A. and Adamson, Hans Christian. *Tragedy at Honda*. New York: Chilton Company, 1960.

Lonsdale, Adrian L., and Kaplan, H. R. *A Guide to Sunken Ships in American Waters*. Arlington: Compass Publications Inc., 1964.

Lowell, Joan. *The Cradle of the Deep*. New York: Simon & Schuster, 1929.

Lubbock, Basil. *Last of the Windjammers, vol. 1 & 2*. Glasgow: Brown, Son & Ferguson, Ltd., 1975.

Lytle, William M. *Merchant Steam Vessels of the United States, 1807-1868*. Staten Island: Steamship Historical Society of America, 1952.

MacMullen, Jerry. *Paddle-Wheel Days in California*. Stanford, Calif.: Stanford University Press, 1944.

MacMullen, Jerry. They Came by Sea—*A Pictorial History of San Diego Bay*. San Diego, Calif.: Ward Richie Press, 1969.

Martin, Wallace E. *Sail and Steam on the Northern California Coast*. San Francisco: National Maritime Museum, 1983.

McNairn, Jack and MacMullen, Jerry. *Ships of the Redwood Coast*. Stanford, Calif.: Stanford University Press, 1970.

Miller, Max. *I Cover the Waterfront*. New York: Ballantine Books, 1971.

Naval History Division, Department of the Navy. *Dictionary of American Naval Fighting Ships*. Washington, D.C.: U.S. Government Printing Office, 1976.

Newell, Gordon, ed. *The H. W. McCurdy Marine History of the Pacific Northwest*. Seattle: Superior Publishing Company, 1966.

Newell, Gordon, and Williamson, Joe. *Pacific Coastal Liners*. New York: Bonanza Books, 1959.

Pacific Lumber Ships. New York: Bonanza Books, 1960.

Overshiner, Elwyn E. *Course 095 to Eternity*. Elwyn E. Overshiner, Santa Rosa, Calif. 1980.

Taylor, John C. *German Warships of World War I*. Garden City, New York: Doubleday and Company, 1970.

Thomas, Lowell. *Raiders of the Deep*. Garden City, New York: Doubleday, Doran, and Company, 1928.

United States Department of Commerce and Labor. *List of Merchant Vessels of the United States*. Washington, D.C.: 1888 to 1978.

Wheelock, Walt. *Ferries of the South*. Glendale, Calif. La Siesta Press, 1964.

Wiltsee, Ernest A. *Gold Rush Steamers of the Pacific*. Lawrence, Mass.: Quarterman Publications, 1976.

Wright, E. W., ed. *Lewis and Dryden's Marine History of the Pacific Northwest*. Seattle: Superior Publishing Company, 1967.

Periodicals

American Neptune. Various Dates.
Daily Alta California. 1853, 1854.
Daily California Chronicle. Various Dates.
Illustrated Daily News (Los Angeles). Various Dates.
Los Angeles Examiner. Various dates.
Los Angeles Times. Various dates.
Noticias, vol. 5, no. 3. Santa Barbara Historical Society.
Overland Monthly, April 1917.
Pacific Marine Review. Various dates.
San Diego Herald. Various dates.
San Diego Union. Various dates.
San Francisco Chronicle. Various dates.
San Francisco Examiner. Various dates.
San Pedro News-Pilot. Various dates.
Santa Barbara Daily Independant. Various dates.
Santa Barbara News–Press. Various dates.
Santa Monica Outlook. Various dates.
Steamboat Bill of Facts, Journal of the Steamship Historical Society of America. Various dates.
The *Greenock Telegraph and Clyde Shipping Gazette*. Various dates.
The *Marine Engineer*. Various dates.
The *Morning Press* (Santa Barbara). Various Dates.
Ventura Free Press. Various dates.

Articles

Anderson, Dick. "There is Gold on the Winfield Scott," *Skin Diver Magazine*, September 1969, pp. 28–31, 65.

Bell, Bob. "The Wreck of the Valiant," *Dive Magazine*, 1967, pp. 40–44.

Bruton, Al. "The El Rey," *Discover Diving*, May/June 1987, pp. 6–10.

"Wreck Alley," *Discover Diving*, November/December, 1987, pp. 23–24.

Call, Asa Cyrus. "Diary," California Historical Society manuscript, December 5, 1953.

Cardone, Bonnie J. "California Shipwrecks," *Seafarers Journal of Maritime Heritage*, Volume I, 1987, pp. 171–174.

Cardone, Bonnie J., and Giles, Steve. "Olympic II," *Skin Diver Magazine*, June 1984, pp. 104–106.

———. "U.S.S. Koka," *Skin Diver Magazine*, January 1985, p. 62.

Cross, E.R. "Dynamite, Danger and Dollars," *Water World*, January 1956, pp. 28–29, 43–45.

Delgado, James P. "The Wreck of the S.S. Winfield Scott," *The Pacific Historian*, Volume XXVII, Number 2, Summer 1983.

Giles, Steve, and Cardone, Bonnie J. "U.S.S. Gregory," *Skin Diver Magazine*, September 1984, pp. 112–113.

Giles, Steve. "Catalina's Wreck of the Valiant," *Skin Diver Magazine*, February 1987, pp. 134–139.

————."Treasure from a Forgotten Warrior," *Skin Diver Magazine*, September 1984, pp. 28–29, 42.

————."S.S. Avalon," *Skin Diver Magazine*, November 1984, pp. 110–111.

————."U.S.S. John C. Butler," *Skin Diver Magazine*, October 1984, p.88.

Hanauer, Eric. "Retrieving the Retriever," *Skin Diver Magazine*, April 1988, pp. 152–156.

Lawson, Steve. "The Olympic II," *Porthole*, Volume 19, Number 6, June 1988, pp. 3–6.

McPeak, Ron H., and Glantz, Dale. "Harvesting California's Kelp Forests," *Oceanus*, Spring 1984, p. 19–26.

Miller, Glenn E. "Ghostly Gold," *Skin Diver Magazine*, March 1967, pp. 26–28.

Pierson, Larry, and Clark, Bob. "A Two Ton Gift to History," *Skin Diver Magazine*, March 1973, p. 24.

Smith, Patrick. "A Lady in Distress," *Skin Diver Magazine*, January 1977, p. 64–65, 70–71.

————. "Marineland Mystery Wreck," *Skin Diver Magazine*, May 1986, pp. 120–121, 130–133.

————. "Popular Shipwrecks of Southern California," *International Diver's Guide*, edited by T. O'Keefe 1975–1977

————. "The Fallen Star," *California Diver*, March/April 1985, p. 32–35.